Craftworkers in Nineteenth-Century Scotland

Making and Adapting in an Industrial Age

Stana Nenadic

EDINBURGH
University Press

Edinburgh University Press is one of the leading university presses in the UK. We publish academic books and journals in our selected subject areas across the humanities and social sciences, combining cutting-edge scholarship with high editorial and production values to produce academic works of lasting importance. For more information visit our website: edinburghuniversitypress.com

Edinburgh University Press Ltd
The Tun – Holyrood Road
12 (2f) Jackson's Entry
Edinburgh EH8 8PJ

First published in hardback by Edinburgh University Press 2022

Typeset in 10.5/13pt Sabon by
IDSUK (DataConnection) Ltd,
and printed and bound by CPI Group (UK) Ltd, Croydon, CR0 4YY

A CIP record for this book is available from the British Library

ISBN 978 1 4744 9307 9 (hardback)
ISBN 978 1 4744 9308 6 (paperback)
ISBN 978 1 4744 9309 3 (webready PDF)
ISBN 978 1 4744 9310 9 (epub)

Contents

List of Figures   iv
Preface   v

Introduction: Craftworkers Today and in the Long
    Eighteenth Century   1
1 Edinburgh and the Luxury Crafts   27
2 Industrial Crafts: Glasgow and Beyond   52
3 Rural Craft in the Lowlands and Highlands   79
4 Tourism and Craftwork   107
5 Country-house Building and Furnishing   133
6 Exhibiting Craftwork   159
7 Amateur Craft   186
Conclusion: Evaluating the Craft Economy   212

Bibliography   233
Index   250

Figures

1.1   Hamilton & Inches, goldsmiths and silversmiths.
      George Street, Edinburgh, *c*.1895   35
2.1   Workshop of a handloom weaver. Lanark, *c*.1910   58
2.2   Cutting and engraving shop. Holyrood Flint Glass Co.,
      Edinburgh, *c*.1860   66
3.1   Wheelwright's shop. Fala Dam, Midlothian, *c*.1890   83
3.2   The carpenter and his wife. Invercrearan Estate,
      Argyll, *c*.1860   87
3.3   Hugh Miller, geologist, writer and stonemason, *c*.1845   92
3.4   Robert Davidson, blacksmith. Stobs Castle, Roxburghshire,
      c.1895   94
3.5   Danny Thompson's cabinetmaking workshop. Tain, *c*.1890   99
4.1   Euphemia Ritchie, silversmith, outside her shop. Iona, *c*.1900   118
4.2   Robert Foubister and his daughter Lizzie making
      Orkney chairs, *c*.1910   125
5.1   Craftsmen working on Mar Lodge, Aberdeenshire, *c*.1900   152
6.1   Shetland and Fair Isle knitters at the Edinburgh
      International Exhibition, 1886   174
6.2   T. M. Ross, plumber of Haddington, pipework, *c*.1886   179
7.1   'Household Industry in Tain Previous to 1850', *c*.1865   189

Preface

This book is the product of many years of thinking about craftworkers and the things they made as well as a three-year research project titled 'Artisans and the Craft Economy in Scotland c.1780–1914' for which I was awarded a Leverhulme Trust grant in 2013 (RPG-2012-247). I am grateful to the Leverhulme Trust for supporting the work and am delighted to acknowledge the contributions made by research associates Dr Sally Tuckett (now of University of Glasgow) and Dr Keren Protheroe (now of Sanderson/Morris & Co. Archive), and project-linked research student Dr Sarah Laurenson (now of National Museums Scotland).

As we worked on the project, we visited many places in Scotland and beyond to see examples of nineteenth-century craftwork and numerous people have been generous with their time and expertise. They include Helen Edwards at City of Edinburgh Museums; Lorna Hepburn for the National Trust for Scotland at Hill House; Kirsty Archer-Thompson at Abbotsford; Mariella Crichton Stuart at Falkland Palace; curators or archivists at Kellie Castle, Lauriston Castle, Kinloch Castle and Mount Stuart; and staff at Kirkcaldy Galleries, the John Gray Centre in Haddington, Falkirk Museum and Archive, and Glasgow Life. Staff at the National Monuments Record of Scotland, National Records of Scotland, National Library of Scotland, Scottish Life (NMS), Signet Library, Incorporated Trades of Edinburgh, Orkney Library and Archive, V&A Archive of Art and Design, British Library and London Metropolitan Archive were especially helpful.

Mairi MacArthur shared her knowledge of jewellers Euphemia and Alexander Ritchie of Iona. The descendants of David Kirkness, Orkney chair maker, allowed me to see some of the photographs and business records that they own. Colin Fraser of Lyon & Turnbull shared his enthusiasm and expertise in Scottish silverwares. Insights gained from the contemporary craftsmen and craftswomen who contributed to the Leverhulme project through allowing workshop visits, giving interviews and participating in public events have been enormously valuable. They include Naomi Robertson and Jonathan Cleaver, tapestry makers at the Dovecot Studios; Peter Macdonald, tartan weaver; Dan Coughlan, handloom weaver and Curator of Textiles at Paisley Museum and Art Gallery; Fiona McIntosh, dyer and screen printer; Bryony Knox, silversmith; Dorothy Hogg, jeweller; the silversmiths, chasers, engravers and apprentices at Hamilton & Inches; Tommy Steel, carpenter and workshop manager at the Grassmarket Community Project; Neil Fyffe, furniture maker and woodcarver; Paul Tebble of The Meadows Pottery and George Young of St Andrews Pottery; Chris Topp of Topp & Co., blacksmiths and architectural metalworkers; Fraser Waugh of Edinburgh Cast Metals; and stonecarvers at Hutton Stone Ltd, who whilst working on the McEwan Hall restoration project at Edinburgh University, kindly showed us their work on site.

Numerous colleagues at Edinburgh University have shared their interests and expertise on craftworkers in the past or in nineteenth-century Scotland. They include in particular Aaron Allen, Tanya Romankiewicz, George Wilson Smith and Richard Rodger. Kacper Lyszkiewicz designed the Leverhulme project website and exhibition. A conference at the end of the project in 2016 brought many experts together and generated much fruitful discussion. Participants included Janice Helland, Clive Edwards, Annette Carruthers, Stephen Knott, Sally Rush and George Dalgleish.

In a few places, this book draws on research that has already seen the light of day in earlier published form, though the material involved and my thinking about it is much developed. I am grateful to Edinburgh University Press and my co-author Sally Tuckett, for allowing me to use illustrations in several chapters drawn from 'Artisans and aristocrats in nineteenth-century Scotland', *Scottish Historical Review*, 95:2 (2016), 203–29. Oxford University Press have allowed me to use details on design schools in Chapter 2 from my essay 'Designers in the nineteenth-century Scottish fancy textile industry: Education, employment and exhibition', *Journal of Design History*, 27:2 (2014), 115–31. Birlinn/John Donald have allowed me to use material in Chapter 1 from my essay 'The spatial and social characteristics of craft businesses in Edinburgh's New Town, *c*.1750–1850', in C. Godard Desmarest, ed., *The New Town of Edinburgh: An Architectural Celebration* (Edinburgh, 2019).

My ability to bring this book to its final form has been aided by research sabbatical leave granted by the School of History, Classics and Archaeology at the University of Edinburgh and latterly by a Leverhulme

Major Research Fellowship, which has developed my interest in craft businesses into a related study on the business of art in Scotland *c*.1700–1900. I remain fascinated by the world of craft making and its new manifestations in areas like craftivism. I enjoy making things as an amateur – not very well, I admit, but that doesn't matter – and I love seeing and holding and owning beautiful things made by other hands, many now long forgotten. While writing this book, I acquired two things that for me capture the magic and eloquence of nineteenth-century craftwork. I purchased the front panel of an embroidered waistcoat which had been worn by a Glasgow textile manufacturer in August 1822 when he visited Edinburgh to see the famous visit by King George IV. Mounted in a frame shortly afterwards, the wearer's name and the occasion are recorded on the back, but not the name of the embroiderer whose exquisite design composed of high summer motifs – butterflies, flowers and wheat sheaves – perfectly executed in colourful thread on pale yellow silk, was a fitting celebration of a great event. Did the wearer know the name of the embroiderer? Probably not, since the garment was almost certain purchased through a tailor in Glasgow with the embroidery work subcontracted to a specialist workshop and from there to a homeworker. Yet the name of the wearer – which is recorded here and there in archives that tell us he went bankrupt a few years after the royal visit – his taste and even his capacious girth, live on in a piece of clothing, beautifully fashioned by an unknown hand and framed for posterity. A second thing, a gift from a friend, is a small spoon carved from sycamore wood, probably made at home in the evening by a handy country labourer sometime round about 1900. The shank is worn and it is a wonder it has survived so long without breaking. Perhaps it was made for sale, or for a gift or just to use in the family. Similar spoons are still made today and sycamore, or ash, or elder is also fashioned by craftsmen and craftswomen into modern kitchen wares. And, of course, embroiderers are still making beautiful clothing to modern designs. As I say at the end of my study, the craft economy and the craftworkers who sustain it have as much relevance in the twenty-first century as they had in the past and they and the things they make are constantly evolving. Long may it remain so.

Introduction: Craftworkers Today and in the Long Eighteenth Century

THERE IS A SIGNIFICANT interest in artisans and craft production today, articulated through evolving theory on workmanship and the meaning of 'things', debates on the role of craft traditions within changing national and global identities, and explorations of craft's moral value in an age of 'fair trade'.[1] Craft for the masses is ubiquitous on the high street and exhibitions of modern craft attract wide public interest. This study of Scotland's craftworkers and craft economy in the nineteenth century builds on contemporary questions and approaches to explore artisan production and adaptation in the first industrial age, along with the individuals, families and communities that generated a vibrant craft sector. The book is timely because our understanding of the nineteenth-century craft economy has been stuck in a conventional intellectual paradigm for decades, largely shaped by narratives of decline in the face of modernisation. The vibrancy of craft making today offers new insights into what has gone before, as do the many cultural commentators of the last 20 or so years who have sought to explain the phenomenon.

CRAFTWORKERS TODAY

In 1997, design theory specialist and exhibition coordinator Peter Dormer offered one of the first important scholarly reinterpretations of the meaning and value of craft. Argued through a mostly twentieth-century historical lens and drawing contrasts between the craftsman or craftswoman and the artist, Dormer and fellow writers charted the shifting status of practitioners, the challenge of technology and the difficulties of writing about crafts.[2] Dormer's observation that craft relied on 'tacit knowledge' and was a way of doing things rather than talking or writing about them usefully contextualises some of the later flourishing of craft writing. Building from this, interest amongst contemporary makers in the making process – either through an exploration of their own work and engagement with materials or by exploring significant craftworkers in the past – has emerged as a popular genre. Of the former, Peter Korn, a noted furniture maker, explored connections between himself, the materials in which he works and his personal history in *Why We Make Things and Why It Matters*.[3] Woodworker David Esterly, reflecting on his own creative process, interrogated the genius of his seventeenth-century predecessor Grinling Gibbons.[4] The ceramicist Edmund de Waal traced the history of porcelain, written as a journey through space and time, a sort of pilgrimage to encounter a lifelong obsession that has shaped his art.[5] Grayson Perry, celebrity potter, through his 2011 British Museum exhibition and book titled *The Tomb of the Unknown Craftsman*, paid homage to the many wonderful things made by unattributed hands over the centuries that are preserved in our museums.[6] The idea of skill and expertise which transcends individual areas of practice and gets close to understanding what the craftsman or craftswoman in the past thought of themselves is examined in practitioner narratives such as these and in a recent examination of the idea of the 'expert'. Written by a surgeon, who links his haptic medical expertise to craft skills such as lacemaking, the emphasis here is on the business of 'doing' and the acquisition of tacit knowledge, which speaks to the present but also to the historical emphasis on craftworker training via apprenticeships and the long path to 'mastery'.[7]

Cultural, sociological and theoretical understandings of craft, and craftsmen and craftswomen have advanced as never before in the last 20 years, though the history is long and can be traced to the writings of Ruskin, Morris and Arts and Crafts theorist practitioners in the second half of the nineteenth century. Sociologist Richard Sennet, known for his work on urbanism, examined craft as a way of practice and being, a basic human impulse to do things well for itself. He makes connections between materials, values and the practices of work ranging across time and different cultural contexts.[8] Sennet's *Craftsman* is a moderniser rather than a traditionalist stuck in the past, who adapts to and shapes change in production processes rather than merely falling victim to them. The latter, as historians have shown, was one of the dominant narratives of craftworkers themselves, who were ever looking back to a lost golden age. Most recent conceptual writers have argued otherwise.[9] Foremost among these, with a foot in museum curation and design history, is Glenn Adamson, whose influential books include a craft anthology that is widely used by students.[10] Also in the field of education is Christopher Frayling's

collection of essays and lectures from a long career that highlights semi-
nal craft writers and institutions of the early twentieth century that still
influence today, from George Sturt's elegiac musings on the passing of an
age, exemplified in *The Wheelwright's Shop*, to the modernist interwar
influence of the Bauhaus movement.[11]

Academic research and writing have flourished through specialist
publications, notably the *Journal of Modern Craft* founded in 2008. Historians have become interested in objects and making, particularly those
rooted in the cultural history of the eighteenth century, at the point when
handmaking fine goods for a luxury market exploded and collided with
new technologies.[12] Art historian Tanya Harrod's contribution, through
her widely praised biography of Michael Cardew, uses the individual and
his ceramics, made in interwar Britain and post-war west Africa, as a
lens to view society and its conflicts, and builds on her earlier *The Crafts
in Britain in the Twentieth Century*.[13] Though not tied to individuals
nor valorised, aspects of craftwork undertaken by women have been
revealed as formative of identity and women's place in society. This idea
started with feminist art historian Rozsika Parker in her influential *The
Subversive Stitch: Embroidery and the Making of the Feminine*, which
explores the tension between needlework as an agent of female subservi-
ence whilst simultaneously offering an avenue for personal creativity.[14]
Then there is the meaning of the things themselves, their intrinsic beauty
or value and the rewarding link between the maker and the owner, as
explored by Glenn Adamson.[15] Basketry has been studied as a medium
for memory and belonging.[16] A recent anthology has asked why ceramics
are important and explores the phenomena as culture, industry, art and
display.[17] Meanwhile, a group of historians at the University of Glasgow
led by Lynn Abrams have been looking at Scottish knitting past and present, as culture and economy.[18]

Alongside an efflorescence of writing about craft, craft making is
recognised as a key component in the modern economy, connected to
contemporary issues such as fair trade and globalisation.[19] Organisations in Britain that represent craft as employment and explore its economic potential and social meaning are led by the Crafts Council, a
charity established in 1972 with government support, whose purpose
is to 'inspire making, empower learning and nurture craft businesses'.[20]
They commission regular studies and reports and act as an advocacy
body. Contemporary political issues such as sustainability are included
in their agendas, as they are in Craft Scotland and similar organisations
in other countries. The Heritage Crafts Association is another British
advocacy body. It has a rural focus, champions endangered crafts and

highlights the role of heritage visitor attractions in keeping skills alive. Popular television programmes, notably 'The Repair Shop', filmed by the BBC at the Weald and Downland Living Museum in West Sussex, show loved but broken objects brought back to life by craftworkers, tell stories of what things can mean for owners and promote a gentle anti-consumerist message.

There are links between craft practice and politics. Craftivism is a manifestation of a belief that craftwork represents a social philosophy capable of bringing about subversion and change and is often linked to environmental issues or social justice campaigns.[21] The phenomenon known as 'yarn bombing' is a colourful and widespread form of such activism, mostly undertaken by women.[22] Craft making as psychological well-being and an avenue for personal growth is reflected in professional as well as amateur motivations.[23] Indeed, the idea of craft and 'whole-ness', a form of cultural and psychological connection, has driven craft revivals in Britain as elsewhere.[24]

Though many craftworkers in the past wrote about their lives and experiences, it was rare, in contrast with craftworkers today, to see them reflecting on the psychological or cultural or haptic meanings attached to what they made. Weavers, as explored in later chapters, are an exception as are those craftsmen such as Hugh Miller, stonemason and geologist, who moved from making to writing for a living and was profoundly interested in stone above all other things, its history and materiality.[25] Another characteristic of craftsmen and craftswomen in the past that further differentiates them from those of the present revolves around the centrality or otherwise of personal creativity. Since the later nineteenth century, when the Arts and Crafts movement took hold, craftwork as a form of creative expression was privileged over handwork as copying or replication, where it was skill not art that was important. This tension has been highlighted in the conceptual literature of Adamson amongst others and accounts in some respects for the importance the early design schools or training regimes placed on copying to perfect technique, rather than originality which now dominates.[26] The craftsman or crafts-woman today who merely copies is not valued, whereas in the past the perfect copy was usually the main objective, as when, for instance, a cabinetmaker's workshop made a matching set of dining room chairs or stonecarvers worked from pattern books.

We live in a world that is interested in craftworkers and handmade things and historians have followed the zeitgeist to explore what this meant in the past. Yet it is important to remember that the meaning of craft today is different to the past because the meaning is constantly evolving. As usefully stated in a recent editor's introduction to a special edition of the *Journal of Modern Craft,*

> Craft in its broadest sense is an endlessly shape-shifting concept, a word with almost too many associations. Craft practice all over the world has been repositioned under colonialism, has responded to tourism, has found a context in the art and design world, has abandoned or adapted skills in response to industrialization, or has found its place within industry.[27]

CRAFTWORKERS IN THE PAST

We can start with definitions. What is a craftworker? He or she creates an entire artefact – or significant part of it – usually from start to finish, using manual skills acquired through formal systems of training. In the past, when they were normally termed 'artisans' and almost always male, their careers and identities were embedded in hierarchical structures of practice and prestige ranging from the apprentice, via the journeyman, to the master craftsman, and they belonged to local representative bodies, the guilds or trades houses, that regulated training, wages and prices.[28] Artisans had qualities in common with professionals and the practical, materials-focused professions such as architects or surgeons had close relationships with artisans, having evolved from craft-trained groups such as master masons or barbers.[29] In the nineteenth century female craftworkers, though high in skill, were mostly low-paid and clustered in textiles and clothing.[30] Craftworkers were mobile, moving within and between countries with skills that found ready markets elsewhere. Many were employed in small firms, often in what is now termed the 'creative industries' and this aspect of recent business history has attracted scholars, as it also attracts policy interest today.[31]

Academic discussion of the nineteenth-century craft economy and the life and work of artisans in Scotland and beyond is caught between two polarities. For the first half of the century, it is subsumed within a dominant literature, informed by economic and labour history, whose main preoccupation is with deskilling and the concomitant radicalisation of craftsmen as their ways of life and incomes were swept away by new technologies and factories.[32] By the mid nineteenth century, according to this literature, the crisis of craft had generated a new political consciousness, but the craftworker, his community and his product had all but vanished, as illustrated, famously, in the fate of Paisley shawl handloom weavers in the 1840s.[33] According to one account, 'by 1830 . . . traditional skilled craftsmen had lost much of their independence and, as markets altered and expanded they found themselves becoming permanent wage-earners tied to capitalist merchants and manufacturers who dictated their pace and pattern of work'.[34] Of course, changes were real and dramatic for individuals and communities, since an artisan trained in one skill could rarely shift into another, but, as has been suggested with reference to European craftsmen in contexts of later-industrial modernisation, there is a long-held 'myth' of decline among artisans and belief in each generation that their forebears lived in better times.[35] Ideas of a past 'golden age' fuelled discontent and political activism and shaped contemporary and later interpretations of the losses that attended industrial change and that is elegiac in character.[36]

The analysis of craft and craftworkers in the later decades of the nineteenth century mostly lies within another dominant literature, informed by art and design history, whose preoccupation is with the Arts and Crafts movement. This is generally seen as an elite aesthetic and quasi-political phenomenon devoted to countering the 'dehumanising' effects of industrialisation, decrying the inferior character of machine-made goods and expounding arguments for social progress through craft production, the latter mainly taking the form of middle-class men and women producing expensive goods for wealthy customers.[37] The relationship between the long-established and flourishing craft economy and the Arts and Crafts movement is rarely explored in this literature, though some of the great Scottish Arts and Crafts building projects clearly made use of jobbing craftworkers who worked to contract for designers of all stripes without apparent concern for the deeper aesthetic or sociopolitical meanings ascribed to such design.[38]

The underpinning narrative in both literatures is that the modern industrial world destroyed the craft economy, replacing it with machine-made goods for the masses and studio-made craft-art for a moneyed few. There are, of course, more subtle analyses of the nature of economic change. One of the more influential argues for a nuanced interpretation of mass production versus craftsmanship, which takes the form of 'flexible specialisation' manifested in the persistence of small artisanal firms well into the twentieth century.[39] Whilst Marxian explanations of industrial dualism – mass production alongside petite bourgeois firms – see the latter as a residual and declining phenomenon, the more positively framed recent economic approach allows the possibility of technical sophistication and market flexibility among artisan-based workshops. The latter is confirmed by detailed sectoral studies. In certain areas of intense industrial production, such as the Turkey red printed-cotton textile industry which had some of the largest factories in Scotland in the mid and later nineteenth century, big businesses retained complex relationships with craftsmen and an adaptive local craft economy.[40] Moreover, studies taking a business-history approach to the creative industries in areas like jewellery making further underline the importance of small firms with complex craft traditions making use of market information and new demand to evolve and flourish in the face of changing technologies and factory organisation.[41]

The history of Scottish artisans in nineteenth-century politics and the labour movement is well charted.[42] Yet their cultural and social role is little understood, the nature of craft skills and products rarely merits attention and there have been no attempts to assess the value of craftwork for Scotland as a whole.[43] This was not the case amongst contemporaries in the nineteenth century, when craftworkers were esteemed and their expertise encouraged long before the Arts and Crafts movement and in ways that are now largely forgotten. Museum formation and the exhibition movement provide illustrations. The Industrial Museum of Scotland, founded in 1854, was a permanent public institution for acquiring and displaying craft-made artefacts from across the globe, particularly with the intention of showing how raw materials were converted into the 'necessities and luxuries of life' and offered displays that juxtaposed handwork with machine production. The exhibition activity of the Edinburgh Industrial Museum was paralleled by another initiative, the creation of a Scottish Art Manufacturers Association in 1855, which partly built on the inspiration of the Great Exhibition of 1851, but also derived from a longer tradition of exhibitions of fine Scottish-made goods.[44] The international exhibition movement – so often associated with the celebration of modern technology – is further testimony to the survival and appreciation of craftworkers at home and abroad, with the Artisans Courts often making up the largest body of exhibits.[45] Working exhibits of craftsmen and craftswomen in traditional dress were especially popular with exhibition visitors.[46] Craftwork as a vector for traditional values and design purity and the appealing sense of 'permanence' and authenticity that attached to craftwork was also embedded in contemporary understanding.

Despite a well-documented cultural presence, the dominant historical narrative that has shaped our understanding of nineteenth-century craftworkers is that they were declining in numbers, earnings and social status, replaced by machines and factory hands, with just small groups of specialists remaining here and there. This long-held and tenacious view is challenged in the book that follows. But before examining a process that is best described as a creative and adaptive response to technical change as opposed to slow extinction, it is useful to look at what the world of the Scottish craftworker comprised in the eighteenth century.

Of course, the economy was not static and the craftworker's environment was one of constant evolution.[47] Yet there were continuities with the past that were important for identity and community, particularly the urban corporate structures that underpinned the different crafts and gave status and authority – the trades houses as they were called in Scotland, equivalent to guilds in England or Europe, or livery companies in London – alongside the system of training through apprenticeship that these bodies controlled. The different incorporated crafts that constituted the trades house of Scottish towns were formed in medieval times, with most gaining their independent charters in the early modern period as towns as centres of production became central to national economic success.[48] Edinburgh and Glasgow led the way in the movement towards incorporation but smaller places followed, with skilled workers forming representative bodies to control their collective interests.[49] They built headquarters for administration and sociability, and engaged in elaborate display on public occasions through formal dinners, religious observance and processions. The numbers of individuals involved was not large compared with the urban population as a whole and some crafts were bigger and more powerful than others. In early modern Glasgow, for instance, the largest group of craft burgesses was the 'clothiers', made up of tailors, dyers, drapers and others who handled textiles and clothing, whereas metalworkers were much fewer.[50]

With their numerous incorporations and control of urban trade, craftworkers engaged in local politics and office holding and maintained charitable structures to look after their own poor, be it sick members of the craft, their widows and children, or unmarried daughters. As the example of Edinburgh's locksmiths reveal, senior craftsmen and their representative bodies were a central feature of urban social control.[51] They were also subject to effective systems of internal policing in the interests of stability.[52] Craftsmen were 'men' first and foremost, arrived at an adult estate and with a distinct masculine identity articulated through clothing and behaviour. Part of that masculine status resided in the capacity to set up a household and maintain a family, with skilled men invariably marrying the daughters of similarly skilled men. Master craftsmen, with their own workshops, were a corporate and social elite. Lesser craftsmen, younger or without the resources to set up in business, were destined for a life as 'journeyman', travelling to make a living or working as an employee. Master craftsmen sealed their status and reputation through pride in work, family respectability and fiscal probity. They also had the right to train apprentices in the skills and culture of the craft.[53] It is no surprise that the freemasons, another masculine corporate phenomenon that rose to prominence throughout Europe in the eighteenth century, attracted large numbers of craftsmen.

With few professionals and what were later termed white-collar workers, early modern Scottish craftsmen had privilege and they protected their positions jealously. But even at its height the craftworker's world was shifting as the broader consumption environment evolved with new commodities or fashions. This could generate local conflicts and realignments, as in early-eighteenth-century Edinburgh when the Incorporation of Barbers, with rights to use knives to shave beards and heads, clashed with unincorporated wigmakers and hairdressers, whose fashionable skills and relationships with elite male customers gave rise to demands for the right to shave their clients and cut as well as dress hair, which the barbers resisted.[54] There was conflict too between cabinetmakers and upholsterers, the first skilled in techniques involving wood and the second in textiles – a tension heightened by growing elite demand for comfortably upholstered furniture.[55] In both examples the protagonists sought to protect market position – what modern economists term 'occupational licensing' – and in both the tides of change elsewhere ultimately rendered such local disputes irrelevant as the capacity to exercise market control was undermined by urban expansion, new occupations and free-market thinking.[56] Skilled workers in emerging areas of urban production were less subject to corporate control than older craft groups. The system of apprentice training that underpinned the craftsman's identity and culture was weakened and shortened. Indeed, men who had not been formally apprentice trained and not registered as 'freemen' were increasingly able to establish themselves in workshops, as the case below of James Watt in Glasgow in the 1770s reveals.

The authority vested in craft organisations did not collapse overnight, it was vigorously defended and in many ways these bodies thrived in the nineteenth century and beyond, though their roles were increasingly founded on ritual and networking or administration of their charitable funds. An iconic Scottish novel of the early nineteenth century, John Galt's *The Provost*, first published in 1822, is testimony to the survival of small-town craft institutions and associated local politicians, though rendered as comic archetypes. Though formalised apprenticeship training overseen collectively was on the wane, reduced in length and fractured by growing volatility which meant that apprentices were more likely to move between masters at the end of the century than at the beginning, nevertheless apprentice contracts were still registered into the early twentieth century.[57] None of this experience was unique to Scotland. For historians of eighteenth-century London, apprenticeship and the associated impact on the London economy has generated considerable scholarly interest alongside research into the lives of adolescents, their migration patterns, wages and workplace relations.[58] Running parallel with pre-occupations with apprentices, there has also been a sustained scholarly debate on the decline of craft guilds in London and whether this was good for or detrimental to the modernising economy.[59]

A further feature of the Scottish craft economy in the early eighteenth century that is worth noting, for it formed the backdrop to numerous improvement initiatives, is the fact that it operated in relatively primitive ways focused on the production of pedestrian or low-value goods. The comparative poverty of Scotland coupled with well-developed international trade with Europe meant that consumer luxuries were more easily purchased abroad than made at home and consequently the craftsmen who made such goods were rare in Scotland. This was particularly true of fine textiles, clocks and watches, or ceramics which figured significantly in Scottish import on the eve of Union.[60] Certain high-skill sectors did exist in Scotland, foremost being the goldsmiths and silversmiths. But goldsmiths, who were few, with many having gentry family connections, were part of a system of government finance as well as makers of fine goods and were often trained in London or Paris. An example is furnished by George Heriot, remembered today as philanthropist and founder of a notable Edinburgh school, but also active as 'Goldsmith to the Crown' and who spent most of his later life living in London alongside the Stuart court.[61] Or there was James Ker in the mid eighteenth century, a wealthy man of landed background who made exceptionally fine wares for the aristocracy and served as MP for Edinburgh.[62] It is not surprising, perhaps, that this elite craft was passed from father to son throughout the nineteenth century.

NEW CRAFT SKILLS

Modernisation in the Scottish economy was slow following the Union of 1707 and when it did occur it was frequently the product of concerted or planned endeavours.[63] In a situation mid century where many areas of craft making were underdeveloped and produced low-value goods, but with a national imperative to develop the country in the wake of the damaging Jacobite rebellion, it is no surprise that attempts were made to 'implant' modern consumer crafts. A well-documented case concerns the pottery industry in Glasgow.[64]

Pottery production in mid-eighteenth-century Scotland mostly comprised simple earthenware jugs and bowls for domestic use made by semi-skilled country potters who also made tiles and bricks in small workshops near to natural clay deposits. With a basic range of glazes and limited decoration, such wares served the everyday needs of Scots rich and poor and were distributed to customers via country markets or travelling salesmen. Fashionable pottery and china were imported from elsewhere and sold by city merchants.[65] With demand for the latter rising, certain well-placed Scottish businessmen seized the opportunity to grow a new industry through persuading skilled workers to move to Scotland from England and Europe.

A letter written in March 1748 by Glasgow-born Robert Dinwiddie, a great colonial merchant then living in London, to his brother Laurence in Glasgow, a tobacco merchant and later Lord Provost, describes how he had just hired a 'master potter' to come to Glasgow to set up a delftware pottery in the city, the first of its kind in Scotland, for the production of fashionable tin-glazed tableware of the sort produced in Holland or London and in London-owned small workshops in Liverpool and Bristol. He had given the potter, John Bird, 12 guineas for the journey northwards, to buy a 'horse, boots etc' because the man would not travel by sea for fear of drowning. Arrangements for employing other skilled workers as journeymen, including some from Delft in Holland and for recruiting local apprentices were also put in place. All of this was to be kept a secret, 'for the trade [in London] are combined together not to employ any person that attempts to bring a new manufactory to any other place'.[66] According to Bird's testimony to a later court case, he was promised an annual salary of £60 and would get coals and candles for his family plus a sixth share of the profits. Part of the attraction offered by Dinwiddie was that 'a person with a family might live a great deal cheaper there [in Glasgow] than in London and might save money'.

John Bird, in his mid thirties, had served a seven-year apprenticeship and then acted for seven years as clerk and manager for a pottery works in Lambeth making white-and-blue decorated dishes and plates, ointment pots and drug jars, punch bowls, mugs and cups, candlesticks, chamber pots, salts and urns.[67] Once in Glasgow, he was joined by his wife and younger brother, an apprentice pot painter, and a brother-in-law, also a pot painter. Further skilled labour was hired from England, contracted for five years and paid at Liverpool rates, which were greater than those paid to Scottish country potters but less than in London. The artisans met together in a local pub and formed what they termed a 'potters box society', effectively a friendly society for sickness benefit, with a subscription of 6d per week. Apprentices were recruited in Glasgow and indentured to the works and not Bird as master potter, a condition that caused discord which compounded other problems. Indeed, Bird's experience in Glasgow was disastrous. He suffered ill health, he hired too many pot painters and not enough turners to keep them busy and his first firing failed. He was sacked and returned to London but subsequently pursued a court case against his employers for what we would now term 'unfair dismissal', which he won and in the process the details of this putative investment in a new area of craft enterprise in Scotland, along with the early years of the works and its complex structures of different skills and processes, was revealed.[68]

Despite the early struggles and court case, the Delftfield pottery soon commenced production suitable for sale and export and in the later 1750s, now competing effectively with Staffordshire cream ware, it diversified into tin-glazed stoneware. It had lucrative specialist lines in decorated punchbowls and table services embellished with monograms or coats of arms for the status-conscious Scottish gentry. Within a few years of founding, the locally trained took up the reins of production and most of the English workforce drifted away, some back to London, Bristol or Liverpool, or to Dublin, where several London potters had established works. The business remained in Dinwiddie family ownership into the 1770s and was then taken over by new partners including William Young, an apprentice trained there in the 1760s (possibly by one of the London craftsmen) and manager from the 1770s.[69] Another with an interest in the firm in this generation was James Watt, the celebrated inventor.

Greenock-born James Watt was first employed in his father's Glasgow business as shipwright and chandler. He was too old for a proper apprenticeship when he went to London in 1755, but through a Scottish-born telescope maker, James Short, he was able to get informal training from a watchmaker and then a mathematical instrument maker. Watt returned to Glasgow in August 1756, where, in the absence of formal apprentice training, he found it hard to set up as an instrument maker but got employment at the university through family connections. From 1759, with a shop in the Saltmarket, he had both journeymen and apprentices and made and sold mathematical and musical instruments and Birmingham-type metal 'toys'. In 1764 he acquired an investment interest in the Delftfield pottery, making a practical contribution through research and experiments in clay, furnace construction, flint-grinding machines, glazes and designs.[70] He lived in a house alongside the pottery for several years and combined trips beyond Scotland, including to London, with his own and the pottery business. For instance, in 1768 he visited London to register a steam-engine patent, but also purchased examples of English wares to take home for copying and hired skilled hands.[71] When undertaking his own business interest in steam engines for mines, he wrote to his Glasgow partners about clay and mineral deposits in different places in England. He maintained a friendly correspondence with Josiah Wedgwood and was involved in the recruitment of another wave of skilled English pottery workers in the early 1770s, this time from Staffordshire, who were dismissed once they had trained up the apprentices. An advertisement in the *Glasgow Journal* on 13 May 1773 stated –

> NOTICE: The Delftfield Company beg leave to inform the public that their apprentices having now learned the art of manufacturing Yellow Stone, or Cream coloured Ware, they have dismissed those strangers they were at first obliged to employ at high wages to teach them. They are thereby enabled to serve their customers at lower prices than formerly, and they flatter themselves with better wares . . .[72]

Though leaving Glasgow to live in London, James Watt retained his interests in the firm. By the later eighteenth century the works was flourishing and employed 40 to 50 people, mostly apprenticeship trained.[73] There were other modern potteries in Glasgow and along the shores of the River Forth near Edinburgh. Delftfield was sold in 1822, advertised as follows and the firm then merged with a bigger undertaking nearby:

> POTTERY FOR SALE. The Partners of the Delftfield Company, being desirous of retiring from business, will be glad to dispose of their Property, bounded by the Canal and near to the Basin of the Monkland Canal. The Houses, Workshops and Machinery are all in very good order, and a purchaser may enter into possession of a going Works, with a stock of Goods ready for immediate sale.[74]

The Delftfield case highlights the problems that beset attempts to develop a modern consumer-based craft economy in Scotland. London, with its large Scottish population, was a resource – a place where specialist labour or market information were potentially available – but not always easy to navigate and inevitably expensive to access and utilise. Such private initiatives in innovative craft production in Scotland, made by rich businessmen with personal profit as the main objective, were not unique but they were more than matched and exceeded by the endeavours of elite-dominated public bodies to do the same. Foremost amongst the latter was the Board of Manufactures.

STATE SUPPORT FOR CRAFT SKILLS

The Board of Trustees for Fisheries, Manufacturers and Improvements in Scotland was established by Act of Parliament in 1726 to administer several government funds whose purpose was the modernisation of the

Scottish economy through a focus on key sectors where encouragement would complement those of the rest of Great Britain.[75] The primary target was the linen industry.[76] Its activities, overseen by a board of eminent men with a small group of salaried staff, mostly based in Edinburgh, changed from time to time according to government needs and waned in the early nineteenth century. The linen interest was abandoned in 1823 since the industry no longer required outside support or regulation and because prevailing economic philosophies around state interventions were moving decisively towards free markets. The Board's later interventions were cultural in focus and included support for art education and the founding of the National Galleries of Scotland in 1859.[77] Over its long years of existence, the Board committed thought and support to other initiatives for positive change in Scotland, including encouragement for the Borders woollen industry in the early nineteenth century and what they described as 'improvements in general', which included the craft economy.[78]

The first significant development towards the latter was the creation of a design school in Edinburgh in 1760, whose purpose was to train young men in drawing for the decorative trades including textile design.[79] It occupied various premises in the Old Town in its first decades and moved to Picardy Place at the east of the New Town in the early nineteenth century, which was close to a distinctive geographical cluster of craft businesses. With the building of the Royal Institution (later known as the Royal Scottish Academy) on Princes Street in the mid 1820s, the school relocated once more to take advantage of better-appointed teaching rooms and exhibition spaces. At the Board's expense, the design school invested in an impressive cast collection of classical statuary in the 1820s, which generated increased demand on student places for artists and 'those connected with the figured branches of manufacture'.[80] The school had successful branches nearby, notably in Dunfermline in the 1820s to service the needs of the fine linen damask industry.[81] The training offered was considered worthwhile by craft practitioners eager to enhance the skills of their children or workforce and consequently places in the school, which had about 40 students at any time, were at a premium. In January 1800, for instance, petitions were read to the Board's meeting from 'Frederick Rudolph Hay apprentice to an Engraver and Mrs Smeton widow of the late Mr Walter Smeton, coach painter, on behalf of her son Alexander who is to follow that profession, praying to be admitted into the Drawing Academy under Mr Graham, with a Recommendation in favour of each from Sir Wm Forbes'. Both youths were given places.[82]

A second area of Board of Manufactures encouragement for craftwork was in the granting of financial rewards, called premiums or bounties, for innovation and exceptional workmanship. Prizes were advertised in the press and winners announced in similar fashion. By the early nineteenth century, prize categories included hand-woven damask tablecloths and silk handkerchiefs, fine woollens, printed cottons and designs drawn on paper.[83] Premiums were also made following direct petition in writing to the Board and applications were normally followed up by some sort of investigation. On 28 June 1808, for instance, a petition was read from John Begg, described as 'His Majesty's Watchmaker for Scotland', stating that he had made an improvement on the escapement of a watch and that his watch 'when completely timed, will go equally well, if not better than the horizontal, the Liverpool, or Arnolds detached escapement, and can be sold for half the price'. The improvement was referred to 'Professor Playfair', a scientist at the University, for examination and report, who confirmed the device was 'ingenious in a high degree'. A reward of 20 guineas was awarded.[84]

Some applications concerned pedestrian but necessary commodities. This was seen in December 1793 when 'a petition was read from William Rodgers journeyman wright in Edinburgh praying for some reward on account of his having found out the Method of making Sandpaper for polishing Mahogany'. 'Several cabinet makers', who confirmed that the sandpaper was good and as cheap as made in London, gave support. The trustees ordered the Secretary to the Board to investigate 'whether this is a matter of any consequence'. Six months later, having sought the advice of Scotland's first-ranked cabinetmaking firm, Young, Trotter & Hamilton, the Secretary reported that 'tho' it cannot perhaps be deemed of great consequence, yet that it is a necessary & useful article [that no one else in Scotland made] and with regard to the Man that he is industrious and deserving'. He was duly granted a premium of £10.[85]

Linked to both the prizes and petitioners and an area of growing activity from the early nineteenth century, was the role of the Board of Manufactures in the public exhibition of craftwork. Sometimes undertaken in their premises in the Royal Exchange just off the High Street, sometimes in commercial premises and in the Royal Institution on Princes Street from the 1820s, exhibitions were linked to judging for the year's premiums following advertising for submissions through the press. They were modest and short-run events, starting with the judge assessments in late November and available for public viewing over the Christmas weeks. The costs associated with the 'competition for public premiums in Edinburgh' for 1828–9 were given as £2 2s 'paid to J. Smith for three-weeks attendance in the office when the regular doorkeeper had to attend the goods lodged for competition at the Royal Institution rooms', plus £3 15s paid to A. Giles, carpenter, for 'erecting tables, etc, for showing the goods'. Mr Smith, the doorkeeper, was paid £4 4s for 'receiving, sorting, packing and giving out the goods produced in competition' and there were payments also for carriage to the competition and insurance, making a total of £19 6s 5d to cover the costs of staging the event.[86] With the Edinburgh Design School flourishing in its Princes Street premises from the mid 1820s, the Board's role in exhibition activity was extended. The statue gallery attracted interest beyond the students and other hand-crafted objects were acquired for study and design inspiration. A list of some of these was made in March 1850 prior to them being sent to the Government School of Design in Glasgow for exhibition in that city and for loan to the Great Exhibition in London the following year.[87]

Complementary to its design training, exhibitions and financial rewards for individual craftworkers, the Board of Manufactures maintained numerous connections with elite individuals the length of Scotland and abroad in pursuit of its aims, with frequent correspondence on goods to be tried or encouraged and regular petitioning of landowners on behalf of crafts people and manufacturers.[88] This was evidenced in the 1840s in correspondence with Sir Grant Suttie of Prestongrange near Edinburgh regarding supplies of his high-quality estate clay for manufacture in Prestonpans into fine handcrafted and engraved ceramics in the style of Neapolitan wares, an industry that the Board sought to develop.[89] Sir John Stuart Forbes of Pitsligo, a noted agricultural reformer, corresponded with the Board on the same subject, sending reports from Porta Ferma in Rome on how the technique was practised.[90] Scottish aristocrats and nobles travelling abroad commonly looked for products that might be developed in Scotland, sending samples to the Board of Manufactures with suggestions. One of these was Lady Hope of Pinkie House, Musselburgh, who in 1844 sent a sample of worsted velvet plush and another of a 'sort of tapestry' article.[91]

A prominent banker and man-of-business, who was also a patron of the arts and Board of Manufactures trustee, Gilbert Innes of Stow, illustrates another connection between craftworkers and the Board. Innes was often on the lookout for new Scottish art or craft talent to promote and found such in Thomas Campbell, a young apprentice-trained marble cutter working for John Marshall, marble cutter of Leith Walk in Edinburgh, who was fitting a fireplace in Innes's house. Being struck by the youth's ability and intelligence, Innes paid for Campbell to further his training in London and supported him in studies in Europe and in his early career in London.[92] There was reciprocity in this patronage, of course, because Campbell acted as Innes 'man of business' when in Europe in the 1820s, also carrying out commissions for the Board. The latter becomes apparent in a letter sent to Innes from Rome in March 1821, with an enclosure directed to 'Mr Thomson, the Secretary' regarding a present of a carving from the great sculptor Canova, which was proposed as a gift for 'the academy'.[93]

The Board of Manufactures made critical interventions in the early development of the nineteenth-century craft and industrial economy in Scotland, but the Board was not without its critics and it was subject to parliamentary scrutiny due to excessive expenditure in the 1820s. An 1830 report of a Committee of Inquiry, made at the behest of the House of Commons, revealed excessive sums of public money going into the pockets of its employees in salaries, travel costs and free housing. It was stated that the Board's business had 'been conducted at an expense disproportionate to the revenue paid out, and to the extent of the duties performed by its officers'. There were also questionable investments in the Edinburgh Botanic Gardens that had no obvious connection with the Board's mandate. Given the Board's shrinking role once linen regulation had ended, it was thought appropriate that employee numbers and expenditure be reduced.[94] Had the committee looked carefully at the records, they might also have observed the degree to which the Board of Manufactures sometimes operated for the benefit of the relatives of its employees and trustees. This was evident in February 1794 when John Guthrie, son of James Guthrie, the 'Board's late Secretary', wrote that,

> having now completed his apprenticeship to the business of an Engraver, he wishes to go to London either to follow it there, or to proceed to India for that purpose – And praying that the Board would add to their former kindness by allowing him a sum necessary for carrying him to London & discharging some little debts which has contracted for Cloaths & other necessaries.[95]

The Board granted him £30 on top of the earlier award, stating, 'if that is not enough the secretary can add £10 more'.

SCOTTISH CRAFTWORKERS AND LONDON

The Board of Manufactures received and supported frequent requests, such as the one above from John Guthrie, to cover the costs of travel to London to practice a skilled craft. They also encouraged craftworkers to move from England to Scotland to develop the textile industry and the craft economy more generally, providing many grants to that end. For craftsmen at an early career stage, London represented a pool of training opportunities that had much appeal for parents who were eager for their children to get on life. The first notable guide to apprenticeship training and the associated business opportunities in the capital city was written by a Scotsman living in London, Robert Campbell, whose *London Tradesman*, first published in 1747, outlined the costs of apprenticeship and the skills necessary to make a success in a range of trades. It provides a good insight into new craft specialisms associated with the modern consumer economy in London in areas such as fashionable furniture and upholstery, ceramics or house decoration.[96] In the seventeenth century, apprentices travelled great distances to get training, including young Scotsmen gravitating towards London. But as the eighteenth century advanced and smaller urban places evolved to provide local, cheaper training, migration fields shrank and fewer adolescent Scots made such lengthy journeys and where they did it was usually to train with a family member.[97] Such was Duncan Verner, son of David Verner, a professor at Marischal College Aberdeen, who was apprenticed in 1740 to his maternal uncle Duncan Campbell, an indigo merchant and dyestuff maker in London.[98] Having a teenage son so far from home was frequently challenging. David Verner visited London in 1744 to try to sort out problems with Duncan, who was three years into the apprenticeship and beginning to run wild in the city, to his uncle's despair. Verner travelled by boat from Leith and spent ten weeks in London. Sadly, but not uncommonly, the apprenticeship collapsed and Duncan, still a teenager, set off to make his fortune in the West Indies instead, where he soon disappeared from the family record, almost certainly due to early death from disease.[99]

The cost of travelling to London was expensive, as were London apprenticeships and this had to be set against the benefit derived from being trained in the great city. The first *Edinburgh Directory* to give fares for the coach to London cited two routes in 1800 – one going via Berwick, Newcastle and York costing £7 17s 6d and the second, via Cornhill and Newcastle, costing £6 16s 6d. Both offered one coach per day and the journey took several days, with additional accommodation costs.[100] Poorer men without the funds for transport, tramped and hitch-hiked, often travelling in company for safety. Robert Mylne, the Edinburgh-trained architect, son of a builder with whom he served an apprenticeship, hitch-hiked across Europe in the mid eighteenth century in order to spend time in Rome for his training before returning to work in London. Whilst abroad, he maintained himself by giving drawing classes.[101] Due

to cost and distance issues, it was not uncommon for Scots who undertook apprentice training in England with the objective of eventually
working in London to do this in stages as a form of step migration.
Samuel Kevan, from a farming background, travelled from Wigtown
in south-west Scotland to serve an apprenticeship with his brother in
north-west England as mason and slater in the later eighteenth century.
This training was cut short by family problems, but he still had London
as his objective. He meandered southwards via Liverpool, Staffordshire
and Shropshire, working in various capacities on the way mostly as a
labourer, before ending in London where, with the weakening system of
artisan regulation, he returned to the building trade to eventually become
a master slater.[102]

Travel from Scotland to London for apprenticeship training had
clearly declined by the second half of the eighteenth century, but moving
to London to improve your skills, business status and income potential
'post-apprenticeship' was still important and increasingly so, as John
Guthrie's petition to the Board of Manufactures reveals. Scots had a
long history of migration to London, travelling south for social life
and leisure, politics and patronage and for employment, particularly
in the arts, professions and international trade.[103] Many having moved
to London remained there, but there were numerous others who visited for short periods, going 'in and out' to advance their particular
interests. The cost of this was not inconsiderable, hence the frequent
petitions to the Board of Manufactures. The connection with London
for craft-skills development and business-contacts formation, with the
intention that these be exploited back in Scotland, is illustrated in an
advertisement in the *Aberdeen Press and Journal* for 16 October 1805.
It relates to the career of William Jamieson, jeweller, who was trained
in Aberdeen by James Gordon from 1793 to 1800. He then went to
London to get further experience over six years as a journeyman 'in one
of the first Working Jewellers Shops of the Metropolis' before returning
to enter a co-partnership with George Roger, goldsmith and jeweller
of Broadstreet, Aberdeen, who had taken over James Gordon's workshop premises and retail business. Jamieson's London-acquired skills
and associated social polish as a fashionable jeweller, along with his
London connections, were an important feature of the new partnership: 'Mr Jamieson, before leaving London, settled correspondence with
some of the most eminent Houses in the city, so that regular supplies of
silver and plated work, in the newest and most approved stile, can be
depended on.'[104] The importance of London as a source of fashionable
goods is indicated elsewhere in early-nineteenth-century advertising,

as in the following from the *Caledonian Mercury*, placed by Robert Morton, Edinburgh jeweller and silversmith:

> New Jewellery & Plate Manufactory.
>
> Robert Morton, no 14 Princes Street, has the pleasure of acquainting the public that the very extensive purchases made by him when in London, Sheffield and Birmingham, is now arrived, and form the first selection for elegance and variety in Great Britain.
>
> Silver Tea Sets, New and Rich Plated Goods of every description, particularly dishes with covers in sets. Dining and Supper Services, double plated and edged with stout silver gadroon sufficiently strong to stand use for half a century . . .[105]

By the early nineteenth century, the relationship between Scottish artisans and London post-apprenticeship training and contacts was well established. Certain Scottish firms and individuals made extensive use of London supply networks and design copyright registration in London was employed to protect their creative interests. Big London-founded craftworking firms had Scottish branches by the 1820s. The London connection was cultivated throughout Scotland but was particularly marked in Edinburgh, with its burgeoning production of craft-made luxury consumer goods for elite markets. This is explored in the next chapter.

Notes

1. Glenn Adamson, ed., *The Craft Reader* (Oxford, 2010); Eberhard Bort, 'Review: Scottish Arts and Crafts', *Scottish Affairs*, 63 (2008), 163–9; Edward S. Cooke, 'Rural industry, village craft: The politics of modern globalized craft', Peter Dormer Lecture at the Royal College of Arts, London, 2009.
2. Peter Dormer, ed., *The Culture of Craft: Status and Future* (Manchester, 1997).
3. Peter Korn, *Why We Make Things and Why It Matters: The Education of a Craftsman* (Boston, 2013).
4. David Esterly, *The Lost Carving: A Journey to the Heart of Making* (London, 2012).
5. Edmund de Waal, *The White Road: Journey into an Obsession* (London, 2015).
6. Perry's exhibition and original installation was remounted in 2020.
7. Roger Kneebone, *Expert: Understanding the Path to Mastery* (London, 2020).
8. Richard Sennet, *The Craftsman* (New Haven and London, 2008).
9. Glenn Adamson, *The Invention of Craft* (London, 2013), chapter 4 'Memory'.
10. Adamson, *The Craft Reader*.

11. Christopher Frayling, *Craftsmanship: Towards a New Bauhaus* (London, 2011).

12. Kate Smith, *Material Goods, Moving Hands: Perceiving Production in England, 1700–1830* (Manchester, 2014).

13. Tanya Harrod, *The Last Sane Man: Michael Cardew: Modern Pots, Colonialism and Counter Culture* (New Haven, 2012); Tanya Harrod, *The Crafts in Britain in the Twentieth Century* (New Haven and London, 1999).

14. Rozsika Parker, *The Subversive Stitch: Embroidery and the Making of the Feminine* (London, 1984).

15. See Glenn Adamson, *Fewer, Better Things: The Hidden Wisdom of Objects* (London, 2018).

16. Stephanie Bunn and Victoria Mitchell, eds, *The Material Culture of Basketry: Practice, Skill and Embodied Knowledge* (London, 2020).

17. Kevin Petrie and Andrew Livingstone, eds, *The Ceramics Reader* (London, 2020).

18. 'Fleece to Fashion: Economies and cultures of knitting in modern Scotland', AHRC funded project, 2018–21; Lynn Abrams, 'Knitting, autonomy and identity: The role of hand-knitting in the construction of women's sense of self in an island community, Shetland, c.1850–2000', *Textile History*, 37:2 (2006), 149–65.

19. Susan Luckman and Nicola Thomas, *Craft Economies* (London, 2017).

20. See Crafts Council website, www.craftscouncil.org.uk (last accessed 15 February 2021).

21. Craftivism: Gentle Protest, BBC Radio 4, 'Four Thought', first broadcast 23 September 2020; Anthea Black and Nicole Burisch, eds, *The New Politics of the Handmade: Craft, Art and Design* (London, 2020).

22. Alyce McGovern, *Craftivism and Yarn Bombing. A Criminological Exploration* (London, 2019).

23. Sinikka Pöllänen, 'The meaning of craft: Craft makers' descriptions of craft as an occupation', *Scandinavian Journal of Occupational Therapy*, 20:3 (2013), 217–27.

24. Jackson Lears, 'Art for life's sake. Craft and the quest for wholeness in American culture', *Journal of Modern Craft*, 12:2 (2019), 161–72.

25. See Chapter 3.

26. Adamson, *Invention of Craft*, 141–3.

27. Tanya Harrod and Miriam Rosser-Owen, 'Introduction: Middle Eastern Crafts', *Journal of Modern Craft*, 13:1 (2020), 1–5.

28. Shelagh Ogilvie, *The European Guilds: An Economic Analysis* (Princeton, 2019).

29. Stana Nenadic, 'Architect-builders in London and Edinburgh c.1750–1800 and the market for expertise', *Historical Journal*, 55:3 (2012), 1–21.

30. Stana Nenadic, 'Gender and the rhetoric of business success: The impact on women entrepreneurs in the later nineteenth century,' in Nigel Goose, ed., *Women's Work in Industrial England c.1700–1900* (Hatfield, 2007).

31. *Business History Review*, 85:2 (2011), special edition, 'The Creative Industries in History'; Morris Hargreaves McIntyre, *Consuming Craft: The Contemporary Craft Market in a Changing Economy*, Crafts Council Report, 2010.
32. Iorwerth Prothero, *Radical Artisans in England and France, 1830–1870* (Cambridge, 1997).
33. T. C. Smout, *A Century of the Scottish People, 1830–1950* (London, 1986). For artisan alienation, see Bert de Munck, 'Artisans, products and gifts: Rethinking the history of material culture in early-modern Europe', *Past and Present*, 224:1 (2014), 39–74.
34. W. Hamish Fraser, 'The working class', in W. Hamish Fraser and Irene Maver, eds, *Glasgow Vol. 2: 1830–1912* (Manchester, 1996), 300.
35. Geoffrey Crossick, ed., *The Artisan and the European Town, 1500–1900* (London, 1997).
36. Vanessa May, 'Belonging from afar: Nostalgia, time and memory', *Sociological Review*, 65:2 (2017), 401–15; John D. Rosenberg, *Elegy for an Age: The Presence of the Past in Victorian Literature* (London, 2005).
37. Elizabeth Cumming, *Hand, Heart and Soul: The Arts and Crafts Movement in Scotland* (Edinburgh, 2006); Annette Carruthers, *Arts and Crafts Movement in Scotland* (New Haven, 2013); Imogen Hart, *Arts and Crafts Objects* (Manchester, 2010).
38. Carruthers, *Arts and Crafts*, considers several architects and their craftsmen; Annette Carruthers, 'William Craigie of Kirkwall and the furnishing of Melsetter House, Hoy', *Regional Furniture*, 16:1 (2002), 108–20.
39. Charles Sabel and Jonathan Zeitlin, 'Historical alternatives to mass production: Politics, markets and technology in nineteenth century industrialization', *Past and Present*, 108 (1985), 133–76; Stana Nenadic, 'The small family firm in Victorian Britain', *Business History*, 35 (1993), 86–114.
40. Stana Nenadic and Sally Tuckett, *Colouring the Nation. The Turkey Red Printed Cotton Industry in Nineteenth-Century Scotland* (Edinburgh, 2013).
41. Francesca Carnevali, 'Fashioning luxury for factory girls. American jewelry, 1860–1914', *Business History Review*, 85:2 (2011), 295–317; Francesca Carnevali, 'Golden opportunities: Jewellery making in Birmingham between mass production and speciality', *Enterprise and Society*, 4:2 (2003), 248–78.
42. W. W. Knox, *Industrial Nation: Work, Culture and Society in Scotland, 1800–Present* (Edinburgh, 1999).
43. On the Highlands, see Janice Helland, *British and Irish Home Arts and Industries, 1880–1914: Marketing Craft, Making Fashion* (Dublin, 2011).
44. Stana Nenadic, 'Industrialisation and the Scottish people', in T. M. Devine and J. Wormald, eds, *Oxford Handbook of Modern Scottish History* (Oxford, 2012), 405–22.
45. Jeffrey Auerbach and Peter Hoffenberg, eds, *Britain, the Empire and the World at the Great Exhibition of 1851* (Aldershot, 2008).

46. Stana Nenadic, 'Exhibiting India in nineteenth-century Scotland and the impact on commerce, industry and popular culture', *Journal of Scottish Historical Studies*, 34:1 (2014), 67–89; Saloni Mathur, *India by Design. Colonial History and Cultural Display* (Berkeley, 2007); Helland, *British and Irish Home Arts and Industries*; Peter H. Hoffenberg, 'Promoting traditional Indian art at home and abroad: *The Journal of Indian Art and Industry*, 1884–1917', *Victorian Periodicals Review*, 37:2 (2004), 192–213.
47. See Aaron Allen, *Building Early Modern Edinburgh. A Social History of Craftwork and Incorporation* (Edinburgh, 2018).
48. Michael Lynch, ed., *The Early Modern Scottish Town* (London, 1986).
49. James McGrath, 'The medieval and early modern burgh', in T. M. Devine and Gordon Jackson, eds, *Glasgow. Vol. 1 Beginnings to 1830* (Manchester, 1995), 17–62; Michael Lynch, *Edinburgh and the Reformation* (Edinburgh, 1981).
50. McGrath, *Glasgow*, 53.
51. Aaron M. Allen, *The Locksmiths Craft in Early Modern Edinburgh* (Edinburgh, 2007).
52. K. Tawny Paul, 'Credit, reputation and masculinity in British urban commerce. Edinburgh c.1710–70', *Economic History Review*, 66:1 (2013), 226–48.
53. Stana Nenadic, 'The rights, rituals and sites of business, 1650–1820', *A Cultural History of Business Vol. 5* (Bloomsbury, forthcoming, 2022).
54. *Information for the Hair Dressers in Edinburgh: Against the Incorporation of Barbers*, Second Edition, 7 March 1758. Pamphlet reproduced in *Econ Journal Watch*, 15:3 (2018), 382–96.
55. Signet Library Pamphlet Collection details these disputes. Francis Bamford, 'A dictionary of Edinburgh wrights and furniture makers, 1660–1840', *Furniture History*, 19 (1983), 1–137.
56. Morris M. Kleiner, *Licensing Occupations: Ensuring Quality or Restricting Competition?* (Michigan, 2006).
57. See for example, Rodney R. Dietert and Janice Dietert, 'The Edinburgh Goldsmiths: Biographical Information for Freemen, Apprentices and Journeymen', Cornell University c.2010.
58. Alysa Levene, 'Honesty, sobriety and diligence: Master-apprentice relations in eighteenth- and nineteenth-century England', *Social History*, 33 (2008), 183–200; Chris Minns and Patrick Wallis, 'Rules and reality: Quantifying the practice of apprenticeship in early modern England', *Economic History Review*, 65:2 (2012), 556–79; William Farrell and Tim Reinke-Williams, 'Apprentice migration to early modern London: A four nations approach', Paper to Economic History Society Annual Conference, Cambridge, April 2016.
59. See S. R. Epstein, 'Craft guilds in the early modern economy: A discussion', *Economic History Review*, 61:1 (2008), 155–74.
60. Richard Saville, *Bank of Scotland: A History, 1695–1995* (Edinburgh, 1996), table 4.1.

61. Stuart Handley, 'Heriot, George (1563–1624)', *Oxford Dictionary of National Biography* [ODNB], 2004.

62. William Irvine Fortescue, 'James Ker, Member of Parliament for Edinburgh, 1747–1754', *Book of the Old Edinburgh Club*, New Series, 10 (2014), 17–44.

63. For an overview see Bob Harris and Charles McKean, *The Scottish Town in the Age of Enlightenment 1740–1820* (Edinburgh, 2014).

64. Signet Library, 'State of the Mutual Process. John Bird late of London, Potter and Robert Dinwiddie, Merchant in London, Laurence Dinwiddie and Patrick Nisbet, Merchants in Glasgow and Robert Finlay Tanner There, 1 November 1750'. Also, 'The Petition of Laurence Dinwiddie, Merchant and Late Provost of Glasgow, Patrick Nisbet Merchant and Robert Finlay Tanner There, and Robert Dinwiddie Merchant in London. Proprietors of a Delftware Factory Lately Set up in Glasgow. 8 January 1751'.

65. See David H. Caldwell and Valerie E. Dean, 'The pottery industry at Throsk, Stirlingshire, in the 17th and early 18th century', *Post-Medieval Archaeology*, 26 (1992), 1–46.

66. Signet Library, 'State of the Mutual Process. John Bird and Robert Dinwiddie', 16–17.

67. Brian J. Bloice, 'Norfolk House, Lambeth. Excavations at a Delftware kiln site, 1968', *Post Medieval Archaeology*, 5 (1971), 99–159.

68. Signet Library, 'State of the Mutual Process. John Bird and Robert Dinwiddie'.

69. James Clelland, *The Rise and Progress of the City of Glasgow* (Glasgow, 1820), 93; George Haggarty, *Glasgow Delftfield Ceramic Resource Disk 18th Century Earthenware and Creamware*, National Museum of Scotland, 2014.

70. Jennifer Tann, 'Watt, James (1736–1819)', *ODNB*, 2004.

71. Richard Hills, 'James Watt and the Delftfield Pottery, Glasgow', *Proceedings of the Society of Antiquaries of Scotland*, 131 (2001), 375–420, 395.

72. Cited in Hills, 'James Watt and Delftfield', 389.

73. Lorna Weatherill, *The Pottery Trade and North Staffordshire, 1660–1760* (Manchester, 1971), 52–3 gives data on works sizes.

74. *Glasgow Herald*, 2 August 1822.

75. National Records of Scotland [NRS]. NG1. Board of Manufactures, General and Manufacturing Records, 1727–1930.

76. Alasdair J. Durie, *The Scottish Linen Industry in the Eighteenth Century* (Edinburgh, 1979).

77. Duncan Thomson, *A History of the Scottish National Portrait Gallery* (2011).

78. *Report of a Committee of the Trustees for the Encouragement of Manufactures in Scotland, to the said Trustees, within the last Six Months; Containing A Statement of the Establishment, Funds, and Expenditure of the Board.* Ordered by the House of Commons, 27 April 1830.

79. J. Mason, 'The Edinburgh School of Design', *Book of the Old Edinburgh Club*, 27 (1949), 67–97.
80. *Report of a Committee of the Trustees*, Appendix 22.
81. Stana Nenadic, 'Designers in the nineteenth-century Scottish fancy textile industry: Education, employment and exhibition', *Journal of Design History*, 27:2 (2014), 115–31.
82. NRS. NG1/1/30. Board of Manufactures, General and Manufacturing Records, 1727–1930. Minutes, 22 January 1800.
83. See *Edinburgh Advertiser*, 7 December 1804.
84. NRS. NG1/1/32. Board of Manufactures. Minutes, 22 June 1808, 23 November 1808.
85. NRS. NG1/1/28. Board of Manufactures. Minutes, 18 December 1793, 8 June 1794.
86. *Report of a Committee of the Trustees*, Appendix 38.
87. NRS. NG1/3/27. Board of Manufactures. Letter to C. H. Wilson, Esq., Director of the Government School of Design, Glasgow, 1 March 1850.
88. Stana Nenadic and Sally Tuckett, 'Artisans and aristocrats in nineteenth-century Scotland', *Scottish Historical Review*, 95:2 (2016), 203–29.
89. NRS. NG1/3/26. Board of Manufactures. Minutes, 26 September 1840.
90. Ibid., 4 April 1840.
91. Ibid., 31 January 1844.
92. Helen E. Smailes, 'Campbell, Thomas (1790–1858)', *ODNB*, 2004.
93. NRS. GD113/5/30. Papers of the Innes Family of Stow. Letter, 31 March 1821.
94. *Report of a Committee of the Trustees*, 10.
95. NRS. NG1/1/28. Board of Manufactures. Minutes, 22 February 1794.
96. Robert Campbell, *The London Tradesman: Being a Compendious View of All the Trades, Professions, Arts, both Liberal and Mechanic now Practiced in the Cities of London and Westminster* (London, 1747).
97. Farrell and Reinke-Williams, 'Apprentice migration'.
98. NRS. RH15/69. Duncan Campbell, Indigo Merchant. Business papers and correspondence. Campbell returned to Edinburgh in his later career to set up a 'blew' works making dyes and bleaches, where he took on further apprentices.
99. NRS. RH15/69/5. Duncan Campbell papers.
100. *Edinburgh and Leith Directory*, 1800, 48–9.
101. Nenadic, 'Architect-builders'.
102. British Library. Additional Manuscript 42556, fol. 2. Diary of Samuel Kevan (1764–1836), Journeyman of Southwark; Jerry White, *A Great and Monstrous Thing: London in the Eighteenth Century* (Cambridge, MA, 2013), 99.
103. Stana Nenadic, ed., *Scots in London in the Eighteenth Century* (Lewisburg, 2010).
104. *Aberdeen Press and Journal*, 6 October 1805.
105. *Caledonian Mercury*, 3 January 1807.

1

Edinburgh and the Luxury Crafts

THE CRAFT SECTOR IN Edinburgh was similar to that in many major cities, including Glasgow, with large numbers of service crafts in the building trades embracing masons and joiners, the clothing crafts such as tailors and dressmakers and the food crafts including bakers and butchers. But the city also had a distinctive craft profile shaped by its role as a centre for elite housing and consumption, and in providing educational and professional services. By the mid nineteenth century Edinburgh was a tourist destination and a transport intersection for visitors travelling to other places in Scotland, which also supported the craft economy.

One area of craft focus was printing and engraving. In 1841, the *Post Office Directory* listed almost 10 per cent of business entries as connected in some way with paper, prints, books and stationery.[1] The equivalent figure for Glasgow was 6 per cent, with a detailed comparison revealing more high-skill engravers and fine book printers and binders in Edinburgh than Glasgow.[2] This configuration of craft activity in the capital, which grew to prominence in the eighteenth century, was waning by the 1860s as technologies for generating printed images changed and factory production became the norm. The sector in 1911 accounted for 4 per cent of businesses listed in the *Directories* for both cities, marking a particularly dramatic fall in Edinburgh where the absolute as well as the relative numbers of artisans declined. The printing industry remained important in Edinburgh and print workers were still a craft-trained elite, with important centres of female skilled labour in some firms.[3] But workplaces were mostly large and other than in bookbinding, few craftworkers were self-employed or workshop based.

The metal and machinery crafts were found in both Edinburgh and Glasgow in large numbers, though their presence, numerically and relative to other sectors, was greater in the latter than the former. The precious-metal crafts were important in both cities and saw a rising percentage of *Directory*-listed local businesses relative to total populations, going from 8 to 11 per cent in Edinburgh between 1841 and 1911 and 7 to 11 per cent in Glasgow. However, the makeup of these businesses and associated craft communities differed, reflecting the distinctive configurations of the populations they served. In Edinburgh, there were large numbers of silversmiths making tableware and presentation pieces, along with fine jewellery makers, all serving an established middle class and elite market. In Glasgow, by contrast, growth in the sector was driven by small-scale watchmaking firms, mostly working with bought-in components for sale to working- and lower-middle-class men.[4]

The clothing crafts, a sector dominated by female dressmakers and milliners was similarly prominent in both cities.[5] In Edinburgh in 1841, 42 per cent of *Directory*-listed firms were clothing related. Even in 1911, when consumer demand was increasingly met through the ready-made trade, 31 per cent of Glasgow businesses were concerned with dress in one form or another. The detail embedded in these figures is revealing and casts further light on the social configurations of the two cities, with Edinburgh having larger numbers of 'hatters' than Glasgow, along with court dress and uniform makers, largely catering for elite masculine needs. The clothing crafts collectively represented some of the key skills that were found in Edinburgh and cut across different business areas, as seen, for instance, in the 'hatter' trade. The hats that were made for rich men at this time were constructed from beaver and other animal skins, which was a different type of materials-based craft to that seen in women's millinery where felted wool or straw were usual. The Edinburgh 'hatter', whose materials were expensive, was aligned with other makers of fine goods in skins and leather such as glovers and shoemakers, bookbinders or trunk makers.[6] There were few hat makers of this sort in Glasgow.

Familiarity with and manipulation of specific materials is one of the primary features of craft identity, with skilled men and women trained in the haptic understanding of the basic materials on which their trade was based. Craftsmen educated through apprenticeships in one area retained their materials-focus despite changes in the things they made because it was the materials that gave them their skills. An illustration is provided by the production and sale of fancy leather and wood travelling cases, with interiors made up of individual components in glass, silver, ivory or tortoiseshell, which was a niche trade in Edinburgh and in other cities associated with a large elite or tourist market. The genesis of companies who produced such goods could be complex and varied. The firm of

W. & J. Milne of 126 Princes Street, in business from 1844 to c.1905, were celebrated 'box makers' who registered patents for some of their products.[7] The founder-owners had craft skills developed over several generations of family involvement in leather bookbinding and pocket-book making and therefore focused their workshop activities in these areas, buying in components such as glass or silverwares from other suppliers. Another firm producing similar high-quality boxes but with a different craft and material at its heart, was that of Thomas Johnston of 42 Hanover Street who advertised in the 1830s and 1840s and were best known as 'diamond paste and razor strop manufacturers'. Their portable dressing cases were aimed at male customers and were described as particularly suited 'to the tourist and the angler' and contained 'all that is requisite for comfortable shaving'.[8] Yet another firm in the 1850s who made 'Ladies and Gentleman's Travelling Dressing Cases' along with 'Travelling and Tourists Writing Cases, Flasks and Sandwich Boxes', was that of J. Stephenson of 13 Leith Street, whose advertising also proclaimed they were 'Comb Manufacturers to Her Majesty'.[9] High-quality combs were made of ivory or tortoiseshell. The firm of Wilson, Walker & Co. of Leeds, who made fine dressing cases which were sold in Edinburgh, came from a different direction. They exhibited at the 1851 Great Exhibition, where they were prizewinners, but their stand in Class 16 'Leather, Saddlery, Boots and Shoes' mostly comprised worked leather, chamois and certain industrial applications such as 'roller leather for silk and cotton spinning'.[10] They were mainly leather processors and carvers, taking supplies of hides from big tanning centres such as Bermondsey in London and selling on to specialist leather-goods makers like W. & J. Milne in Edinburgh.

Fancy boxes were covered with tooled or gilded leather, but the carcasses were made of wood and in many it was decorative elements comprising fine wood veneers and inlay that gave them beauty and appeal. These sorts of fancy boxes were the work of cabinetmakers and Edinburgh was notable for its numerous producers of fine furniture by cabinetmakers and upholsterers. The wood-based craft sector was equally important in Edinburgh and Glasgow, with the relative numbers of firms equivalent and consistent over the century. In both cities, 12 per cent of *Directory* listings were in the wood-based trades, but again the detail shows a nuanced story with a preponderance of the fine end of the craft in Edinburgh compared with the larger proportion of joiners and wrights in Glasgow. Alongside the Edinburgh cabinetmakers was an important niche trade, that of carvers and gilders who worked on small furniture items, interior décor and mirror and picture frames.

This range of craft producers with a focus on luxury furnishing goods for wealthy customers, reflected the evolution of the city as a centre for elite residence. This in turn owed much to the mid-eighteenth-century political decision to build a 'new town' housing development befitting a national capital.

CRAFTWORKING IN THE NEW TOWN

The early history of Edinburgh as a centre of court and church and with easy links to Europe and London was associated with the development of the luxury crafts. These were dominated by gold- and silversmiths, who acted as bankers to the Crown and established traditions of fine metalwork that survived and thrived into the nineteenth century and beyond. Skilled tradesmen and artists from the continent commonly visited Edinburgh and nearby country houses to undertake such specialist work as the elaborate painted interiors that were fashionable in the seventeenth century and some then remained in Scotland. The departure of the court to London, from 1603, taking a tranche of Scotland's elite to England, coupled with civil war and economic depression, undermined high-end craftwork, though there were short-lived attempts by pre-Union government to encourage skilled Picardy weavers to settle in the capital and develop fine textile making. There were similar initiatives in the 1720s.[11] The situation in Edinburgh in the early eighteenth century was one of enduring stagnation. Yes, the craft elites dominated the city as an administrative and economic entity and provincial gentlemen visited Edinburgh to furnish their country houses and purchase clothing and plate, but much of what they acquired was imported from London and Europe with the quality of craftwork in the capital city similar to that of country areas. So, when gentry families sought to own fashionable sets of dining chairs at a fraction of the price charged in London, they would borrow a London-made example from a richer kinsman and have it copied locally by craftsmen with skill equal to those in the capital.[12]

Mid-eighteenth-century Edinburgh was noted for its poor urban environment, the legacy of incoherent building over centuries and want of investment in infrastructure. The Jacobite rebellion and its aftermath reinforced a sense of backwardness and crisis. The need for a concerted initiative to change Edinburgh's fortunes was widely accepted and this began in 1752 with the publication of a visionary blueprint for transforming the capital. Edinburgh's first New Town was designed to stimulate national prosperity through investment in commercial infrastructure and elite housing and thereby bring about a 'spirit of industry and improvement'. The model was London and the context decades of economic decline and physical deterioration.

> The meanness of Edinburgh has been too long an obstruction to our improvement, and a reproach to Scotland. The increase of our people, the extension of our commerce, and the honour of the nation, are all concerned in the success of this project.[13]

Building the first New Town from the 1760s, and then the second and third 'new towns' in the early nineteenth century, gave unprecedented opportunities for expansion and skill development in the different branches of the building crafts along with house decorators, glaziers and fancy-metal smiths. Cabinetmakers were in demand, along with painters, gilders and print engravers for room decoration. Ceramic and crystal glassmakers and domestic textile designers and weavers saw business increase as the wealthy flocked to Edinburgh for residence and consumption. Industrial and high-technology firms developed lines of fine crafted production for New Town houses, such as the Carron Iron Works near Falkirk, which in addition to its output of cannon balls and iron girders, also made ironwork for decorative railings, rainwater goods and especially its registered fire grates and stoves, elegantly designed, with matching fenders and fire irons.[14] Housing provision and workshop space for the 'better class of artisan', mainly in the secondary streets and lanes, were integral to the New Town plan of 1752, which meant that Edinburgh's craft community not only flourished on the opportunities provided by servicing the wealthy who gravitated to this purpose-designed suburb, they also lived and worked there.[15]

The attractions of a New Town location for craftworkers, though complex and varied, were rooted in the pressures generated by expansion of people and workshops in the Old Town, with its ancient tenements and crowded back lanes. Edinburgh's Dean of Guild Court records are full of complaints over the inappropriate use of tenement flats for workshop production, with noisy machinery and polluting materials that inconvenienced domestic residents and threatened buildings.[16] In June 1782, for example, John Dundas, Clerk to the Signet living in Parliament Close, raised a complaint about a wright's shop:

> The petitioner owns one of the uppermost flats and his complaint is against Andrew Baxter, journeyman wright, who has rented one of the garrets above him and works there, occasionally at night by candlelight. He cites the Police Act as prohibiting such work in garrets. Having challenged Baxter he refuses to 'give over'.[17]

Dangerous stoves and illegal chimneys were a particular cause for concern, as revealed in January 1809 when several residents of a Mylnes
Court tenement, just off the High Street, lodged a complaint against
Alexander Martin, a plasterer engaged in the interior decoration trade,
who 'about two years ago, placed a stove for preparing stucco in his
premises, situated below all three of the petitioners. The stove stands on
the floor but has a pipe to conduct the smoke to a chimney.' The Dean
of Guild was sufficiently impressed by the seriousness of the situation
that the plasterer was ordered to remove the offending stove.[18] Printers
were another concern, as seen in complaints against Grant & Moire in
Paterson's Court in 1792 because of large vats of oil and open fires that
were used in the business. Or, more alarming still, a complaint of 1770
against Mr Esplin, wallpaper printer, in Bell's Wynd whose equipment
in a building described as 'weak and frail' was threatening to bring the
tenement crashing down.[19]

Anxieties such as these were well founded, as hundreds of residents
and dozens of business owners found on the night of 15 November 1824
when a great fire broke out in a large tenement in Old Assembly Close,
near Parliament Square. It started in the printing office of the engravers
James Kirkwood & Sons when an unattended pot of linseed oil, being
heated in preparation for making copperplate printing ink, burst into
flames and quickly spread into adjoining buildings.[20] Over the next four
days, numerous business premises and flats were destroyed, 13 lives were
lost and hundreds rendered homeless. On finding themselves burned out
of their premises, James Kirkwood & Sons, a large and successful firm,
quickly relocated to South St Andrew's Street in the New Town, where
they were based for twenty-five years.[21] The founder of the firm, Robert,
came from Perth, where he may have been trained and was in business
in Edinburgh, a guild brother and then burgess, from 1786. He was succeeded by his son James in 1820, the latter apprentice trained in London
to the engraver James Heath – 'engraver to the King' – who ran a significant workshop and training academy and was noted for topographical prints. The firm of Kirkwood & Sons had a complex portfolio that
included map and banknote engraving. They held large stocks of 'super-
fine writing papers and ruled ledgers and account books'.[22] The grand-
son of the founder established a branch of the firm in Dublin in 1826,
where he developed a line of marine and military prints.[23] The firm took
some of their Scottish skilled workmen to Ireland, including Thomas
Knox, the principal assistant and manager. Several Kirkwood apprentices, including William Murphy, apprenticed in 1812 and a burgess
in Edinburgh from 1839, established successful engraving firms.[24] As a

centre for print production and engraver training, businesses elsewhere recruited skilled labour in Edinburgh. A *Scotsman* advert of 16 February 1825, placed by Samuel Tompkin of Sheffield, illustrates: 'Engraver Wanted. A steady person, qualified to engrave in good style, plain and ornamental, writing, vignettes etc.'

A second firm that suffered in the 1824 fire was that of Robert Scott & Sons. Robert Scott was born in Lanark in 1777 where his father was a skinner. He was apprenticed to the Edinburgh engraver and printer Alexander Robertson in 1787, at his premises in the Luckenbooths, and trained at the Board of Manufactures design school. After the fire, Scott moved his large workshop to 65 Princes Street where, for over 20 years he produced prints of Scottish country seats and other notable buildings for the *Scots Magazine* and employed many assistants and apprentices. Two of his sons were trained in the business in the early 1820s, also attending design-school classes. Both made their careers in London.[25] The fire of 1824 was an opportunity for positive relocation for big firms like those of Scott or Kirkwood, but for smaller undertakings it was disruptive and damaging. Charles Thomson, engraver and copperplate printer, provided an account of the impact when he advertised in the *Scotsman*.

> Charles Thomson, engraver, regrets that, in consequence of the late calamitous Fires, he has had occasion twice to remove his Work Shops: and begs to mention, that he is now to be found at No. 19 SHAKESPEARE SQUARE, immediately behind the Theatre Royal. C.T. desires to apologise to his employers for the disappointment they have met with, and now respectfully informs them, that he is ready to receive their further orders, which he will endeavour to execute with promptitude and accuracy.[26]

Thomson moved several times thereafter before returning to the High Street in 1834.[27]

Fires were not the only reason for moving to the New Town. For most, it was proximity to elite customers and opportunities to advance an enterprise begun elsewhere that prompted relocation, as illustrated by John Steell, carver, gilder and print seller. Steell, born in 1779, arrived in Edinburgh in 1806 having run a business in Aberdeen, advertising his removal in the press and announcing he was commencing in Leith offering 'house and ship carving, gilding and print selling in all their various branches'. He also sold paper, articles for ladies' fancywork and artist materials.[28] Within a couple of years, Steell relocated to the foot of Calton Hill on the eastern fringe of the New Town, where he also had a house and at the height of his success *c.*1815 he occupied premises at 34 Princes Street, Edinburgh's premier shopping street. Two years later, his business was in crisis, which he attributed to losses made on portrait prints and inaccurate estimates for the time involved in major interior carving commissions. Taken into a bankruptcy, Steell moved to a cheaper shop and workshop in Leith Street, where he employed a shop man, three workmen and eight apprentices, the latter an unusually large group of junior workers paying for their training.[29] His was a major business with almost £8,000 due to creditors and c.£2,000 owed in unpaid debts, many from fellow Edinburgh engravers and publishers. His main creditor was the Calton Society of Incorporated Trades, of which he was a prominent member. Another was W. R. Ackermann of London, a notable print retailer and supplier of artist materials. Steell's business activity is apparent from the 'stock in trade', which included large numbers of British and Dutch prints for sale, gilded frames and mountings, mirrors and mirror frames, carved pieces, chimney ornaments, artists' materials, paints, brushes, pencils, sketch books and all manner of paper, plain and fancy. Steell survived sequestration and remained active as a 'carver and gilder', moving back into the New Town at Hanover Street and then North St David's Street by the early 1830s. In 1838, now semi-retired, he was living again at Calton Hill and gave evening classes in 'ornamental modelling' at the Edinburgh School of Arts for the Instruction of Mechanics.[30] Steell's son, who trained as a carver and gilder alongside his father, was the sculptor Sir John Steell, famous for public art such as the 1846 memorial statue of Walter Scott on Princes Street.[31]

Areas close to the New Town were densely settled with craft businesses like those of John Steell, particularly, as in this instance, to the east around Calton Hill, Greenside, Leith Street and Shakespeare Square, which also gave easy access to the Old Town via North Bridge. But it was in the secondary streets of the New Town itself – notably Rose Street and Thistle Street – where the first New Town plan made specific provision for artisans. An advertisement of 1827 for the sale of properties in Rose Street reveals the proximity of domestic and commercial space, as well as the rentals charged: 'Premises, no. 86 Rose Street consisting of – 1st, Shop, two rooms etc possessed by Mr Steele, tinsmith, rent £26. House below, possessed by Mr Horsburgh, shoemaker, rent £5 10s; workshop below, possessed by Mr Roxburgh, cooper, rent £4 10s.'[32] Next door, at 88 Rose Street, was a shop, two rooms, plus a bakehouse and cellar rented annually for £25 with a house behind, along with a bakehouse, entered via 90 Rose Street, at a rent of £12. The purchase price for the first building was £460 and £500 for the second. Like similarly overcrowded buildings in the Old Town, with a mix of workshops and houses, fires in Rose Street were commonplace, though less damaging

Figure 1.1   Hamilton & Inches, goldsmiths and silversmiths. George Street, Edinburgh, c.1895. © HES.

due to newer building materials and easier access for fire engines. 'Early yesterday morning a fire broke out in a back lane in Rose Street, in the tenement occupied as workshops by Mr Sommerville, painter, and Mr Hislop, dyer. The engines were soon on the spot and the fire was got out without doing much damage.'[33]

The most prestigious New Town commercial streets were Princes Street and George Street and though retail premises dominated the street fronts, many firms also maintained workshops for their craftsmen with obvious economic benefits to be had when these were close to warerooms. An example is illustrated in an advertisement of 1827 for 'a large front double shop or wareroom, with a large workshop behind' which was available to rent. The workshop, 75 feet long, was 'well lighted, both from side and sky-lights' and deemed suitable for 'a cabinetmaker, upholsterer [or] printing office etc . . . such premises are not always to be found, having both workshop and warehouse connected'.[34] Such proximity was clearly desirable for management and because many proprietors were also practising master craftsmen, active in apprentice training and bench work. Moreover, craftsmen were routinely called into the shop for customer advice and customers visited workshops to see commissions in progress. But having the two together could create problems around the exposure of genteel customers to noxious manufacturing processes and working men whose numbers could be considerable. For instance, John Taylor & Co., sometimes styled 'Cabinetmakers to the Queen', with retail and workshop premises in West Thistle Street in the 1820s, moving to 109 Princes Street by the 1840s, employed 90 men and four apprentices at the census of 1851.[35] Problems around customer–worker contact were resolved through entrances on separate streets, as is detailed in an account of an overnight theft of goods worth £600 from the premises of David Hodges, a high-quality jeweller and silversmith specialising in tableware. The business occupied a front shop at 11 George Street with a basement below 'which he uses as a workshop', the latter entered from a lane behind George Street, via a door onto a common stair 'through which the tradesmen enter to their work', thus avoiding the elegant wareroom. Security was maintained between the shop and workshop, but a suspect customer had asked to see the workshop and in the process of being shown round was thought to have devised a way of undertaking the theft via the back door in the lane.[36]

The extent of some craft-based businesses in the New Town's principal streets can be seen through insurance records as well as employee numbers. At the east end of Princes Street, on the corner with North Bridge, was a notable building comprising the warerooms, workshop and stores of William Trotter, the famous cabinetmaker, who was also a leading figure in the town council and Lord Provost during the 1820s.[37] The premises of the firm, then known as Young, Trotter & Hamilton, were insured through the London-based Sun Alliance company and in 1792 the business comprised utensils and stock in the warehouse valued at £900; mirrors valued at £100; utensils and stock in the workshop valued at £1,000 and timber in the yard valued at £100 – making a total valuation of £2,100. This was similar to insurance valuations for major textile manufacturing concerns.[38] Celebrated for its furniture as well as the spectacular shop, which had complete furnished rooms displayed, the business was a tourist attraction, detailed as a place to visit when in Edinburgh in Thomas Dibdin's *Tour in the North Counties of England and in Scotland* (1838).[39] Insurance records, compiled by provincial agents working for London firms, provide further insights to Edinburgh's craft businesses. In 1791, Angus McKennon, upholsterer, took out an insurance policy with Sun Alliance that listed his tenement in Bristo Street with a value of £100; tools and stock at £200; workshops and sheds adjoining his tenement at £50; timber in the yard at £200; and stock in his shops in Adams Square and South Bridge at £350, with further domestic goods also valued, making a total of £1,000 for insurance purposes.[40] John Corri, an instrument maker and sheet-music seller who occupied the first storey of a tenement on the west side of Bridge Street in the 1790s, had stock in his shop worth £1,000.[41]

FURNITURE MAKING

Cabinetmakers, the finest of the wood-based craftsmen, were a large and consistently important group in Edinburgh, supplying bespoke luxury furnishings for elite consumers as well as maintaining large stocks of made-up furniture and upholstery for retail through their shops and warehouses. The first in terms of reputation and innovation in the first half of the nineteenth century was William Trotter, mentioned above. Few records survive for his business, but a firm of equal size which encountered bankruptcy and generated a court record, gives insights into how such enterprises and their owners related to customers. David Gullan, cabinetmaker and upholsterer of Musselburgh, a small town a few miles to the east of Edinburgh and connected to the Edinburgh market, was sequestered for bankruptcy between 1813 and 1815.[42] Born in 1763, he was the son of John Gullan, a wright in Musselburgh[43] and related to a William Gullan, a wright in Thistle Street, Edinburgh, in the early nineteenth century. In addition to trade-related activity his family were significant property owners in Musselburgh. Little is known about David Gullan prior to sequestration, though he is recorded as a subscriber to Thomas Sheraton's *The Cabinetmaker and Upholsterer's Drawing Book* in 1793, when, as an apprentice-trained craftsman aged 30, he appears to have been extending his design credentials as maker of fine furniture.[44] The character of David Gullan's business and the furniture he made can be gauged from details contained in the sequestration records. Typical of the period, his domestic premises, with a byre for a cow and pigs, were on the same site as his workshop and wood yard. The commercial premises comprised –

1. 'ware room on the first floor', which contained some furniture items but was largely given over to carpets and rugs and textiles for making and covering upholstery.
2. 'feather garret above the shop' containing feathers and hair for stuffing.
3. 'wareroom upstairs' containing considerable quantities of made-up furniture, mirrors and framed prints.
4. 'counting room' with a 'glass case filled with hardware articles', plus a clock and a double desk with two stools. Elsewhere were listed a series of business books comprising mainly daybooks, starting in June 1797 and sasine records connected with his property holdings.

5. 'woodyard' containing wood in various lengths and breadths dominated by mahogany and some chestnut.
6. 'joiners shop' with six benches and 'wood for tent beds in the process of working'.
7. 'cabinet makers shop' with 11 benches and various items in the process of being made including two knife cases and a dozen chairs.
8. the 'west loft adjoining the wood yard', which was filled with old furniture.
9. the 'east loft' also with older items being stored.
10. the 'shade and saw pit in the park in front of D. Gullans dwelling house' where there was a variety of types of wood in storage. [45]

The value of the furniture in the warerooms was itemised and given a total of £643 3s 8d. The most valuable single item listed was a 'mahogany secretary & bookcase' at £12. Two sets of mahogany dining tables were valued at £14. There was a 'convex mirror' at £6. Forty mahogany chair frames were valued at £20 and three dozen bamboo chairs at £12 12s. The carpeting, given as 620 yards, was valued at £62 and 150 yards of 'passage carpeting' was valued at £15. There were 200 'pieces of paper' worth £15. Amongst the quantities of hardware items, the most valuable was a set of locks at £10 10s. Much of the stock, such as the carpeting, mirrors or bamboo furniture was bought in from elsewhere, as reflected in the numerous and geographically wide list of creditors. They included John Broom & Sons of Kidderminster, carpet makers, owed £345 4s 3d; and Stanton & Wilcoxon of London, looking-glass makers, owed £205 5s 10d. The Edinburgh creditors included brass founders, rope makers, carvers and gilders, lacemakers and other cabinetmaking firms who were part of Gullan's subcontracting network. Most of the made-up furniture was listed in multiples, suggesting a large holding of ready-to-purchase items for immediate delivery. In addition to chairs, it was small and fashionable pieces that were kept in the greatest quantities, such as '16 square bason stands, mahogany', worth £7 12s in total; or '7 ladies work boxes' at £2 2s for the lot; '4 mirrors with gilt frames' at £11 and '7 mirrors with mahogany frames' at £2 16s. Other multiples included dressing glasses with swing frames; dressing glasses with drawers; portable desks; bedroom candlesticks; oval trays; tea chests; knife cases; fire screen poles and footstools. Amongst the textiles were 100 yards of moreen, a heavily ribbed cotton or wool used in upholstery and 70 yards of Manchester stripe, a cotton used for loose covers, along with 40 yards of green linen, probably for window blinds.

David Gullan not only made furniture, he also, in common with other big cabinetmaking firms, offered a whole-house decorating service, the latter evident from the rolls of wallpaper he had in his warerooms along with sets of 'papered window cornices'.[46] Both before and after the sequestration, his name was listed in local newspaper advertising of 'houses for sale' as someone who acted as a 'house agent', charged with showing potential purchasers around domestic property in Musselburgh, which was doubtless a useful device for gaining future customers.[47] It was his service as a bespoke house furnisher and decorator that resulted in cash-flow troubles, leading to sequestration, as the following letter from a Highland nobleman, given in evidence at the court case, reveals.

Portobello, 6 Febry 1812. Mr David Gullan Sir, Before we proceed further in the business of furnishing Rosehaugh House, I consider it better to inform you on what terms I can purchase furniture from you. As to the painting and papering the house that shall be paid for at Martinmas 1812. The furniture to be paid one half the amount in July 1813 years and the other half at the same time the following year. The amount will be so large that I cann't to a certainty assure of earlier pays. The furniture to be delivered at your own risk in Rosehaugh House. My carts will be ready to carry the furniture when ever it arrives at Avoch Bay. I am offered the like terms from some of your profession, but as Lady McKenzie wishes you to have a preference I tender you the first offer. If these terms are agreeable to you, please to inform me by letter – Should you accept of my proposals, both Lady McKenzie and myself rely on the articles being of the very best quality. I am Sir, your most humble servant. Signed James McKenzie.[48]

Gullan noted with his signature at the end, 'Answered the letter and accepted the terms although distant payments.'

The letter was sent from Portobello, between Edinburgh and Musselburgh, which was a fashionable seaside and health resort. Sir James McKenzie of Scatwell was there with his wife who was pregnant with their first child.[49] McKenzie had recently inherited Rosehaugh House north of Inverness following the death of his father.[50] He was in his early forties and spent many years in Jamaica as a planter and military provisioning agent. Later he was MP for Ross-shire. His wife had also been in Jamaica and was a Highland heiress in her own right, but neither had secure incomes, though they owned extensive properties.[51] The furniture supplied by David Gullan was valued at above £2,000, a significant sum and McKenzie's payments were tardy. But though pursued for bankruptcy largely due to the McKenzie contract, David Gullan's business was sound; he survived the crisis and continued in partnership with George Gullan, his son, to his death in 1827. George Gullan was listed in the same cabinetmaking workshop through to the mid 1830s. Thereafter the premises were occupied by George Primrose, manufacturer of haircloth for upholstery, and the property, advertised for sale in 1840, was described as 'three tenements with a garden or area behind . . . which are extensive and well suited to manufactory or public work.'[52]

Gullan's firm, like that of William Trotter, was unusually large with workshop premises sufficient for almost 20 craftsmen when fully employed. More typical of the cabinetmaking sector in the first half of the century was the workshop occupied by James Dowell, whose business was sequestered in 1829. James Dowell, born in Caithness in 1793, was active in Edinburgh as a cabinetmaker and upholsterer in the 1820s.[53] He operated from premises built as a coach house in Thistle Street, behind St Andrews Church at the east end of George Street, where he also had his home, and before that from a nearby tenement at 41 Hanover Street.[54] He paid annual rent of £27 5s for the house and workshop.[55] His bankruptcy was precipitated by a serious fire, reported in the press in May 1828, resulting in the loss of the 'greater part of the furniture in progress'.[56] The sequestration revealed a modest domestic part of the building – just two rooms and a kitchen – with the contents of this and the workshop valued at £68 4s. A simple working space comprised a wood yard, a 'workshop above the dwelling house', a loft for storage above that and an 'engine house' containing a turning lathe and tools. The wood was worth £31 4s. At the sequestration it was noted,

> The Trustee informed the meeting that a considerably part of the stock of wood etc belonging to the bankrupt had been partially wrought up into various articles of household furniture which if sold in its present state would produce very little and much below its intrinsic value and the labour bestowed upon it. He therefore had employed the bankrupts apprentices at a weekly wage for sometime past in completing these articles by which considerable benefit was decreed on the Estate.[57]

The items in the workshop included 'nearly a dozen chairs blocked out, back legs awanting', valued at 18s; 2 loo tables, unfinished, valued at £3 1s 6d; 2 bookcases, unfinished, valued at £2 5s; and 2 armchairs, unfinished, valued at £1 4s. He had three 'working benches', along with a tool chest and 'a lot of working tools'. There was a turning lathe and tools in the 'engine house', which together were among the most valuable part of the estate valued at £4 10s. In addition to the wood in the wood yard, which was dominated by mahogany, there was also a 'stove and pipes for the workshop'. Another set of furniture belonging to the estate and not yet paid for, was identified as 'articles at Mr Reid's no. 5 Newington Place' comprising an easy chair, a small easy chair, a tea caddy, a dining table, a dressing table and bed steps. These latter, fully made up and delivered to a client in a middle-class suburb to the south of Edinburgh, were valued together at £20 2s.[58]

Though he continued in his original business and premises in Thistle Street for a short while after bankruptcy, Dowell shifted his activity towards furniture valuation for second-hand sales, a common secondary activity amongst cabinetmakers and then worked full-time as an auctioneer, mainly selling household furniture, pictures and antiques. His later firm, known as Dowell & Co., with showrooms in George Street, was highly successful and survived into the mid twentieth century. That he flourished as an auctioneer is testament to his enterprise and luck, for he was in the right place with premises in central Edinburgh at a time when the market for high-quality second-hand furniture was rising, a consequence of rapid expansion in elite and middle-class housing, and financial instability in 1830s and 1840s. James Dowell, now wealthy, was a town councillor for many years and in later life owned a townhouse in fashionable Royal Circus. His *Scotsman* obituary made no mention of his life as a craftsman, or his bankruptcy.[59] This is a typical advertisement from Dowell's early career as auctioneer, listing the highest quality furniture and effects of a finer sort than he ever made himself:

SALE OF EXCELLENT HOUSEHOLD FURNITURE, FRENCH WARDROBE, EIGHT-DAY CLOCK, PIANO-FORTE, CHAIR-BED and other effects to be SOLD by auction at 30 South Castle Street on Friday the 1st June.

An excellent assortment of FURNITURE consisting of Mahogany Sideboard, Spanish Wood Dining Tables, Haircloth Sofa and Chairs, Rosewood Diningroom Tables, Chairs and Sofa; Register Grate and other Grates, Fenders and Fire Irons, elegant Four Post Bed and Bedding, Tent Beds and Bedding, Chests of Drawers, Cheval Glass, Dressing Glasses, Carpets, Basin Stands, Bookcase and Drawers, China, Crystal and Table Stone, and Kitchen Articles.

Sale at 11 o'clock forenoon.

JAMES DOWELL, Auctioneer, Thistle Street, 23 May 1832.[60]

As a small-scale cabinetmaker with his own workshop and apprentices, but limited stock and no retail premises, James Dowell probably worked as a subcontractor for others from time to time. Bigger undertakings relied on an ability to increase their skilled workforce or subcontractors according to the flow of business, hence their geographical clustering. Another example of a New Town sequestration, viewed through the wages book, gives insights into how such complex relationships operated.[61] James Watson was a cabinetmaker and upholsterer with a substantial business, known as Watson & Co., which operated from warerooms and workshops in various premises in George Street from c.1830 to 1853. [62] His *Directory* listing also included mention of an undertaking business run in conjunction with the cabinetmaking concern – a common combination of interests. In his early commercial life, Watson lived in a house in Young Street, though later he occupied a flat above his business at 121 George Street. [63] The reasons for the sequestration are unclear, though it is possible that ill health leading to death in 1851 was a contributory factor. The wages book for Watson & Co. covers the period from 1844–52, including a year or so after Watson had died. [64] It offers details of payments for individual cabinetmakers, upholsterers, polishers, turners, apprentices and 'sewing room women'. The index lists 65 individuals termed 'cabinet makers' and 19 'upholsterers', all coming and going from the workshop, though most were only employed for short periods. One of them, a cabinetmaker called James McCallam, was employed throughout the years covered by the wages book. He had the highest wages listed and was probably the foreman. The sewing room women were a shifting group, but one, Ann Boak, was listed throughout and given her higher wages, was probably the forewoman.

The wages for most of the workers were fixed for a 60-hour, six-day week ranging from 25s for the foreman; 16s or 19s, varied according to skill and seniority, for the cabinetmakers; 15s for the upholsterers and polishers; and 5s or 6s for the apprentices, who worked a shorter week of 48–54 hours. Many of the skilled workers were also paid at piece rates, including those who in some periods were on weekly contracts. The weekly-employed men occasionally worked for longer hours and were paid overtime. The sewing room women, whose hours were unspecified, ranged in payments from 8s per week for the forewoman to 5s–6s for the others. With a shifting group of employees, many short-term, it is hard to gauge how many were in the workshop at any time, but a rough estimate suggests ten men, two apprentices and two female sewers. With short hours the norm, it is assumed that many also worked for other cabinetmaking firms or supplemented their earnings with other forms of work.

In addition to the wages paid and the hierarchies of workers involved in such a firm, the wages book offers insights to what was being made by Watson & Co. and some of the customers are listed. For example, John Brown, cabinetmaker on 16s per week, was in regular weekly employment throughout August 1848. In September he was on piecework with weekly hours ranging from 34 for the week at the start of the month and just 3.5 hours in the last week of the month. In early October he was paid for making specified objects, as follows –

A birch 4ft tent bed (for stock)	9s.6d
6 folding trunk stands (for Mr Burnett)	10s.6d
A birch French bed (for stock)	15s
A mahogany four post bed (for stock)	£2.15s
A rosewood pillar and claw for marquetery tabletop (for L.B. Hare Esq.)	9s.6d
2 ditto (for stock)	19s
A Grecian ottoman on rosewood mouldings and ball, lifting top (for Sir Robert Houston)	6s
A rosewood Elizabethan cross leg stool 21x30 inches (for Alexander Haig Esq.) [65]	12s

Payment for these items together, all undertaken between 6 and 13 October came to almost £6, which is a larger sum than John Brown commonly earned in a week, but he was acting on a subcontracting basis, possibly from a workshop of his own and employing lesser workers or apprentices to help. From 13 October onwards and for many months thereafter he returned to hourly paid work, with another burst of subcontracting for specified items in June 1849. Subcontracting such as this gives an insight into labour flexibility in the cabinetmaking trade, with skilled men sometimes working for themselves and sometimes for others, underlining the advantages of geographical concentration. The records also show the range of items commonly carried in stock by a fashionable George Street firm.

FURNITURE MAKING AFTER 1850

As the sector evolved through technical and market changes, including the wide introduction of steam power from the 1870s, there were changes too in the character of the entrepreneurs who dominated cabinetmaking. In the early nineteenth century, the typical business owner was an apprentice-trained craftsman who had progressed through the traditional stages to running his own workshop where he played a hands-on role in making fine furniture. But as businesses evolved such practical expertise was not enough and those other skills that were always part of the repertoire of the successful cabinetmaker, such as design, marketing and financial management, superseded the technical command of materials and haptic knowledge of making techniques.

In some instances, it was design that took the lead. The firm of Morison & Co., with retail premises in George Street and a workshop and stores in Gorgie in industrial west Edinburgh, provides an example. This celebrated late-Victorian cabinetmaking firm was established in the town of Ayr *c.*1808 by apprentice-trained craftsman Matthew Morison. It first migrated to Glasgow under the ownership of the founder's son and by the early 1860s was trading in Edinburgh. The firm was acquired by one of the works managers, William Reid, who was also trained at the bench and it was he who established the George Street premises which became the flagship site. There was a later branch in Manchester. There were two sons of this family in the third generation, both born and raised in Edinburgh's west end. They were practical men of business, but their route into cabinetmaking was different to that of their father, for they were sent to London for an art and design training and then travelled in Europe. On returning to take over the business, William R. Reid junior developed his own expertise in interior design schemes involving fine furniture made in historic, particularly French, neoclassical styles, which were in fashion. The firm worked with the notable architects of the day such as Robert Lorimer and supplied major corporate clients including the Royal Institution. Reid married the daughter of one of his business partners, a specialist in domestic plumbing, and together this educated, cultured and wealthy couple purchased and renovated Lauriston Castle in Cramond near Edinburgh, furnishing it with a mix of antiques and modern Morison & Co. wares designed in antique styles.[66]

Morison & Co. made handcrafted furniture for elite customers with conservative tastes. It was also well known for its commercial interiors and fittings, particularly first-class railway carriages, one of its most lucrative lines. The firm's owner in the third generation was childless and on reaching middle age sold the business to a London company in 1902 and retired to his antiques and collections, though William R. Reid did dabble for a time in architectural design.[67] Other notable later-nineteenth-century cabinetmaking firms in Edinburgh were similarly led by designer-entrepreneurs with a good knowledge of materials and making techniques but driven mainly by an eye for the market and an innovative aesthetic. Scott Morton & Co. and Whytock & Reid were both 'art furnishers', the former also notable woodcarvers, with strong associations with the Scottish Arts and Crafts movement. The firms worked closely with notable architects on house-furnishing schemes and Scott Morton & Co. was additionally famed for its commercial interiors for offices and luxury liners made in Glasgow's shipyards.[68] William Scott Morton, born in Lanarkshire in 1840, was the son of a wheelwright and joiner who also made furniture. He trained as a designer and architect and with his younger brother John, a mechanical engineer, set up in business in 1870 as a cabinetmaking and interior-design firm. Their workshop was in industrial west Edinburgh at Tynecastle and the offices in St Andrew Square. The Morton brothers had a strong socialist orientation, they were highly concerned with the welfare of their craft employees and espoused the moral value of handwork. Much of the output was bespoke, but the firm also had its more commercialised lines of business, including the production at Tynecastle of heavily embossed wallpaper which they called 'Tynecastle Tapestry', which was run as a separate undertaking. The brothers supplied designs for carpets produced by Templetons of Glasgow and for domestic iron wares manufactured by the Falkirk Iron Company. The firm survived through three generations, had branches in London and Manchester in the twentieth century and was taken over by Whytock & Reid in 1958.[69]

Many owners of craft businesses put high store by their design expertise or business acumen and as their companies evolved the distance between themselves and the workforce increased. Not all craftsman-entrepreneurs were talented designers or marketing men and the other feature of changing business profiles was the growing emphasis on management skills. Even in the eighteenth century in big cities like London, there was a trend towards two types of apprenticeship reflecting the importance of business knowledge. The first, of the conventional sort, involved training in the practical skills and techniques of the trade and the second, more costly and also more strictly controlled by the apprentice master, included practical skills developed alongside the business and financial skills and insights that were necessary to found, maintain and expand a business.[70] If a business developed, the latter increased in significance and hand knowledge or attainment, whilst necessary for credibility on the shop floor and for talking with clients, declined in importance. Another notable Edinburgh cabinetmaking firm of the second half of the nineteenth century illustrates this point. John Taylor & Sons was founded in Edinburgh in 1825 with premises in West Thistle Street and then Princes Street, where they had extensive retail premises with a workshop and offices behind, and later establishing a more extensive workshop – the Rosemount Cabinetworks – to the west of the city centre close to Haymarket railway station. They began as makers of artists' supplies and picture frames, became furniture makers and upholsterers, offered undertaking services and were house content appraisers and auctioneers. Mid century, the founder, John Taylor, who was a wright by training, born in Perthshire, employed 90 men and four apprentices, including his son, an apprentice cabinetmaker. There was a workforce of 300 by the 1890s. The firm survived well into the twentieth century and was highly innovative in its business practice, product lines and market understanding. By the early twentieth century it operated as a house letting and sales agent.

Its specialist lines in fine billiard tables and associated scoreboards, cues and other types of leisure-related furniture for the wealthy, which were developed from the 1880s, saw it through the difficult interwar years and beyond to 1945 when it ceased trading.[71]

CRAFTSMAN AS EMPLOYER AND EMPLOYEE

The last case highlights the fact that the world of the craftsman (and to an extent also the craftswoman) was divided between those that owned businesses and employed others and those who were employees.[72] It was always thus, though the language for describing such structures had changed, as had narratives regarding communities of men of similar training and values.[73] In the eighteenth century, when old systems of training were starting to wane, there was still an expectation of 'traditional hierarchy' within the skilled trades as the apprentice trained, one of a small and privileged group in any setting, served his time in a workshop, progressed to journeyman working for others and eventually became a master in his own right, with a workshop, apprentices and journeymen to command. This signalled established adult status and came with a place in the system that ordered the trade and its rights and authorities and in the governance of the towns where they operated. Career progression was a normal expectation, though, inevitably, many men never advanced to master status through the want of opportunity and the financial means to set up a workshop, and some small masters also worked on a casual or subcontracting basis for others. But what was always a pyramid-like structure with a few big masters at the top and many juniors at the base, became flatter and more divided as employment structures and technologies of craft production changed over the course of the nineteenth century.

The annual *Directory* for Edinburgh gives insights into continuities in the numbers of firms in the cabinetmaking and upholstery sector, but a close look at employment data from census records casts nuanced light on some the changes taking place in relationships between masters and men. In the census of 1841 for the city of Edinburgh and Leith, when the *Directory* for the year listed 187 individuals or firms under the 'wood and furniture trades', there were 1,194 cabinetmakers and upholsterers (counted as a single trade) enumerated as individuals and a further 209 woodcarvers and gilders. Amongst the cabinetmakers detailed in the census, 22 per cent were youths of less than 20 years old and amongst the woodcarvers and upholsterers it was 32 per cent. On average, it appears that businesses in this area employed five people per firm – a figure that is broadly consistent with the case illustrations above. Firms typical fell in a range of two to ten employees, with flexibility achieved for bigger businesses through subcontracting and piecework.[74]

By 1911, on the eve of the First World War, the trade had changed significantly in some of its areas, which is reflected in the census listings of occupations. Cabinetmakers were now enumerated separately from upholsterers and French polishers – that is, the finishing trades connected with furniture making.[75] And these different parts of what had formerly been a single craft area (albeit, undertaken by workers of different skill levels and reward) had very different organisational structures. Cabinetmakers in Edinburgh, according to the 1911 census, were made up of 72 employers, 620 employees and 33 described as working on their own account. This meant that the average size of an employment unit among cabinetmaking firms was seven individuals, all men. Again, there would have been a range and, as we have seen, there were some large firms in Edinburgh, but the figure is little different to what was usual mid century. The upholsterers were, however, different since here there were 20 employers listed in the census, for a male work force of 430 and 215 women, making an average workforce per employer of 30 individuals. Moreover, upholsterers, in addition to employing large numbers of adult women, equivalent to about a third of workers, also employed large numbers of young males in their teens. This was a classic factory-type workforce and though some upholsterers possessed skill, the training and consequent identities of these workers was not craft-defined. French polishing, which employed many women, was also characterised by large units, with an average of 55 employees per Edinburgh employer in 1911, though some almost certainly worked in smaller units for cabinetmakers, probably undertaking piecework. Woodcarvers and gilders, often linked to 'art manufacturers' in other materials and who were always identified as a distinct area of the wood trades, with 13 employers and 178 employees, almost all male, had an average workforce of 14 per employer in 1911. But this was also the trade that was most likely to generate self-employment, with 32 individuals in Edinburgh describing themselves as working on their own account.[76]

In short, what we see in this data is some evidence of continuity – particularly at the highly skilled end of the wood and furniture crafts, in cabinetmaking and in carving and gilding, which were doubtless sustained by the particular character of the market in Edinburgh for high-quality wares using the finest materials. But there was also deskilling in some of the finishing trades, where the materials were less valuable and the market wider, as it was for upholstery and French polishing, the latter designed to give a fashionable high gloss to woods of all value using a combination of shellac and abrasion and involving only limited technical competence in the polisher.[77]

The implications for employer and employees were significant. Owner-entrepreneurs were still heavily invested in an identity that embraced the core crafts and key haptic skills that exemplified their businesses where a high-skill workforce and bespoke output remained the norm – and this was evidenced through their membership of trades bodies and espousal of values associated with the Arts and Crafts movement, as in the case of Scott Morton & Co. But the identity and ambitions of the apprentice-trained but employed cabinetmaker or lesser-skilled upholsterers or polishers, who could never expect to progress to employer status, was articulated differently – through trade-union organisations and working men's clubs. Though they had features in common with eighteenth-century craft organisations and communities of interest, these new representative bodies, in addition to advancing a self-improvement and education agenda for the individual, were also party political in their collective ambition. They sought changes in relationships between masters and men through improved employment practices and payments, and favoured socialist agendas for the benefit of workers more generally. The next chapter, focused on industrialising Glasgow, explores these themes further in an urban situation where the craftsman was secondary to the factory worker.

Notes

1. The date reflects the point at which *Post Office Directories* are easily matched with printed census abstracts. Further comparisons between Edinburgh and Glasgow are discussed in Chapter 2.
2. Bill Bell, ed., *The Edinburgh History of the Book in Scotland vol. 2: Ambition and Industry, 1800–1880* (Edinburgh, 2007), Part 1.
3. See Sian Reynolds, *Britannica's Typesetters. Women Compositors in Edwardian Edinburgh* (Edinburgh, 1989).
4. Sarah Laurenson, 'Materials, Making and Meaning: The Jewellery Craft in Scotland, c.1780–1914', PhD thesis, University of Edinburgh, 2017.
5. Stana Nenadic, 'The social shaping of business behaviour in the nineteenth-century women's garment trades', *Journal of Social History*, 31:3 (1998), 625–45.
6. For background, see Giorgio Riello, 'Nature, production and regulation in eighteenth-century Britain and France: The case of the leather industry', *Historical Research*, 81 (2008), 75–99. An insight into processes involved in men's hat making is given in 'New Patents Lately Enrolled. Mr William

Hance's (Tooley Street) Method of rendering Beaver and other Hats Water-proof', *Monthly Magazine or British Register*, 23:157 (June 1807), 466. Beaver skins were imported from Canada.

7. National Archives. Registered Design no. 17619. Class 3: Wood, bone, ivory etc. 25 November 1884. 'Protection sought for the shape of the bowl and the pattern thereon.' W. and J. Milne, Dressing Case Makers.

8. *Scotsman*, 3 August 1833.

9. *Edinburgh Post Office Directory*, 1855.

10. *Official Catalogue of the Great Exhibition of the Works of Industry of All Nations* (1851), 86. Wilson, Walker & Co. of the Sheepscar Leather Works (sometimes called the Spanish Leather Works) was founded *c.*1825 and continued into the twentieth century.

11. Vanessa Habib and Helen Clark, 'The linen weavers of Drumsheugh and the linen damask tablecloth woven to commemorate the visit of George IV to Scotland in 1822', *Proceedings of the Society of Antiquaries of Scotland*, 132 (2002), 529–53.

12. See Stana Nenadic, *Lairds and Luxury. The Highland Gentry in Eighteenth-Century Scotland* (Edinburgh, 2007).

13. 'An account of a scheme for enlarging and improving the city of Edinburgh and for adorning it with certain public buildings and other useful works', *Scots Magazine*, (August 1752), 369–379, 375.

14. David Scott Mitchell, 'The Development of the Architectural Iron Founding Industry in Scotland', PhD thesis, University of Edinburgh, 2013.

15. A. J. Youngson, *The Making of Classical Edinburgh 1750–1840* (Edinburgh, 1966).

16. Joe Rock, Annotated Catalogue of the Edinburgh Dean of Guild Court, Architectural Plans, 1700–1824. Box 1782/24. www.google.com/site/edinburghdeanofguild (last accessed 15 February 2021).

17. Ibid., Box 1782/24.

18. Ibid., Box 1809/11.

19. Ibid., Box 1770/12; 1777/10; 1787/22; 1792/2.

20. Alyssa Jean Popiel, *A Capital View: The Art of Edinburgh* (Edinburgh, 2014), 43.

21. See National Library of Scotland [NLS] Scottish Book Trade Index. James Kirkwood.

22. *Scotsman*, 1 November 1817.

23. *A Dictionary of Irish Artists* (1913).

24. NLS Book Trade Index. James Kirkwood.

25. Ibid., Robert Scott.

26. *Scotsman*, 11 December 1824.

27. NLS Book Trade Index. Charles Thomson.

28. *Aberdeen Journal*, 21 May 1806; *Caledonian Mercury*, 2 August 1806.

29. NRS. CS96/415/1. Sequestration of John Steell, Gilder and Print Dealer, Edinburgh. Sederunt books 1819–25.

30. *Caledonian Mercury*, 8 October 1838.
31. R. E. Graves, revised by Robin L. Woodward, 'Steell, Sir John Robert (1804–1891)', *ODNB*, 2004.
32. *Scotsman*, 20 January 1827.
33. *Scotsman*, 13 May 1826.
34. *Scotsman*, 14 April 1827.
35. National Portrait Gallery [NPG], British Artists' Suppliers, 1650–1950, John Taylor (1802–53); *Scotsman*, 20 August 1851.
36. *Scotsman*, 20 January 1830, 'Extensive Robbery'; *Scotsman*, 18 March 1846, Death Notice and 'Sale of Gold and Silver Watches, Silver Plate and Jewellery at no. 11 George Street.'.
37. Stephen Jackson, 'William Trotter, cabinetmaker, entrepreneur and Lord Provost, 1772–1833', *Book of the Old Edinburgh Club*, New Series, 6 (2005), 73–90.
38. London Metropolitan Archives [LMA]. MS 11936–7. Sun Insurance Company Registers, 1792. Vol. 345. Policy 572037.
39. Francis Bamford, 'A Dictionary of Edinburgh Wrights and Furniture Makers, 1660–1840', *Furniture History*, 19 (1983), 1–137, 115–16.
40. LMA. MS 11936–7. Sun Insurance Registers, 1792. Vol. 342. Policy 572032.
41. Ibid., Vol. 340. Policy 572023.
42. NRS. CS96/1246. David Gullan, Cabinetmaker, Musselburgh. Sederunt Book, 1813–15.
43. Inveresk Parish Church Monumental Inscriptions.
44. Bamford, *Edinburgh Furniture Makers*, 68.
45. NRS. CS96/1246. David Gullan. Sederunt, 18–30.
46. Ibid., 32.
47. For example, *Caledonian Mercury*, 18 January 1823.
48. NRS. CS96/1246. David Gullan. Sederunt. 88–9.
49. *Edinburgh Annual Register*, 5:2 (1812), 28.
50. The house was built in the 1790s and demolished a century later.
51. Biography of Sir James Wemyss McKenzie, 5th Bt (1770–1843), of Scatwell and Suddie, Ross, from *The History of Parliament: The House of Commons 1820–1832*, edited by D. R. Fisher, (Cambridge, 2009).
52. *Scotsman*, 26 August 1840.
53. *Scotsman*, 12 December 1857, Obituary; National Library of Scotland. MS, Acc 7603. Records of Dowells Ltd, Auctioneers, Edinburgh. Introduction.
54. *Scotsman*, 3 January 1824, sales notice, details the 'joiners shop', then occupied by Dowell. It is described as a coach house and stable with a 40-foot frontage.
55. NRS. CS96/452. Sequestration of James Dowell, Cabinetmaker, Edinburgh, 1829–31.
56. *Scotsman*, 24 May 1828.
57. NRS. CS96/452. Sequestration of James Dowell, 63–4.
58. Ibid., 63.

59. *Scotsman*, 12 December 1857.
60. *Scotsman*, 30 May 1832.
61. NRS. CS96/204. James Watson, Cabinet Maker, Edinburgh. Wages Book 1844–52.
62. *Scotsman*, 2 July 1851.
63. *Directory* entries show his business at 89 George Street for a few years, then 145 George Street, finally settling at 121 George Street.
64. Despite sequestration, the business was run as a going concern and sold on that basis. After Watson & Co. ceased trading, the premises were occupied by another cabinet-making firm, R. Simpson. *Directory*, 1853–4.
65. NRS. CS96/204. James Watson. Wages Book, 64.
66. J. A. Fairley, *Lauriston Castle. The Estate and its Owners* (Edinburgh, 1925).
67. *Dictionary of Scottish Architects* [DSA]. William R. Reid (1854–1919).
68. Christine M. Anderson, 'Robert Lorimer and Scott Morton & Company', *Regional Furniture*, 19 (2005), 43–68.
69. National Record of the Historic Environment in Scotland holds the extensive uncatalogued business records, correspondence and sales catalogues of Scott Morton & Co. and Whytock & Reid; *DSA*, William Scott Morton (1840–1903).
70. Nenadic, 'Rights, rituals and sites of business'.
71. Jennifer M. Ide, 'John Taylor & Son, Manufacturers Edinburgh', *Mauchline Ware Newsletter*, 2011.
72. On women's firms, see Stana Nenadic, 'Social shaping of business behaviour'.
73. For background, see Geoffrey Crossick, ed., *The Artisan and the European Town, 1500–1900* (Aldershot, 1997).
74. Census of Scotland, 1841. Abstract of Answers and Returns published in *Accounts and Papers*, vol. 26, 1844.
75. Census of Scotland, 1881. *Report*, vol. 2. 1883.
76. Ibid.
77. For background, Clive Edwards, *Victorian Furniture: Technology and Design* (Manchester, 1993).

2

Industrial Crafts: Glasgow and Beyond

GLASGOW, A GREAT INDUSTRIAL CITY, expanding rapidly from the later eighteenth century, was successively identified with factory-based cotton textiles, iron and steel production, engineering and shipbuilding. By the later nineteenth century, as widely celebrated by contemporaries, Glasgow was also associated with an extensive empire trade through its merchant and agency houses. Though accounts of Glasgow give prominence to industrial, technical or commercial achievement by great men of industry – alongside the associated diseconomies of labour exploitation, popular dissatisfaction and collective protest – there was also a strong presence in the city of traditional craft trades, and craftsmen and craftswomen. Cabinetmaking flourished in Glasgow with firms of similar characteristics to those in Edinburgh. There was a fine silver industry with traditions of craftwork in areas like silver engraving. Scientific instrument making and watch- and clockmaking were notable. The Glasgow international exhibitions from the 1880s gave prominence to craftwork and celebratory publications such as the 1891 *Glasgow and Its Environs: A Literary, Commercial and Social Review*, though focused on 'leading mercantile houses and commercial enterprises', included craft businesses and their founders.[1]

The character of craft making in Glasgow can be gauged through Post Office directories and census abstracts, comparing 1841 and 1911 and drawing parallels with what has already been shown for Edinburgh. In terms of directory advertising, Glasgow routinely exhibited a wider range of business types than Edinburgh, a product mainly of the large and complex industrial economy in textiles, metals and engineering – sectors that were largely absent in Edinburgh. Of absolute numbers, the largest sector in both cities was dress and clothing, though firms in Glasgow were more likely to be male owned and serving a middle-class and ready-made market than the predominantly bespoke and elite female trade that exemplified Edinburgh. And, as the relative numbers of clothing-making concerns increased in Edinburgh through to 1911, those in Glasgow fell as larger factory units evolved. Typical of the latter was the firm of Lillie & Russell, tailors of Gordon Street Glasgow, who employed over 80 skilled workmen as cutters and tailors, with many more semi-skilled women on the payroll. They specialised in ready-made goods as well as habit making, some of it bespoke, for yachting, clerical and military orders.[2]

Furniture making retained a consistent profile amongst advertising businesses in the Post Office directories in both cities, though the numbers of employees expanded more rapidly in Glasgow as factory production and firm size increased. In 1911, the furniture sector represented 12 per cent of businesses in Edinburgh and 13 per cent in Glasgow, though the absolute number of firms in the latter was almost twice that of Edinburgh. Metals and machine making in Glasgow comprised nearly 20 per cent of advertising businesses, compared with about 10 per cent in Edinburgh. Precious metal concerns, along with clock- and watchmaking businesses, were of rising importance in both cities, with a relatively equal presence of about 11 per cent of advertisers by 1911, compared with 8 per cent in 1840. The expansion was due to growth in middle-class demand for personal luxuries and though the Glasgow business class and Edinburgh's professionals had different cultural identities and modes of dress, they equally favoured the pocket watch and chain as primary adornment for the successful man, and rings, necklaces or brooches for women.

Despite parallels, the character of small businesses in Glasgow was different to those found in Edinburgh, even in sectors where craft skills survived into the twentieth century. Glasgow workplaces were likely to have bigger numbers of employees per employer than commonly seen in the capital. In cabinetmaking, for instance, in 1911 the average size in Edinburgh was seven workers per firm whilst in Glasgow it was 13. Edinburgh had relatively more skilled cabinetmakers working on their own account than was ever seen in Glasgow. In the secondary furniture trades a similar comparative profile prevailed. French polishing firms were large, industrialised concerns in both cities, but in 1911 those in Glasgow had workforce units more than twice the size of those in Edinburgh, with an average of 113 employees. By contrast, upholsterers, carvers and gilders worked in business units of similar size in both cities, reflecting the relatively low levels of mechanisation or opportunities for economies of scale that these crafts presented, even as late as 1911. A Glasgow firm of note was Strattan & Mackay, described in the 1890s as

'decorative upholsterers, cabinet and art furniture makers' with premises at 92 Woodlands Road in the west end of Glasgow.[3] Both partners
were termed 'eminently practical men'. John Crosby Strattan had been
employed for many years by the big furnishing firm of Wylie & Lochhead
and was also the foreman upholsterer for Thomas Murray of Sauchiehall
Street, before setting up in business with John Mackay who had 'attained
[his] position as a tasteful and practical cabinet-maker through experience gained in several of the first-class houses in Glasgow'.[4] Furniture
and fittings for commercial customers were also distinctive to Glasgow.
C. L. Dobbie & Son was a ship, ornamental and architectural carving
and gilding firm of Paisley Road, who employed a 'large staff of skilled
designers and workmen' in the 1890s and specialised in carved figure
heads for ships and yachts.[5] George Taggart & Co., based at the North
British Wholesale Cabinet and Upholstery Works in Glasgow, employed
over 200 'skilled hands' engaged in semi-mass production using mechanised cutting and sawing with some limited deployment of traditional
craft techniques.[6]

The sector in Glasgow most associated with small craft units was that
of the goldsmiths, silversmiths and jewellers, with seven workers on average in each workplace in 1911, along with watch- and clockmakers, with
six workers per average workplace. Larger craft enterprises existed, however, such as that owned by Robert Scott, manufacturing and wholesale
jeweller of 8 Buchanan Street, who employed a staff of 30 trained jewellers in the early 1890s producing the 'most exquisite ideals of jewellery-
making art'.[7] Scientific instrument making was a notable area of craft
production in Glasgow with strong connections with chemicals-based
industry, with medicine and also with shipbuilding. Like jewellery or
watch- and clockmaking, scientific instrument making was increasingly
dominated by English centres using a mix of factory production and craft
manufacture to supply standard components for use in workshops elsewhere. Yet there were some notable scientific instrument makers in Scotland and in Glasgow the fine end of the sector was sustained by demand
from the engineering and nautical industries as well as the burgeoning
consumer goods market. The number of firms was always small, with an
average of just 16 in Glasgow in the second half of the century and 12
in Edinburgh.[8] Many operated as individuals with one or two apprentices and diversification into making goods outside the normal defini-
tion of scientific instruments was normal, as in the case of Alexander
Dick, active in Glasgow from 1828 to 1843, a specialist in land-surveying
instruments who also advertised wirework and made mine safety lamps.[9]
Instrument makers who employed glassworking skills commonly moved

into the growing optician's trade and retail of goods made elsewhere was normal amongst these smaller makers.[10] A notable and long-established Glasgow firm was that of Gardner & Co., who advertised as 'opticians to her Majesty, spectacle manufacturers, mathematical and philosophical instrument makers' and operated from prestigious retail premises at 53 Buchanan Street in the 1870s. They catered for both the non-specialist and the professional market, with stock lists and advertising literature including magnifying glasses, barometers, opera glasses, telescopes as well as hydrometers, sextants and quadrants.[11]

The leading firm of Whyte, Thomson & Co., nautical instrument makers and 'compass adjusters' in Govan, a family firm across three generation, had a staff of 'seventy skilled mechanics' in the early 1890s. A frequent exhibitor and prizewinner at international exhibitions, holder of numerous patents and exclusive contracts with both the Admiralty and commercial shipping lines like Cunard, the firm employed craft-trained artisans and specialist technical designers.[12] Another specialist Glasgow firm connected with the city's seafaring traditions was that of Duncan McGregor, a nautical instrument maker from 1844, operating from premises close to the Clyde docks, who began his working life as a ship chandler in Greenock. A range of products were made by this firm, with compass adjusters advertised by the 1860s and chronometers by the 1870s. A branch of the firm was established in Liverpool in the 1880s and most of the manufacturing moved south. They were enthusiastic exhibitors at international exhibitions in Britain and abroad, registered several patents and enjoyed lucrative naval contracts. With new communication technologies in the 1890s, the firm made ships' telegraph machines. The founder died wealthy and his sons were gentlemen entrepreneurs who were members of bodies such as the Royal Geographical Society and Royal Scottish Society of Arts.[13] However, the glory days of Scotland's scientific instrument makers, when they were also inventors and involved in scientific research and learned societies, was mostly gone by the early nineteenth century.

Other areas of craft production, such as pottery and ceramics, were contained within larger industrial units, where specialist staff undertook commissions or art pottery making for the elite end of the market, alongside mass production for the middle and lower market. Consequently, the average workplace size in this sector in Glasgow in 1911 was large at 94 workers. The relationship between large industrial workplaces deploying new technologies for mass production, alongside the parallel survival of craftworkers, some employed within the factory and some acting as subcontractors in satellite workshops, is best represented by the textile industry. Textile production exemplified Glasgow's first engagement with modern industry, though by mid century it was in relative decline as economic momentum shifted to metals. But though part of a passing world, the textile industry with its family-workshop traditions and potential for creative engagement with the product was still celebrated in Glasgow. And though it had been quickly and bitterly industrialised in the first half of the nineteenth century, a memory of craft skill and autonomy embodied especially in the handloom weaver was retained and valued.

HANDLOOM WEAVERS: AN ARTISAN ELITE

Handloom weavers were the largest single group of skilled craftworkers in Scotland in the first half of the nineteenth century and their changing fortunes in the face of mechanisation and the rise of factory production has attracted the interest of generations of historians. We know a lot about their lives, training and working conditions because of the numerous public enquiries into weaver unemployment and poverty that occurred in the 1830s and 1840s and because the weavers themselves wrote about their experiences and formed mutual organisations with rules and records to protect their interests.[14]

Handloom weavers were frequently classed as 'outworkers' – a term that is a product of the factory age – and worked at foot-powered looms in their own homes or nearby workshops, a practice that continued throughout the nineteenth century, particularly in rural districts or in specialised areas of production, alongside the rise in power looms and weaving factories. One who described his experience was William Hammond, an Irish-born pattern weaver in Glasgow from the 1840s, who moved back and forth between handloom and factory weaving and was also an active member of the Calton District Handloom Weavers Trade Union. In common with many others, he had moved to Glasgow with family members, including a sister who was married to a beamer in a weaving factory, though also in common with others, the sister and her husband left Glasgow for America in search of better opportunities.[15] William Hammond remained and prospered, and in the later nineteenth century had his own small weaving shop, working on the ground floor and living in a flat above.[16] Another account of what a handloom workshop might comprise was given in a later-nineteenth-century description by an elderly handloom weaver in Glasgow, 83-year-old William Muir of 30 Somers Street in Bridgeton, who was one of the last to remember the famed weaver-poet Robert Tannahill and his Paisley workshop.

Tannahill wrought in a 'four-loom' shop belonging to his widowed mother, and one of his fellow-workers was 'Black Peter', who recovered the poet's body from the 'hole' besides the canal. The second was one John Archibald; the third old Muir does not presently remember. Peter Burnett, or 'Black Peter', was a West Indian, and came to Tannahill's father's shop when a boy.[17]

Weavers like Hammond or Tannahill were celebrated for their rich cultural and political life in Scotland as elsewhere and during the late-eighteenth- and early-nineteenth-century 'golden age', when wages were good, they were able to gain an education, buy books and engage in various forms of cultural production, such as poetry or song writing and natural history research.[18] In 1819–20 there was a monthly publication in Glasgow titled *The Weaver's Magazine and Literary Companion* that sought to represent the interests of the craft. It included poetry, biography and curiosities, along with accounts of the state of the trade in the different categories of weaving. There were letters from readers reflecting on their experiences and court cases related to weaver–employer relations were reported. The magazine included an essay titled 'How far has the invention of Weaving contributed to promote the happiness and improve the condition of Man?'[19] This itemised the value of weaving for dress, national prosperity, health and the 'promotion of human happiness'. The article also praised the intrinsic activity –

> Weaving, though not ranked as a science, is certainly a business that requires much study. To devise the possible ways into which yarn may be disposed; the various effects that such combination will produce; to arrange colours in all their tasteful variety in damask and figured silks, and muslins, gives a pleasure to the minds of those that are capable of accomplishing it.[20]

The tone in describing the art and craft of the weaver is philosophical and historical, with the weaver represented as educated and respected. Even later in the century, when times were harder, some handloom weavers maintained these traditions, as with William Hammond, who was heavily involved in secular education in Glasgow, as well as trade union politics, and was a leading figure in the Bridgeton Rambling Club which dominated his recollections when they were published in 1905 and of which he was the last surviving member.

Weavers were famed for their sense of community and collective organisations that protected their interests and rights, a product of physical concentration in weaving villages and city districts and the legacy of strong incorporated status in centuries past.[21] Some weavers worked in small groups and although the weaving itself was typically a one-person job, there were certain processes that required more than one pair of

Figure 2.1 Workshop of a handloom weaver. Lanark, *c*.1910. Postcard. © The Royal Burgh of Lanark Museum Trust.

hands, such as setting up the warp. Harness weavers in Ayrshire, for instance, would take their warp yarn to a beaming house, where the beamer and two or three weavers would wind the warp onto a beam, which was then carried back to the weaving shop and put on the loom.[22] Assisting one another with warping, which often took place in the evening so as not to impinge on weaving time, was a chance for weavers to socialise. Although the work was unpaid, bread, cheese and whisky were usually supplied, the latter leading one commentator to note that weavers were often unfit for work the next day.[23] Some saw the independence of the home-based weavers as one of the main attractions of the craft, since by working at home weavers could be surrounded by their family (who were usually employed in some part of textile manufacturing) and could keep their own hours and be as 'idle or busy' as they pleased.[24] But this, of course, was simplistic and weavers themselves often noted the physical demands of the work and the long hours necessary to support their families. They worked 13 or 14 hours a day, sometimes longer, in the summer starting at 6 a.m. with short breaks for breakfast and dinner and working late into the night.[25]

Less usual than the individual home-based or journeyman weaver, but still evident in Scotland mid century, were some of the larger weaving businesses who employed handloom weavers in a factory setting. William Wilson & Son of Bannockburn was one of the foremost tartan manufacturers of the eighteenth and nineteenth century, supplying the fashion industry and the military.[26] In the 1780s the firm had 12 handlooms on the business premises near Stirling, with purpose-built living accommodation for their in-house weavers, as well as employing outworkers in their own homes. As the business grew, they invested in a new, water-powered mill to cope with demand. Built in 1822 on the banks of the Bannock Burn, this was a three-storey building with large windows and space for multiple handloom weavers as well as mechanised spinning.[27] This pattern of production survived to the 1860s. And despite the decline of handloom weaving in Glasgow or Paisley, rural handloom weaving survived for decades into the twentieth century.

As a centre of modern industrial production, it is not surprising that many craftsmen in Glasgow turned their attention to technical innovations in weaving from which they hoped to reap financial rewards. It was a practice aided by the ingenuity of many craft-trained artisans and their capacity for independent thinking, a hallmark of the handloom weaver. The records of the Board of Manufacturers, who offered bounties for successful inventions, give insights into a wide range of craftworker initiatives. A typical case is that of Archibald Macvicar, a watchmaker in Glasgow, who in 1796 had invented a 'machine for spotting or brocading Muslin in the loom, which had hitherto been executed in a very imperfect manner by the finger work of children'. His petition for financial reward was accompanied by a 'certificate from a number of respectable Manufacturers, and from a joint Committee of the Merchants & Trades House in Glasgow . . . stating their approbation of the machine as a most ingenious invention'. Macvicar exhibited his machine for the Board in Edinburgh, who asked for more evidence of its utility, with a promise of a premium of over ten guineas if adopted.[28] By the following year, when the invention was demonstrably successful, he had received £30.[29] George Young, an edge tool maker was rewarded in 1817 for his refinements to fly shuttles.[30] Weavers also sought rewards for their inventions, such as this one in 1802, eventually granted a premium of 25 guineas.

> A Petition was read from George McIndoe, weaver in Anderston [Glasgow] stating that he has contrived a Machine which, superadded to a common Loom, weaves Flowers & Sprigs on Muslin, with netting, extending or contracting according to the figure of the flowers, with very little trouble & expense, upon a new & improved plan;– And praying to be rewarded;– And

Certificates as to the ingenuity & usefulness of the contrivance, from several Manufacturers, and from the Deacon & several Master Weavers in Glasgow, being read Ordered upon a motion from one of the Members that Mr Dale be requested to give his opinion of the Machine & whether it be superior to anything else of the kind with which he is acquainted; – And in the meantime it was agreed that five Guineas be paid to Mr McIndoe on account of his expense in coming to town to shew the model of his Machine.[31]

As with any craft, the prosperity of handloom weavers depended on demand for their product and fortunes rose and fell accordingly. William Hammond, who started as a cotton weaver, also wove wool and cotton mixes, including tartan, if the work and materials were available.[32] Others turned to different employments. Peter Burnett, who worked alongside Tannahill the poet-weaver, was raised in service and found work as gentleman's valet when times were hard in the trade.[33] Local landowners gave support and made work during tough times in country districts, but in towns and cities, charity was the main recourse. The fate of weavers was inevitably a troubled one and most commentators observed that weaver poverty was a product of too much labour. It was an easy trade to learn to a basic level and according to one report for the Select Committee on Handloom Weavers in 1834, 'a lad of fourteen may acquire a sufficient knowledge of it in six weeks'.[34] Some wanted to restrict the number of people who entered the trade, to boost the wages of those who remained.[35] But free market philosophies and the rise of factories effectively blocked such protectionist demands. Their dwindling numbers yet still distinctive character was recorded in 1869 by David Bremner, the industrial journalist, mainly with reference to the Borders woollen industry and in 'rural districts where faith in "home-made" stuffs still survives'.[36]

CRAFTWORKERS IN INDUSTRIAL PRODUCTION

Narratives of handloom weaver decline, both in the nineteenth century and since, typically represent the craftworker pitted against a relentless process of industrialisation and deskilling. Yet contemporary accounts and records reveal the many circumstances where craft production survived and evolved in a modernising context and where handwork and machine work co-existed. Evidence of a dynamic relationship between hand and machine is apparent in one of the most advanced and lucrative areas of nineteenth-century Scottish industrial production – the Turkey red printed cotton textile industry.

Turkey red dyeing and printing of mid-price cotton textiles used sophisticated dyeing technologies undertaken in large workplace units that flourished in Glasgow, Dunbartonshire and north-west England from c.1820 to c.1900. It was a highly mechanised industry, yet the sector employed many craftworkers in print-block cutting and factory-based hand printing as well as designers and pattern drawers who normally had close connections with craftsmen through their training.[37] The finest output from the Turkey red printers, even in the later nineteenth century, was produced using wooden hand-blocks, which gave a subtler range of colourways to fabric than possible with machine printing and contained within the technique the evidence that it was produced by hand, which had high value in the primary overseas markets, particularly in India. The India market also generated demand for narrow-woven printed textile pieces produced by handloom.[38] A similar combination of craft and machine work was found in linen tableware production throughout the nineteenth century and in later design-based industries such as linoleum making. The skilled craftworkers involved, who were mostly apprenticeship or design-school trained, were sometimes employed by the factory enterprise, sometimes self-employed, and in other cases worked for smaller firms, often family workshops, doing a mix of subcontracting and their own specialist production.[39]

The pottery industry, a flourishing sector in Glasgow, similarly maintained a skilled-craft element alongside factory production, with the decorative details on the best-quality tableware always applied by hand. Even the more prosaic, mass-produced wares from a large company such as Bell & Co.'s Glasgow Pottery at the Broomielaw, employing about 800 people in 1868 when described by Bremner, were decorated with prints engraved on copper plates, which in turn were produced by craftsmen.[40] Works like this embraced new technologies as they evolved, but also put high store by their 'art manufactures' for the higher end of the market and for exhibition wares. At the first of the Glasgow International Exhibitions in 1888, one of the most prominent displays was that mounted by Doulton & Co. of London, which included craftsmen and craftswomen to demonstrate the different elements of decorative pottery making, all housed in an elaborate Indian-themed pavilion. Up to 20 men were making the pots and several women were there for the painting and carved-design work. The pots found ready customers and such product lines were commercially successful, but the firm's main area of production was in pedestrian domestic sanitary wares such as baths and toilet bowls.[41]

The iron industry was another high-technology sector where skilled craftsmen flourished alongside mass production. The Carron Iron Works near Falkirk was the first coal-based iron smelting company in Scotland. Founded in 1759 on the banks of the River Carron the firm was established as a large-scale manufactory producing goods for a ready and growing market. Armaments, architectural iron work and decorative domestic wares were notable elements in the output.[42] In its early years, Carron depended on the skills and knowledge of a workforce brought in from the iron district of Coalbrookdale in Shropshire. Renowned for expertise in decorative cast iron, the Shropshire men were charged with teaching Carron's local workforce the iron founder's craft, as seen in the early Glasgow pottery industry. Scotland's natural geology, the founders' investment in skills and new technology, and emphasis on good design were all factors in Carron's early success. The first supply of architectural goods from Carron was in 1764, when cast-iron railings were provided for the College of Glasgow.[43] By the 1770s, Scottish architects Robert, James and John Adam were shareholders in the firm. They influenced the style of Carron's decorative work and advanced the firm's commercial interests in London. Under their influence, Carron supplied cast-iron ranges and decorative grates for the private and public rooms of country and town houses throughout Scotland.[44] Plaster and wood were used to create the 'patterns' or moulds for castings and Carron depended on the skills of its carvers to achieve a fineness of execution relative to the limitations of the iron-casting process. George Smith, wright and patternmaker, was one of these craftsmen who signed a 12-year contract with the company in 1817.[45]

In addition to local craftsmen and specialists from the Midlands, Carron employed two generations of the London-based Haworth family to design and carve their patterns. Portraits of King George III and Queen Charlotte were carved by Samuel Haworth to commemorate the Royal Charter in 1773 and were used widely in different types of iron wares. Samuel's son, William, produced classical-style patterns for Carron for 56 years between the 1780s and 1830s.[46] Carron extended its product range in cast- and wrought-iron architectural and decorative wares throughout the nineteenth century, drawing on its own skilled workers, designers and subcontractors in nearby smaller forges and design studios. According to Bremner, 'no establishment in Britain possesses such a valuable collection of patterns for stoves, grates, umbrella-stands, garden-seat, verandas, iron stairs, balconies, and fancy articles – such as inkstands, card-trays, mirror-frames, statuary groups etc'.[47] The firm copyrighted many of its designs. An 1883 sales catalogue illustrates a stock of ornamental goods that included garden furniture, sanitary fittings and stoves for shops and ships.[48] Shop-fitting was a significant business area in Glasgow where Carron had a warehouse at 123 Buchanan Street. Other warehouses were in London and Liverpool.

The almost infinite opportunity for design variation that was enabled by factory-made iron led to fears from the 1850s that public taste would be degraded by superfluous ornamentation. The art critic John Ruskin was not alone in condemning decorative cast iron, a mainstay of Carron's output, as a cheap and vulgar alternative to the hand-worked beauty and structural integrity of wrought iron.[49] By the end of the century a shift in elite consumer preferences can be discerned as the Arts and Crafts movement advocated for the values of simply formed, handmade goods rather than goods that expressed the technical and ornamental possibilities of the mass produced. This led to a resurgent interest in decorative wrought iron that was seen in Scotland in the work of blacksmiths such as Thomas Hadden.

Thomas Hadden was born in 1871 in Hamilton, south of Glasgow, to a metalworking family. He trained at Howgate near Edinburgh and worked for James Milne & Sons in Edinburgh before starting in business in partnership with his brother who was a woodcarver. Hadden's reputation as a skilled art metalworker led to his involvement in numerous prestigious commissions, notably the garden ornaments and railings at Skirling House in Peebleshire.[50] Architectural commissions were a key area of his business. He made gates and railings and more whimsical iron wares including weathervanes and boot scrapers as well as fireplace goods such as fenders and firedogs. The firm survived into the 1950s.[51] His most famous project was the wrought-iron gates designed by architect Robert Lorimer for the Thistle Chapel in Edinburgh's St Giles Cathedral. The chapel was a commission from the Trustees of The Order of the Thistle who wanted to create a meeting place that embodied a nationalist spirit. On awarding the contract to Lorimer, the trustees stipulated that Scottish craftsmen should carry out as much of the work as possible. W. & A. Clow of Edinburgh carved the ornate choir stalls. Phoebe Traquair, artist and decorator, and Whytock & Reid, cabinetmakers, were other Edinburgh contributors. The coloured glass was the work of Aberdeen glass stainer Douglas Strachan.[52]

Another area of the metal industries where a combination of handcraft and factory work existed in parallel is seen in the printing industry. Type founding– the process of making the individual letters that are put together by compositors to form a page of text – began in Scotland with the Glasgow works of Alexander Wilson, who in the 1770s was responsible for the types used by the Foulis Press in the production of beautiful editions of the classics under the patronage of Glasgow University. The punch cutters and engravers who first worked in Scotland were mostly trained in London, but by c.1800 Wilson also employed several

Scottish craftsmen including William Miller, his foreman, who set up his own business in Edinburgh in 1808. Miller joined with his son-in-law, Walter Richard, in 1842 and the firm of Miller & Richard of 65 Nicholson Street became the largest in Scotland employing over 500 'men and boys' by the 1860s. Metal type was made from a mix of lead, tin and antimony. Before type could be made, however, the first operation was to cut a set of punches in fine steel, which was the most skilled element in the type-making process. Many craft-trained punch cutters were self-employed and some of those responsible for Scotland's finest typefaces were London based. In addition to the punchers and type founders, a typical type foundry in the mid nineteenth century also employed skilled craftsmen to make the wooden and brass framework or 'furniture' for setting the types, though, as noted by industrial journalist David Bremner in 1869 in his detailed account of the Miller & Richard's works, the 'division-of-labour principle' was increasingly adopted.[53] Skilled women were also long associated with the book and paper trades, though they were never as well paid as men.[54] Type dressing, sorting and packing was one area of work and also book sewing and cloth binding. Leather binding was normally viewed as a male skill, though it became a notable art-craft practised by women in Glasgow and Edinburgh by the later nineteenth century.[55]

A characteristic of most large-scale industrial employments by mid century was the prevalence of trade union membership which included craftworkers. Bremner's 1869 accounts of the *Industries of Scotland*, which gives so many insights to the integration of hand and machine work, offers insights also to trade union activity in the different sectors. One that drew comment was glassmaking. Scottish glassmaking, for windows, bottles or decorative wares, had a long history traceable to the early seventeenth century but developing rapidly from the early nineteenth century.[56] Abundant raw materials gave Greenock an early start in production of basic glass for bottles, whilst finer crown glass for windows, which employed skilled craftsmen, was made in Dumbarton from 1777 at a works owned by local gentry landowners. Crown glass was first perfected in late-seventeenth-century London and was made using a blowpipe technique, with the glass spun rapidly until a disk has been formed that was then cut into panes. The Dumbarton Glassworks Company supplied most of the quality glass in Scotland *c.*1800–30, with a focus on the Edinburgh market where it maintained an agent and warehouse.[57] The *Statistical Account* for Dumbarton in the 1790s describes a 'considerable crown and bottle glass manufactory, which employs 130 hands'. The 'glass-house men' were said to earn up to 25s a week, which put them on a par with other local craftsmen such as carpenters; they were mostly migrants from Lancashire or London, where glassmaking flourished.[58] At its height, the glassworks employed about 300 men, who, with their wives and children comprised about a third of the local population. But the industry was soon on the wane as machine-rolled plate glass replaced hand-blown crown glass from c.1840. The Dumbarton Glassworks was finally discontinued in 1850 when the brick cones that dominated the skyline were dismantled and the premises, with its river frontage, was given over to a shipyard.[59]

The history of the Verreville Glassworks in Glasgow followed a similar trajectory to that in Dumbarton and for similar reasons linked to market competition. Established in 1776 to produce high-quality flint glass wares mainly for export to America, its glass production gradually decreased in the nineteenth century and ceased altogether in 1842 when the works shifted to ceramics.[60] There was limited-quality glass production in the Glasgow thereafter, other than from a small cut-glass works established in 1832 at St Rollox, though numerous agents for companies elsewhere were established in the city by mid century. These included the notable Birmingham firm of F. & C. Osler & Co., which had showrooms in India and exhibited in Glasgow in 1888, whose agency in Glasgow's Hope Street supplied chandeliers and electric light fittings.[61] Glassmaking in Glasgow was dominated mid century by low-skill mass production of glass bottles, so it is to other places that we look to see the glass-producing artisan and the impact of modern trade unions.

The cutting and engraving shop at the Holyrood Flint Glass Co. in the Canongate area of Edinburgh was for the finishing of quality domestic glass wares using skilled cutting and engraving techniques and had a mixture of machine technologies for powering the cutting wheels combined with apprentice-trained handworkers. As represented in contemporary images and described by Bremner, the workshop was lit from above and contained about 40 wheels attended by as many craftsmen. The same room housed the engravers and their benches, who were fewer in number. The business, which employed over 200 men, was known for its cut-glass decanters and table glasses, along with fruit bowls, vases, glass oil lamps and dressing-table sets. A heavy glass vessel such as a large bowl could take up to 40 hours of work for the cutting stage. The Holyrood company also produced fine glass door handles set with cameo portraits of notable figures of the day and was famed for its elaborately coloured glass jugs, a product of the glassblower's art. The firm made to commission and also for sale through its retail premises in central Edinburgh and was a frequent attendee at the great exhibitions in Scotland.

The owner, John Ford, who succeeded an uncle, was apprentice trained as a glass cutter, making a fruit bowl as his 'apprentice piece'. According to Bremner's account of the skills involved in this sort of work –

> The wheels are fixed in a sort of turning-lathe and are driven by steam, and the variety of patterns that may be produced on them is almost unlimited. The workman rarely makes any attempt at drawing the device on the glass before cutting it. He simply divides the circumference of the article into sections by scratching with a file and guided so far by these marks he trusts to his eye to the rest.[62]

Firms like this, or those in the pottery industry, not only employed craftworkers within their own factories, they maintained close connections with smaller satellite firms acting as subcontractors. Much of the engraving work undertaken from mid century for the Holyrood company was done by workshops in the nearby Abbeyhill area of Edinburgh, which were mainly staffed by Bohemian glass engravers with specialist skills. The latter were especially associated with design innovation in engraving motifs and are credited with the fern pattern that came to exemplify the finest of Scottish engraved glass wares from the 1850s to 1880s.[63]

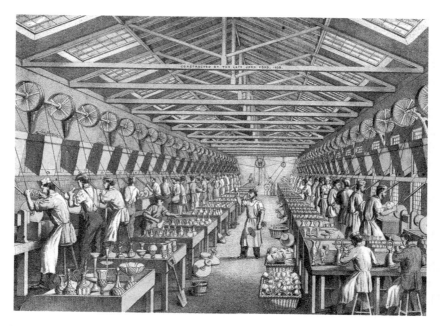

Figure 2.2   Cutting and engraving shop. Holyrood Flint Glass Co., Edinburgh, c.1860. © City of Edinburgh Council Museums and Galleries, Museum of Edinburgh and Private Lender to Museum of Edinburgh.

The glass industry was heavily unionised by mid century, with a national organisation headquartered in Birmingham. The union determined wages and apprenticeship terms, setting a ratio of one apprentice to five journeymen in an endeavour to control entry to the trade in much the same way as the old trades houses of pre-burgh reform days. The glass cutters, as a distinct skill group, had a union organisation of their own with contributions ranging from 1s to 3s 6d per week, which was higher than that of ordinary glassmakers. Glassmakers, who were specialists in glass-blowing techniques, earned from 20s to 38s a week, cutters earned from 20s to 34s per week, and the engravers were the best paid of all earning up to 40s per week, with many also working in self-employed capacities. Apprentices, who served seven years, earned 4s to 5s per week and paid up to £7 entry money when progressing to journeyman. These were good wages and, according to Bremner, employment conditions were mostly healthy, but in the later nineteenth century there were damaging conflicts between the unions and the owners over wages and terms, which threatened the industry.[64]

Bremner was not an overt fan of the unions, pointing to some of their self-defeating conflicts with employers and minutia of workplace practices that undermined effective commerce, though this feature of his published commentaries is perhaps more a product of his perceived readership than personal inclination, since he was himself a leading figure in the National Association of Journalists, his own trade union body.[65] In describing the largest trade union in Scotland, the Amalgamated Society of Engineers, Millwrights, Smiths and Pattern Makers, which prevailed in many areas of the metal fabrication and engineering industries in Glasgow, he highlighted the 'levelling' principle which seemed to rob men of their initiative and ambition to better understand the business. 'One employer' it was claimed, could scarce find an employee in his workforce of 200–300 who could take on the role of foreman, 'whereas, before trades-unions became so fashionable with the men, he could, from a smaller number in his workshops, select at least a dozen fit for the superior post'.[66] But Bremner was also impressed by the fact that men engaged in the engineering trades were, generally, better educated than earlier in the century and for this we can look to the role of the new training bodies including Glasgow's School of Design.

EDUCATING CRAFTWORKERS: GLASGOW'S SCHOOL OF DESIGN

The 1901 Glasgow International Exhibition held in Kelvingrove Park included an exhibition stand, designed by Charles Rennie Mackintosh, for showcasing the work of the Glasgow School of Art. The simple structure echoed the appearance of the recently completed, Mackintosh-designed new art school in Glasgow. Placed in the Women's Section of the Exhibition, the stand was devoted to 'working handicrafts' that included bookbinding, tapestry weaving, woodcarving, lacemaking and basketmaking.[67] These were essentially manifestations of the middle-class Arts and Crafts movement and many of the practitioners involved in the displays were amateurs. Yet the institution, with a history going back to the 1840s, was important for support of the craft economy in the early twentieth century as in the decades before, through part-time and evening training as a supplement to artisan apprenticeship.[68]

Most nineteenth-century craftworkers, as well as designers in textiles, wood or metal, were of working-class background and came to their occupations through apprenticeships, often involving training with a close family member. But Scotland also had a long history of institutional training, starting in 1760 when the government-funded agency, the Board of Manufactures, founded a drawing school in Edinburgh, which was loosely connected with the University.[69] At Glasgow University a few years before, the short-lived Foulis Academy was also created to improve industrial design and the art of engraving.[70] The larger and longer-lived body in Edinburgh, which had a branch in nearby Dunfermline, the heart of linen damask production, was focused on textiles and the decorating trades, the former reflecting the geographical focus in the east of Scotland of fancy textile weaving. Prizes were awarded annually following open competition, but few went to Glasgow craftworkers.[71] By the 1830s, when government was beginning to take an interest in design for manufacturing, the Edinburgh school taught 40 male students annually free of charge and there was intense competition for places. As the Edinburgh textile industry, including fine shawl weaving, slowly ebbed away, the design school was merged with the broader arts-focused Royal Institution (now the Royal Scottish Academy) and its teaching functions evolved into the Edinburgh School of Art, founded in 1858.[72] Yet the aims of the design school concept were still valued and there were hopes in the 1830s that it might form a model for other more effective bodies, particularly in Glasgow, which, with nearby Paisley, was now established as the centre for decorative textile production.[73] The need for such training according to James Skene, secretary to the Board of Manufactures, was prompted by Scottish concern over competition from French designer-weavers particularly in fashionable shawl making. By the mid 1830s, the Scottish shawl industry was dominated by Paisley handloom weavers whose products, even in the Scottish market, was trumped by those from France, which had 'better designs and dyes, and also a school

in Paris dedicated to teaching the design of shawl patterns'.[74] The local
mechanics' institutes sought to fill the training gap with evening classes
in design and in Glasgow among the annual prizes distributed by the
Mechanics Institute, there was a reward in 1844 for 'the best essay on the
benefits likely to be derived from a School of Design'.[75] The opening of
new design schools in Britain began in earnest in the late 1830s, initially
in London with the Government School of Design at Somerset House
and then in the big English manufacturing centres and in Glasgow and
Paisley from the 1840s. Their purpose, according to the founders, was
to raise the artistic credentials of designers and operatives and increase
their numbers as a first step towards addressing European superiority.[76]

Schools of design were popular and grew rapidly, with 3,296 students
across Britain in 1851 and 31,455 by 1855.[77] The Glasgow Government
School of Design was an immediate success, with 360 students registered within six months of opening in 1845. At the inaugural prizegiving
ceremony, held in the Merchant's Hall, there was a public exhibition of
drawings submitted for competition and prizes were awarded for chalk
drawings, the first prize going to Alexander Wilson, pattern drawer; for
outline drawings, the first prize going to Alexander Craigie, plasterer;
for outline drawings by pupils under the age of 16, the first prize going
to Donald McIntosh, an inker in the printing industry; and for outline
drawings by students in the female class, which was awarded jointly
to three competitors, none of them with a defined occupation.[78] Under
the direction of the Lord Provost and various local dignitaries, there
were ambitions from the outset to form a design library and establish a
gallery of paintings, casts and models for the students to use for copying, which mainly came from loans and gifts from local elites, including
Archibald McLellan, whose collection later laid the foundation for the
first public art gallery in Glasgow.[79] By spring 1846, when the school
moved into new purpose-built premises, it was advertising, in addition
to classes in 'elementary and outline drawing', 'designing suited to Metals, Wood, Stone, Pottery: also to Silk, Wool, Cotton, Paper, and Lace.
Painting in Oil, Water, Distemper, Wax, and Frescos. Perspective. Figure
with Anatomy. Architectural Drawing. Modelling from Casts and Original Designs.'[80] The 'morning school' was from 7 a.m. to 9 a.m. every
weekday and evening classes were from 8 p.m. to 10 p.m. The 'public
classes' cost 2s per month and the 'private class', which ran during the
day, cost £1 11s 6d per quarter. The committee that had the oversight of
the Glasgow school was mainly drawn from local industrialists, and in
the early years included a predominance of textile manufacturers headed
by Walter Crum, calico printer as Vice-President; with A. Broadfoot,

delaine manufacturer; Andrew Wingage, shawl manufacturer; Samuel R. Brown, sewed muslin manufacturer; and A. S. Dalglish, calico printer, all serving as board members.

In common with similar bodies elsewhere, the Glasgow design school was partly funded by an annual government grant of £600, but most of the income in the first few years was from donations, totalling over £1,000 in 1853 and student fees amounting to over £400 annually. Most expenditure was on salaries for masters and on the school premises in Ingram Street. There were 785 male students in 1853, mainly undertaking early morning or evening classes in conjunction with employment, though 147 were described as 'schoolboys' and 183 female students, predominantly described as having 'no occupation'. Most students of both genders were in the 15 to 20 years age category, with about a quarter in their twenties. Of the employed male students, the largest group, with 78 individuals, were 'mechanical engineers'. The textile industry was well represented with six calico printing engravers, 24 pattern designers, 53 pattern-designer apprentices and 13 patternmakers – a group which taken together comprised 15 per cent of the total male employed student body and was matched in numbers by students working as clerks and warehousemen, many doubtless also involved in the textile industry.[81]

Design schools in industrial cities such as Glasgow attracted enormous interest from students and the public and provided an education for large numbers drawn from a wide social range including many craftworkers and apprentices, but the impact on design improvement was always questioned. Even in the 1840s, before they were fully instituted, public discussion in Glasgow had dwelt on the challenges to be faced in educating manufacturers in the value of good design.[82] In a public lecture on 'Ornamental Art and Suggestions for its Improvement' given in Edinburgh in 1857, Charles Heath Wilson, formerly associated with design education in London and then head of the Glasgow school, drew attention to the ongoing task at hand:

> For some years we have been trying to improve Industrial Design, by educating pattern drawers and artisans in a knowledge of art . . . but when our disciples pass into the workshop, they have little opportunity of applying the good principles which they have been taught. Good taste and fashion are found to be in antagonism.[83]

It seems that despite the initial interest from industry, there was frequent complaint that business owners were unwilling to give their employees the necessary time to attend classes and improve skills. In Glasgow this was identified as a particular problem for part-time students once they had completed their initial training, because the good state of trade in the early 1850s meant they were required to undertake overtime in the evenings and also because employers were loath to support further training 'on the ground of their drawing too well, and consequently claiming a higher rate of wages at too early a period of their engagements'.[84] Moreover, as numerous commentators observed, for many businessmen 'good design' was unnecessary when 'the only legitimate standard of taste is the demands of the market'.[85]

Arguments for and against the government-funded design schools in Britain remained vigorous throughout the century. Textile manufacturers were mostly unimpressed because the schools did not serve their interests. Elsewhere, however, the link between good design and knowledge of materials, tools and making processes was stressed, as in an account of 1900 where it was stated at a prizegiving, 'they wanted the designer to be the craftsman and to join their classes with the sole object of making himself or herself more accomplished in his or her craft'.[86] Newspaper biographies and obituaries emphasised the role of design school or mechanics' institute training in the lives and successes of notable local craftsmen.[87] In the early twentieth century the Society of Art Masters, representing teachers and leaders of schools across Britain, met annually in London to hear lectures and debate the issues of the day which included, in 1905, 'Is art, as taught in Schools of Art and Art classes, the Art which will benefit the Craftsman?' or 'The Teaching of Art and Craft to the Paris Artisan'.[88] At this stage in the history of design training for craftwork, the Arts and Crafts movement had given new impetus to benchwork in art school training and what was now termed 'art technology' was stressed for the effective uniting of 'skill, invention and craftsmanship'.[89]

The Glasgow Government School of Design changed its name to the Glasgow School of Art in 1853 and as the fine textile industry faded its focus shifted to other areas of training including a growing emphasis on architecture. Yet the connection with craft and manufacture was maintained here as elsewhere in industrial Britain. In 1897, at a point when the enrolment was 562 students, the *Scotsman* reported the prizewinners awarded by the Department of Science and Art of the Committee of the Council on Education in London, including those based in Scottish institutions.[90] The range of industries and crafts represented was wide as were the numbers of named women. Though there were new bodies represented, such as the Glasgow West of Scotland Technical College or Gray's School of Art in Aberdeen, the Glasgow School of Art dominated the list of prizewinners in all categories which included carpets, wallpaper and ceiling decorations, ceramics and architecture.

The schools of art were not the only source of craftsman training. The emergence of technical schools from the 1870s was part of a distinctive alternative trend in the education of artisans, away from design and towards scientific knowledge. The focus, according to a debate recorded in the *Scotsman*, was for 'securing good scientific teaching for all branches of the building and decorative arts, and for the kindred branches of civil engineering, mechanical engineering, and iron founders' work'.[91] This greater hybridity in the world of hand making and the different skill and sectoral trajectories from which the craftsman evolved is illustrated by the craft, science and art of glass staining.

GLASS STAINING AND THE MARYHILL BURGH HALL

The technically complex craft of decorative glass staining flourished in Glasgow at the end of the nineteenth century. A notable business, operating from large premises in Glassford Street, was that of William Cairney, established *c*.1810 and known as John Cairney & Co. from the 1860s, who initially advertised as painters, glaziers and glass stainers, also offered a paper-hanging service and were dealers and agents for crown and plate glass of English manufacture.[92] Stained glass, an increasingly lucrative decorative specialism, was fashionable from the 1840s and there were several notable Glasgow practitioners who influenced the art and its evolution.[93] One of these was Daniel Cottier, who trained in John Cairney's studio, worked on major church commissions in Glasgow and in London, where he was based for most of his career and shaped the development of the later-nineteenth-century aesthetic movement. He also influenced Louis Tiffany, the famed decorative glassmaker in New York.[94] Most of the craftsmen who worked in the field began as painters and decorators, but when demand for stained glass began to rise, particularly for church memorial windows, glass staining, which is both a science and an art, became a specialist field in its own right. Another Glasgow firm, Guthrie & Wells, established in 1852, had a different range of activities including, in addition to glass staining and decorating, working on tiles and mosaics, fabrics, furniture, carpets and parquet flooring.[95] They were particularly noted for furniture made to designs by Charles Rennie Mackintosh, much of it decorated with tiles and stained-glass panels. Andrew Wells, one of the partners in the firm, was trained by Daniel Cottier and so too was another celebrated Glasgow craftsman, Stephen Adam, creator of the Maryhill Burgh Hall stained-glass windows.

The Stephen Adam & Co. entry in *Glasgow and Its Environs* describes an extensive firm, responsible for a prolific output, with 'fine premises' in St Vincent Street, on six floors, with workshops for lead working, a drawing and design studio, a glass painting and staining studio, and kilns for firing, along with a stock room and dispatch office.[96] The census for 1911 noted there were 12 employers in the decorative glass sector in Glasgow with an average workforce of 40 per firm, about a third women. This is a good estimation of the workforce employed by Stephen Adam & Co. at the height of the firm's success. Stephen Adam was Edinburgh-born in 1848 and was initially apprenticed there with the firm of Ballantine & Son, stained-glass makers with contracts in London, including the Houses of Parliament. The family moved to Glasgow and he began studying at the Glasgow School of Art before entering the workshop of Daniel Cottier to complete his apprenticeship. He worked on several Cottier church commissions, a line of work he continued after setting up his own firm, though he also worked on windows for bars and public houses, country houses and commercial buildings.[97] In the 1890s, at the time he featured in the *Glasgow and Its Environs* volume, Stephen Adam was an established figure in the Glasgow decorative arts establishment. He was a writer and lecturer, member of various prominent societies in the city and patron of the Glasgow East End Exhibition for industrial arts.[98] His 'art politics', socialist in orientation, were influenced by the Arts and Crafts movement and he sought to promote the dignity and respect of the craftsman, as a lecture in Edinburgh, reported in the *Scotsman*, reveals.[99] The artisan worker as backbone of the community was celebrated by Stephen Adam and was also depicted in his Maryhill Burgh Hall commission for a series of stained-glass windows to decorate a new public building, opened in 1878, in a growing part of Glasgow.[100]

Maryhill, a north Glasgow suburb that developed on the banks of the Forth and Clyde Canal, had a wide range of businesses and trades concentrated in a relatively small area to take advantage of the transport links. The new burgh hall, created to house police and fire stations as well as a community facility for meetings and elections, was designed by Glasgow architect Duncan McNaughtan and decorated with 20 square stained-glass windows by Stephen Adam, McNaughtan's neighbour in St Vincent Street.[101] Each of the panels represents a different trade or industry typical of the area, ranging from the traditional, such as the blacksmith, to modern industrial workers such as engineers and including lesser professionals such as school teachers along with women involved in the textile industry. There are also woodworkers, transport workers including a wheelwright, a paper maker, glass blower and brick maker. Most of the representations are in contemporary dress and though stylised, the machinery and equipment are also represented in careful detail. It is thought that these images were based on drawings taken in places of work and that some of the faces are portraits. In a few cases, however, particularly those related to the textile trades, both the clothing of the women represented and the machinery, which includes a calico printing press, belonged to the earlier nineteenth century when such industries thrived.[102]

The Maryhill figures are predominantly adult men in their prime, faces adorned with conspicuous whiskers, brawny forearms exposed by rolled-up sleeves and an assortment of headgear typical of their different employments. Their poses are heroic, dignified and focused on the various tasks at hand. They are a celebration of the skilled working man and a few women, mostly involved in trades with lengthy apprenticeships, in much the same way that the great industrial exhibitions of the day were a celebration of the things they made. Widely considered Stephen Adam's greatest achievement in glass and design, the figures represent an unambiguous 'aristocracy of labour' simultaneously looking to the past for its heritage and authority, whilst looking to the future to embrace modernity. Though represented in glass, the panels were part of a phenomenon seen elsewhere in Glasgow and in other great industrial cities, of depictions of skilled working men including craftsmen as an urban archetype. Yet the survival of the world of craft making and craft communities in the nineteenth century is more typically associated with rural places than with great industrial cities such as Glasgow. This forms the subject of the next chapter.

Notes

1. *Glasgow and Its Environs: A Literary, Commercial, and Social Review Past & Present with a Description of its Leading Mercantile Houses and Commercial Enterprises* (1891).
2. Ibid., 220.
3. The term 'art furniture' was coined in London in the 1860s. Clive Edwards, '"Art furniture in the Old English style". The firm of Colinson and Lock, London, 1870–1900', *West 86th*, 19:1 (2012), 255–81.
4. *Glasgow and Its Environs*, 53.
5. Ibid., 164.
6. Clive Edwards, *Victorian Furniture: Technology and Design* (Manchester, 1993); *Glasgow and Its Environs*, 167.
7. *Glasgow and Its Environs*, 46.
8. See D. J. Bryden, *Scottish Scientific Instrument Makers, 1600–1900* (Edinburgh, 1972), 26.
9. Ibid., 23.
10. T. N. Clarke, A. D. Morrison-Low and A. D. C. *Simpson, Brass & Glass. Scientific Instrument Making Workshops in Scotland as Illustrated by*

Instruments from the Arthur Frank Collection at the Royal Museum of Scotland (Edinburgh, 1989), 96–7.

11. Ibid., 169.
12. Ibid., 75.
13. Ibid., 235–44.
14. *Poor Man's Guardian*, 26 December 1835, 'Dreadful condition of the poor handloom weavers'; *Times*, 11 June 1841, 'Destitution among the handloom weavers'; *Morning Post*, 16 December 1843, 'The Spitalfield weavers'; *Times*, 20 August 1835, 'Mr P. Scrope and the handloom weavers'. The latter is an impassioned commentary on suggestions that impoverished weavers should emigrate. *Sessional Papers of the House of Lords in the Session 1840*, vol. 32, 'Handloom Weavers'.
15. Liam Harte, ed. *The Literature of the Irish in Britain: Autobiography and Memoir, 1725–2001* (Basingstoke, 2009), 42–44.
16. William Hammond, *Recollections of William Hammond: A Glasgow Handloom Weaver* (Glasgow, c.1905), 23.
17. *Evening Telegraph*, 20 June 1878. The life of 'Black Peter' (d.1841), a slave-child brought to Glasgow by a merchant, is detailed in various nineteenth-century publications. See *Sketch of the Life of Peter Burnet. A Negro* (Paisley, 1842).
18. Anne Secord, 'Science in the pub: Artisan botanists in early nineteenth century Lancashire', *History of Science*, 32 (1994), 269–315.
19. *The Weavers Magazine and Literary Companion*, 6, February 1819, 1.
20. Ibid., 243.
21. Robert D. McEwan, *Old Glasgow Weavers: Being Records of the Incorporation of Weavers* (Glasgow, 1908).
22. *Ayrshire Post*, 14 July 1916.
23. *Report from Select Committee on Handloom Weavers' Petitions*, July 1835, 28.
24. NRS. GD45/7/6. Papers of the Maule family, Earls of Dalhousie, 1842. Grievances of silk handloom weavers, framework knitters and wood sawyers.
25. *Select Committee on Handloom Weavers*, 42.
26. Sally Tuckett, 'Reassessing the romance: Tartan as a popular commodity, c.1770–1830', *Scottish Historical Review*, 95:2 (2016), 182–202.
27. Geoffrey D. Hay and Geoffrey P. Stell, *Monuments of Industry: An Illustrated Historical Record* (Glasgow, 1986), 68.
28. NRS. NG1/1/29. Board of Manufactures. Minutes, 21 January 1795–19 December 1798, 208; 7 December 1796.
29. NRS. NG1/1/30. Board of Manufactures. Minutes, 23 January 1799–17 December 1800, 38; 6 March 1799.
30. NRS NG1/3/21. Board of Manufactures. Letters, July 1813–October 1818, 471; 10 June 1817.
31. NRS NG1/1/31. Board of Manufactures. Minutes, 21 January 1801–11 December 1805, 137; 26 May 1802.

32. Hammond, *Recollections.*
33. *Life of Peter Burnet.*
34. *Select Committee on Handloom Weavers,* 12–13.
35. Ibid., 12.
36. David Bremner, *The Industries of Scotland: Their Rise, Progress and Present Condition* (Edinburgh, 1869), 166.
37. Nenadic and Tuckett, *Colouring the Nation.*
38. Nenadic, 'Selling printed cottons'.
39. Nenadic, 'Designers in the fancy textile industry'.
40. Bremner, *Industries of Scotland,* 393–4.
41. Supplement to the *North British Daily Mail,* 24 May 1888; *Glasgow Herald,* 23 August 1888.
42. NRS. GD58/16. Carron Iron Company. Catalogues.
43. Mitchell, 'Architectural Iron Founding Industry'.
44. Paul Dobraszczyk, *Iron, Ornament and Architecture in Victorian Britain: Myth, Modernity, Excess and Enchantment* (Farnham, 2014).
45. NRS. GD1/1164. Miscellaneous Papers. Contract between John Stainton Manager of Carron Company and George Smith, 6 January 1817.
46. John Gloag and Derek Bridgewater, *A History of Cast Iron in Architecture* (London, 1948), 299.
47. Bremner, *Industries of Scotland,* 48.
48. British Library [BL]. 1807 a.4 74/1. *Catalogue: Section 1 Stoves, Hearths, & c. Manufactured by Carron Company,* 1883.
49. Dobraszczyk, *Iron, Ornament and Architecture,* 2.
50. Historic Environment Scotland, Thomas Hadden Collection.
51. Elizabeth Wright, 'Thomas Hadden, architectural metalworker', *Proceedings of the Society of Antiquaries of Scotland,* 121 (1992), 427–35.
52. Elizabeth Roads, ed., *The Thistle Chapel within St Giles' Cathedral* (Edinburgh, 2009), provides a full list of the artists and craftsmen.
53. Bremner, *Industries of Scotland,* 141–3.
54. Reynolds, *Britannica's Typesetters.*
55. Lewis F. Day, 'Decorative and industrial art at the Glasgow exhibition', *Art Journal,* September 1901, 273–7.
56. Jill Turnbull, *From Goblets to Gaslights: The Scottish Glass Industry, 1750–2006* (Edinburgh, 2017).
57. John C. Logan, 'The Dumbarton Glassworks Company: A study in entrepreneurship', *Business History,* 14:1 (1992), 61–81.
58. Sinclair, John, ed., *The Statistical Account of Scotland,* 21 vols (Edinburgh, 1791–99), IV, 21–6.
59. Logan, 'Dumbarton Glassworks Company'.
60. Turnbull, *From Goblets to Gaslights,* chapter 1.
61. University of Glasgow, Mackintosh Architecture, Context, Making and Meaning, Osler, https://www.mackintosh-architecture.gla.ac.uk/catalogue/name/?nid=OslerCo (last accessed 18 May 2021).

62. Bremner, *Industries of Scotland*, 382.
63. Peter D. A. Boyd, 'Ferns and pteridomania in Victorian Scotland,' *The Scottish Garden,* Winter (2005), 24–9.
64. Bremner, *Industries of Scotland*, 383–4.
65. *Hampshire Advertiser*, 19 May 1894, David Bremner obituary.
66. Bremner, *Industries of Scotland*, 134–5.
67. Day, 'Decorative and industrial art'; Perilla Kinchin and Juliet Kinchin, with a contribution by Neil Baxter, *Glasgow's Great Exhibitions* (Wendlebury, Bicester, 1988).
68. Nenadic, 'Designers in the fancy textile industry'.
69. For the early history of Scottish design schools see *Report from the Select Committee on the Arts and the Connections with Manufactures, House of Commons Papers*, 1X.1, 1836, 83–95. Evidence from James Skene, Secretary to the Board of Trustees and to the Royal Institution for the Encouragement of the Fine Arts in Scotland.
70. Francina Irwin, 'Scottish eighteenth-century chintz and its design', *The Burlington Magazine*, 107:750 (September 1965), 452–8.
71. *Caledonian Mercury*, 12 December 1822.
72. See D. A. Whyte and M. H. Swain, 'Edinburgh Shawls', *The Book of the Old Edinburgh Club*, 31 (1962), 52–64.
73. For an early history and assessment see, George Wallis, *Schools of Art. Their Constitution, Management etc* (London, 1857). Also, Quentin Bell, *The Design School* (London, 1963).
74. *Report from the Select Committee on the Arts*, 80.
75. *Glasgow Herald*, 20 May 1844. The prize was won by John Cook, pattern drawer of Calton, who was obviously a man-of-parts, for he also won the prize for an essay on 'the circulation of the blood'.
76. *Sheffield & Rotherham Independent*, 25 September 1841. 'Arts of design.'
77. Wallis, *Schools of Art*, 21.
78. *Glasgow Herald*, 15 August 1845.
79. *Glasgow Herald*, 25 April 1853.
80. *Glasgow Herald*, 16 January 1846.
81. *Glasgow Herald*, 25 April 1853.
82. *Glasgow Herald*, 28 December 1846, 'Artist's Soiree and Converszaione. Lecture from Mr Chisholm, pattern drawer'.
83. Charles Heath Wilson, *Remarks on Ornamental Art and Suggestions for its Improvement. A Lecture Delivered in the National Galleries [of Scotland] at the Request of the Committee of Management of the Art Manufacture Association on the Evening of 20 January 1857* (Edinburgh, 1857), 7.
84. *Glasgow Herald*, 28 February 1852.
85. Ibid.
86. *Birmingham Daily Post*, 12 March 1900, 'Municipal School of Art'.
87. *Lincoln, Rutland and Stamford Mercury*, 28 July 1899, 'The Autobiography of Mr T. W. Wallis [carver and gilder]'.

88. *Times*, 4 August 1905.
89. Ibid.
90. *Scotsman*, 25 November 1897; *Scotsman*, 2 February 1897.
91. *Scotsman*, 23 January 1873, 'Proposed technical school for Edinburgh'.
92. *Glasgow Directory*, 1851–2, advertisement, 141.
93. See *Journal of Stained Glass, Scotland Issue*, 30 (2006).
94. Michael Donnelly, *Scotland's Stained Glass. Making the Colours Sing* (1997).
95. Guthrie & Wells advertisement, *Glasgow Building Trades Exchange*, 1898, 183.
96. *Glasgow and Its Environs*, 140.
97. Lionel Gossman, 'Stephen Adam: The Early Years and the Glasgow Studio', www.victorianweb.org (last accessed 15 February 2021).
98. Carruthers, *Arts and Crafts Movement*, 234–5.
99. *Scotsman*, 3 December 1896, 'Mr Stephen Adam on artists and craftsmen'.
100. *Glasgow Herald*, 20 April 1878.
101. Gordon Barr, 'Maryhill Burgh Halls', *Architectural Heritage*, 28:3 (2010) 19–21.
102. *Maryhill Burgh Halls: Historic Stained-Glass Windows*, Maryhill Burgh Halls Trust.

3

Rural Craft in the Lowlands and Highlands

RURAL CRAFT SEEMS TIMELESS and immutable and to belong to life in hamlets, villages or small towns which are often described in nostalgic terms. Rural craft is also commonly connected to the essence of Scottishness (or Englishness) because the materials used in such crafts are native to the landscape, and the people, in their dress or speech, are rooted in vernacular cultures. Sentimentalised ideas about rural or small-town craft were rife in urban, industrial Scotland in the later nineteenth century and are exemplified in the popular Kailyard School of fiction, seen in the work of several successful writers including J. M. Barrie, who modelled *A Window in Thrums* (1890), concerned with the homely affairs of a weaving community, on his home town of Kirriemuir.

One of the best-known commentators on rural life and craft is George Sturt (who published under the name George Bourne) a Surrey wheelwright writing at the end of the nineteenth century and in the first few decades of the twentieth century, who owned a wheelwright business that survived through several generations of his family. His most famous book, *The Wheelwright's Shop*, published in 1923 after he had retired from trade, is an elegy on a changing way of life and craft skills undermined by new technologies and expanding social horizons. The world of the village wheelwright, which he entered in 1884, was 'a "folk" industry carried on in a "folk" method'. The 'eight skilled workmen or apprentices' that he and his father employed, were also eight 'friends of the family' and there was 'no looking far afield for customers'. 'Farmers rarely more than five miles away; millers, brewers, a local grocer or builder or timber-merchant or hop-grower – for such and no others did the ancient shop still cater, as it had done for nearly two centuries.'[1] On the nature of craftworkers in villages, he observed, with that wistful tone for which his writing is known,

> It was of the essence of the old system that those living under it subsisted in the main upon what their own industry could produce out of the soil and materials of their own countryside . . . Amongst themselves they would number a few special craftsmen – a smith, a carpenter or wheelwright, a shoemaker, a pair of sawyers, and so on; yet the trades of these specialists were only ancillary to the general handiness of the people, who with their own hands raised and harvested their crops, made their clothes, did much of the building of their homes, attended to their cattle, thatched their ricks, cut their firing, made their bread and wine or cider, pruned their fruit-trees and vines, looked after their bees, all for themselves.[2]

The narratives that underpin Sturt's writings concern the modernisation of work and rural practices, but also changing mindsets as education and information became more widely available. Sturt was a socialist and this informed his observations.

> For me the probability of a development for our village labourers similar to that of the town artisans is heightened, by recollection what artisans themselves were like, say a quarter of a century ago . . . While they worked by rule of thumb, outside their work they were as full of prejudices . . . They had quite the old attitude towards their employers; quite the old stubborn distrust of innovations in their work. When, however, you turn to their successors, you find a difference . . . they are thinking for themselves and informing themselves.[3]

These 'new' men were eager for their children to do well and move away from manual labour, but they were also 'conscious of a want of that book-learned culture which the practice of their skilled crafts cannot bestow'.[4] With expanded horizons dissatisfaction set in and old ways were abandoned.

Scotland was different by virtue of landscape and prevailing occupations. With a well-established parish school system, it is also possible that the Scottish rural craftsman was better educated than many in England long before the introduction of compulsory state schooling. Yet Sturt's reflections on change in southern England, with the hardships encountered by ordinary people, the narrow and repetitive cycles of work even amongst the craft trained and the tendency for the best to migrate to towns also rings true for rural Scotland. And so too does the array of local craftsmen that served a rural community, though even here it is clear that change was taking place over the course of the nineteenth century, not just at the end, and that proximity to a town and transport linkages was always important for shaping mindsets and opportunities.

FALA DAM AND A SCOTTISH WHEELWRIGHT'S SHOP

The hamlet of Fala Dam in Midlothian 20 or so miles south of Edinburgh, taken together with the nearby straggle of houses at Blackshiels and Soutra, gives us a good indication of life and craftwork in a Scottish rural context. I was about to write 'in a typical Scottish rural context', but there really is no such thing as typical here or anywhere else, since proximity to Edinburgh and a nearby major toll road leading to the Borders and England (today the A68) shaped the character of the place, just as coastal villages or those in coal-mining areas supported their own distinctive craft communities and cultures. Fala today, like many such places in pretty countryside within easy reach of a big city, is almost entirely given over to comfortable housing for a commuting population. Prosperous large farms producing monoculture crops have replaced the small mixed arable and livestock farms that once defined the area. The hamlet and its history are unremarkable, but it is unusual for having generated a legacy in the form of several photographs of late-nineteenth-century village life and craft – including a series of photographs depicting the local wheelwright's shop – and for the rare survival of the contents of one Fala craftsman's joinery workshop and business records.[5]

Fala in the eighteenth century was just a small collection of cottages for a mostly agricultural population, but it grew swiftly in the nineteenth century due to the creation of a new toll road and toll house, designed by Thomas Telford and opened in 1834, giving rise to a coaching inn at nearby Blackshiels, which in turn supported a flourishing blacksmith's business and several wheelwrights. The road transformed the area's fortunes and population. A new school was built and the parish church was redesigned and extended. The population, always small, peaked in the later nineteenth century and then fell, partly because road traffic and especially the cross-country coaching service declined when a new railway line was opened, which bypassed the village. There were 272 people living in Fala Dam at the 1911 census, down from 319 in 1901, made up of 67 families.[6]

In *Pigot's Commercial Directory* for 1825, the listing for Fala and Soutra includes William Oliver, smith, James and Thomas Paterson, wrights, Thomas Robertson, boot and shoemaker, two grocers, a flesher and a baker, a librarian called James Paterson and Agnes Herkes, linen and woollens draper.[7] In 1861, Pigot recorded the arrival of the Broomfield family, proprietors of Blackshiels Inn at the height of its prosperity, who were also shopkeepers, blacksmiths and farmers. There were two shoemakers in Fala in 1861 and three cartwrights, with one also keeping a shop.[8] By 1889, the *Directory* listed blacksmith Charles Herkes, shoemaker Scott Mathieson, a dressmaker, Sarah Spence, three wrights – Walter Stoddart, John Patterson and James Good – James Simpson joiner, plus a baker, a grocer and a photographer, Robert Lothian.[9] The same family names appear throughout the years covered by these different directories, suggesting craft businesses passed from father to son and clusters of complementary trades and shops.

The character of Fala and Soutra and some of its distinctive families is described in an 1892 antiquarian account written by local minister James Hunter. It includes the history of Peter Herkes, the tailor, who died in 1845 and left a charitable bequest of £100, from which two cottages were built to generate a rental income to pay for the education of local children. Peter Herkes was connected to Agnes Herkes, the linen draper, and also blacksmith Charles Herkes – probably husband of the first and father of the second.[10] Robert Broomfield, long active as a blacksmith, was the tenant of Fala Mill farm by 1892 as well as being the occupant of the former Blackshields Inn, which he closed in 1880 and converted into his private residence.[11] Hunter described the modernisation of the parish, which now had a post office, telegraph station and daily connection by post gig to the Tynehead railway station, with fast links into Edinburgh. In 1892 it had a daily coach each way to Dalkeith, the county town eight miles away.[12] As local minister, Hunter was concerned about the morals of the local people and their tendency to 'idleness' – 'The home life and home habits in the whole district around show the necessity of teaching the people Domestic Economy, and how to spend a winter's evening in some easy useful occupation.' To this end, he added, 'the local exhibitions of industrial work have not come too soon', with two of these events having been held in recent times at nearby Upper Keith.[13] He also remarked on the falling population:

> Few villages had had such a rapid decline as that of Fala. It is not now the fourth of the size it was sixty years ago. It had its doctor, policeman, inn, several public houses, shops of various kinds, tailors, joiners and blacksmiths in abundance. Now these have mostly all disappeared, and the closing of the Blackshiels Inn ten years ago, and the stopping of the coach, have left it without stir or bustle . . . During the coaching days the smithy was a place of some importance, there meeting all and sundry, discussing the kirk and market, the laird, the minister.[14]

The thin distribution of once numerous craftsmen in the area is reflected in a *Scotsman* advertisement for 1887: 'Blackshields – house, shop and garden, occupied by late A. Brockie, Millwright and Implement Maker. No millwright in locality: £8; house, 4 apartments, £5.'[15]

Figure 3.1   Wheelwright's shop. Fala Dam, Midlothian, *c*.1890. © National Museums Scotland.

Directories do not suggest as bleak a picture as the one painted by the local minister, for there were new tradesmen listed including the photographer, but clearly the demise of the nearby post road and coaching inn had taken its toll, with Fala now bypassed by the modernising world. The 'left behind', quaint and sleepy character of the village may well account for a series of late-nineteenth-century photographs that record the craftsmen and work activities of the wheelwright's shop which occupied a range of buildings that are now a house. The subject of the images is possibly Walter Stoddart and his workforce of two or three men or boys and the photographer may have been Robert Lothian, who lived locally. The images capture a bucolic scene and may have been intended for tourist postcards at a time in the village's history when the cartwright was slowly slipping into the past as new types of transport took over, much as described by George Sturt in Surrey.

The Fala wheelwright's workshop is shown as a stone-built, pan-tiled structure on two floors with a cottage at one end that was part of a terrace of cottages, shops and workshops. The roof tiles suggest it was constructed in the later eighteenth century. The wide central entrance and opening above reveal the building's specialist functions for storing wood and components of carts and related things such as wheelbarrows, with the yard in front for construction or repair of large vehicles. There was a forge nearby for making the iron components and tyres. A great deal of the work undertaken was probably out of doors, indeed, the dismantled cart that dominates the image is so large it could only have been built in a yard. Three men are visible in the image, which is taken in high summer. Another photograph of the same workshop a few years earlier has four men posed outside holding their working tools, with rolled-up sleeves and aprons. Such craftsmen would have turned their hands to a wide range of activities. This was also the typical experience of the rural carpenter and joiner, as the business records of James Simpson, joiner in Fala, reveals for the years from 1912 to 1921. Simpson's clients included the local school boards, the bowling club and numerous nearby farmers and gentry houses. For Mrs Hodge of Pathhead in 1913, for example, he fitted new castors to a sofa and a bed, put up some blinds and mended a window fastening. He repaired fences, carts and tools, often working in conjunction with the smith. He did finer work such as picture-frame making and offered a coffin-making service.[16] The contents of Simpson's house suggest comfortable, if modest, accommodation.[17]

'OUR GLEN': HIGHLAND CRAFTSMAN

Rural craftworkers, though typically found in villages or hamlets like Fala, were also based in country areas and can be identified through estate records. Landowners, many absent for much of the year, were often heavily involved in the support and promotion of artisans on their estates, partly because this retained a skilled workforce of benefit to their properties, but also, in some areas and the Highlands in particular, because it ensured prosperity in the region and the maintenance of a population in the face of pressure to migrate.[18]

The relationships between craftworkers and local elites was often personal and paternal. A great Highland estate owner, such as the Marquis of Breadalbane, received numerous petitions from his tenants each year seeking patronage or favours, as in November 1791 when Duncan MacCallum, house carpenter and joiner in Morinsh petitioned to be granted the whole croft of Ardveil so that he could keep a kailyard.[19] Landowners also supported industrial activity on their estates with adjacent housing provided, such as the Easdale slate quarries in Argyll, which generated employment for a resident joiner comprising, in 1816, building and repair work for the manager's house and byre as well work on the school for the quarry workers' children.[20] Landowners' charitable activity embraced the welfare of aged craftworkers resident on their estates, as illustrated in 1828 when Margaret MacKay, seamstress, who had taught sewing on Breadalbane's Perthshire estates for decades, petitioned for a better house, 'she being not very stout'.[21] Some of these petitions sought to convince landowners of the importance of keeping them in the district, as in May 1830 when John Robertson, a wright living in the 'factory house' in lower Ballinlaggain in Perthshire, close to Taymouth Castle, stated that he was 'the only experienced wright in the officiary of Taymouth for making farming utencels and has in general to employ four men more then himself in order to serve his customers and to continue his usefulness in the country, he would humbly beg leave . . . [there followed a complex request for the tenancy of a larger landholding nearby that had recently become vacant]'.[22]

Sometimes the traditional relationships between craftsmen working on an estate and other tenants were not to their liking, as in 1835 when four blacksmiths wrote to Breadalbane to complain about the 'antiquated and obsolete custom' whereby they were paid 'a certain specified quantity of barley and oatmeal in proportion to the quality of the lands possessed' by their local customers.[23] In short, payment was determined by the means of the client and not the work undertaken. And it is also clear that some of the petitioning from craftsmen was for help towards the costs of leaving the district and setting up elsewhere, as in 1837 when a number of tenants in the Aberfeldy area lobbied Breadalbane on behalf of the sons of Alexander McDonald, smith in Aberfeldy, to secure the boys with situations in the south to learn the farrier's trade before setting up on their own elsewhere.[24] The last two petitions from the 1830s give insights to evolving relationships with local craftsmen on Highland estates, for though patronage for country-house building remained important and great landlords still influenced employment in nearby small towns, the ambitious rural craftsman was frustrated by localised cultures and limited opportunities and looked elsewhere to advance. By mid century, craftsmen were less likely to be tied to estate tenancies than 50 years before, though some older men remained. Those left behind were often viewed by their noble landlords with fond attachment.

A sentimentalised relationship between artisans and Highland landowners is illustrated in a series of photographs of the Invercreran estate in the Appin area of northern Argyllshire in the 1860s.[25] Set in a deep valley inland from Loch Creran, the estate and the neighbouring property of Fasnacloich was well populated and supported a hamlet with a school, church and post office.[26] Even in the 1790s, at the time of the first *Statistical Account*, when most of the population spoke only Gaelic and emigration was all the rage, the district was well settled with a range of artisans including tailors, shoemakers, carpenters 'and other mechanics', most of them working for day rates plus the cost of their victuals, suggesting that they tended to journey around the extensive parish to the different farms and townships to undertake their work.[27] At the time of the second *Statistical Account* in 1845, this pattern of itinerant work went unremarked and had probably vanished. Greatly expanded by 1845 and clearly having an impact on the local population, was the slate quarry at Ballachulish, which gave employment to significant numbers of joiners and blacksmiths as well as quarrymen.[28]

Traditionally associated with the Campbell family, the Invercreran estate, like many others in the Highlands, had passed into the ownership of another family by mid century, the McCallum Websters, who, though of Highland descent, were mostly employed as civil servants or law officers in Britain and India. The principal owner was matriarch Margaret Kennedy McCallum, who was born near Spean Bridge in 1786 and married Alexander McCallum from Loch Nell near Oban, who made his fortune as a Jamaica sugar planter. The couple lived in London for much of the time and the property passed to a daughter, another Margaret, a great Jamaica heiress and mother of 11 children whose husband, George Webster was Sheriff for Forfarshire.[29] The house in Appin was a much-loved summer retreat for this large, well-connected and educated family.[30] One of their number, Alexander McCallum Webster (1837–1879), a civil servant in India, was a keen amateur photographer who created a unique photographic record of life on the estate during 1866 when he took a long family holiday in Britain. Titled 'Our Glen', the resulting album shows the McCallum Websters and their friends enjoying the usual round of picnics and outdoor games and shooting and fishing that was typical of their class when holidaying in the Highlands. But it also provides a record of others who lived on the estate the year round, including the minister, the schoolmaster, the midwife, domestic servants and an array of estate workers. Many of the latter were photographed in settings connected with their occupations and holding their tools. The individuals are named, with husbands and wives photographed together, and aspects of their lives can be discerned. The road mender, Duncan Rankin, was photographed with his wife Flora, who ran the local post office. The estate gardener, Peter Rankin, brother of Duncan, was also portrayed. All are comfortably dressed. The tailor, unnamed, was photographed with a note stating he was 91 years old at the time and long before, during the Napoleonic Wars, had been a soldier in the 92nd Regiment (the Gordon Highlanders). One of the best dressed of

Figure 3.2 The carpenter and his wife (Mr and Mrs McInnes). 'Our Glen' photo album, Invercrearan Estate, Argyll, *c*.1860. © National Records of Scotland.

the estate-worker couples is the carpenter and his wife, Mr and Mrs McInnes, with the former wearing a watch chain across his waistcoat and carrying a ruler in his hand to indicate his trade. As in this case, most of the skilled, named workers in 'Our Glen' were middle-aged or elderly, with indications that the young and able had moved away to better themselves, some only as far as the slate quarry at Ballachulish, but others further afield. One of these was Duncan Cameron, photographed in 1867 when aged about 15 and described as 'the herd boy', but with a note added to indicate that two years later he left the district to work as a clerk in a Glasgow mercantile house.[31]

Local craftsmen like McInnes the joiner could turn their hands to multiple activities and were valued but as 'generalists' were not the best option for high quality or complex work. A letter of 1821 from the factor at Taymouth Castle to Breadalbane concerning estimates for the cost of making new gates suggested that local workmen should be hired to hang the gates, but that the design and making of the gates and hinges should be left to a joiner and blacksmith from Perth, which would be cheaper and faster.[32] Yet despite this practical eye to efficiency and cost savings, there is much in the 'Our Glen' photograph album to suggest elite paternalistic fondness for the people who worked on estates, particularly among such summer-visiting and wealthy owners as the McCallum Websters, who did not rely on their property for income.

WEAVER, STONEMASON, BLACKSMITH AND PATTERNMAKER

Though there was no such person as the typical rural craftworker, four trades that were seen in large numbers throughout Scotland and were conducted by individuals who left records of their lives, give insights to common experience. Three worked in traditional crafts and the last practised a new specialism connected to the work of the engineer.

William Thom (1799–1848) was an itinerant weaver and sometime poet in Aberdeenshire, who mainly lived in and around the small town of Inverurie, which had a population of about 500 in 1800, rising to c.2,000 in 1845 following the opening of the Aberdeen canal.[33] As described in the 1790s,

> A great part of the townsmen are mechanics, such as weavers, shoemakers, taylors, cart and square wrights, and blacksmiths; and they are all employed in working for the inhabitants of the town and neighbourhood . . . at the same time, they cultivate their small pieces of property, of from one to six acres of land.[34]

Thom's working life as a weaver comprised periods of factory work in Aberdeen combined with semi-rural home-based and itinerant weaving according to the shifting circumstances of the trade. A widower with three children to support, he described his life as a 'customary' weaver in the 1830s and 1840s.

> I occupy two trim little garrets in a house belonging to Sir Robert Elphinstone, lately built on the market stance of Inverury. We have everything required in our humble way; perhaps our blankets pressed a little too lightly during the late severe winter, but then we crept closer together . . .
> [I am] employed seven or eight months yearly in customary weaving- that is, a country weaver who wants a journeyman sends for me. I assist in making bedding, shirting and other household stuffs. When his customers are served, I am discharged, and so ends the season. During that time I earn from ten to twelve shillings a week; pay the master generally four shillings for my 'keep', and remit the rest to my family. In this way, we move on happy enough . . .
> I eke out the blank portions of the season by going into a factory . . . A little job now and then, in the musical way, puts all right again . . .[35]

Thom came to weaving too late to experience the good times of the trade – the 'golden age' – but a memory of those days, highly romanticised, remained a powerful presence in weaving communities. Referring to the last decades of the eighteenth century,

> Then was the daisy portion of weaving – the bright and mid-day period of all who pitched a shuttle, and of the happy one whose luck it was to win a weaver's smile. Four days did the weaver work, – for then four days was a week, as far as working went, – and such a week to a skillful workman brought forty shillings. Sunday, Monday, and Tuesday were of course jubilee . . . Weaving commenced gradually on Wednesday.[36]

Thom's experience was very different and could be volatile in the extreme, despite the rural context in which he worked. The latter is captured in his account of the sudden collapse in fortunes for the village of Newtyle, near Coupar Angus, which had recently sprung up alongside the newly completed Dundee Railway and consisted 'chiefly of weaving-shops and dwellings for the weavers'. The inhabitants were mostly strangers to the place 'and to each other' having been brought from distant places by manufacturers advertising for workers. And when trade collapsed in 1837, they mostly moved away, leaving the families with children behind, including that of William Thom.[37] They too eventually left to tramp the nearby countryside, begging and singing along the way to make ends meet before settling back to weaving in Aberdeen and then 'home' again to Inverurie when trade improved. Though he enjoyed some success as a weaver poet and saw the publication of his *Recollections*, Thom ended his life still working at the loom, stricken with consumption and died in poverty in Dundee in 1848.[38]

Despite such individual circumstances, the rural weaving workforce was considerable and, in many instances, survived and adapted long after the handloom weavers of Glasgow or Paisley had fallen away. Some adjusted their practice by switching from cotton to wool, as in Sanquhar in south-west Scotland in the early 1840s when the Borders woollen weaving and knitting industries took off.[39] Indeed, pockets of rural weaving with specialist product lines survived for decades and by the turn of the twentieth century, with a shift in elite opinion and practice, particularly in the Highlands, it was felt that a craft like handloom weaving should be encouraged and supported for the good of communities. The Scottish Home Industries Association, founded in 1889, was active in assisting inhabitants of the Hebrides in obtaining weaving equipment to produce tweed. Instructors would travel to the islands, offering guidance and advice, and the weavers – like their forebears in the early nineteenth century – worked at looms in their homes.[40] The early twentieth century saw frequent remarks on the passing of the age of the rural weaver long after they were gone in towns, as in this newspaper report of 1929:

> LAST OF THE HANDLOOM WEAVERS. Mr Angus Munro, farmer, South Tullich, Glenaray, died on Saturday at the age of 76 years. When a tenant of Auchnagoul township, Inveraray, he carried on business as a handloom weaver, the products of his loom in the nature of brown crotal cloth, being purchased by H.R.H. Princess Louise and other Royal personages, who had the cloth made into garments . . . Mr Munro was the last handloom weaver in that district.[41]

And occasional accounts were given of weaver communities still surviving in out-of-the-way places, described in the press as if they were exotic lost tribes of the Amazon. Under the title 'Last of Handloom Workers', from 'Our Special Correspondent', the *Daily Mail* in 1931 reported:

> I have found the last of the handloom weavers. Here in this little Scots village, five miles from Paisley, is a colony of twenty weavers who still follow the craft which has been in their families for centuries . . . The average age of the weavers here is 73 years . . . Kilbarchan is one of the few villages of Scotland which is self-supporting and self-contained.[42]

This weaver community, which also featured in a newsreel film of 1926, was made up of tartan weavers crafting an expensive form of wool cloth, 'for hand-woven tartan never loses its colour or its durability'. When the weaving finally ended, a cottage with loom was acquired by the National Trust for Scotland to be a visitor attraction.

Another group of craftsmen who were found in all Scottish country districts were the stonemasons, whose experience in the first half of the nineteenth century can be seen in the recollections of Hugh Miller (1802–56). Miller was a celebrated geologist and writer who began his working life as a stonemason in the small coastal town of Cromarty in north-east Scotland and recorded the circumstances in an autobiography.[43] He was the son of a seafaring man, with uncles variously employed in trades ranging from shoemaker to harness maker, cartwright to stonemason. He described the milieu in which he was raised as one where the skilled man commonly cultivated a range of accomplishments beyond his craft:

> My native town had possessed, for at least an age or two previous to that of my boyhood, its sprinkling of intelligent, book-consulting mechanics and tradesfolk . . . there was a literary cabinet-maker in the neighbourhood, who had once actually composed a poem of thirty lines on the Hill of Cromarty, whose collection of books, chiefly poetical, amounted for from about eighty to a hundred.[44]

Hugh was clever and well educated in the local school but had no ambition beyond what he knew. He was apprenticed to an uncle who was a stonemason, with work mostly comprising quarrying, building and stone cutting. As he explained,

> The husband of one of my maternal aunts was a mason, who, contracting for jobs on a small scale, usually kept an apprentice or two, and employed a few journeymen. With him I agreed to serve for the term of three years; and, getting a suit of strong moleskin clothes, and a pair of heavy hob-nailed shoes, I waited only for the breaking up of the winter frosts, to begin work in the Cromarty quarries – jobbing masters in the north of Scotland usually combining the profession of the quarrier with that of the mason.[45]

After three years he commenced as self-employed journeyman working across the Highlands on farm- and house-building projects during the summer months and going home to his mother's house for the winter for leisure and study. He improved his drawing and geometry to better his chances of good work. In writing about his early career, Miller reflected on the skills of the best men in his craft, regarding them almost as artists for their understanding of the materials with which they worked. One was a man in his sixties called John Fraser.

> Fraser showed me how very much the ability depended on a natural faculty. John's strength had never been above the average of that of Scotchmen, and it was now considerably reduced; nor did his mallet deal more or heavier blows than that of the common workman. He had, however, an extraordinary power of conceiving of the finished piece of work, as lying within the rude stone from which it was his business to disinter it; and while ordinary stone-cutters had to repeat and re-repeat their lines and draughts, and had in this way virtually to give to their work several surfaces in detail ere they reached the true one, old John cut upon the true figure at once, and made one surface serve for all.[46]

When still a young man, Miller travelled south to Edinburgh to find work during the building boom of 1824–5, getting employment on a mansion-house project at Niddry as one of a party of 16 masons, plus apprentices and labourers, mostly engaged to cut mouldings for mullioned windows. He was paid £2 8s fortnightly. But stone hewing, which was dusty, undermined his health and he went home for a while to convalesce before turning to gravestone carving.[47] In 1828 he moved to Inverness and advertised in the local newspaper as a gravestone carver.

After nearly 20 years as a stonemason and with persistently poor health, but a good education and a lifetime of self-improvement to draw on, Hugh Miller trained as bank accountant in Linlithgow and then took

Figure 3.3   Hugh Miller, geologist, writer and stonemason, c.1845. © Scottish National Portrait Gallery.

up journalism in the 1840s as editor of the Free Church newspaper *The Witness*, based in Edinburgh. He pursued studies in geology, natural history, religion, and myths and legends, and published to great acclaim. He also posed for pioneering Edinburgh photographers David Octavius Hill and Robert Anderson in a series of striking portraits which show him with a stonemason's chisel and mallet, leaning on a gravestone, with his sleeves rolled up in typical workman style (though his clothing is that of a middle-class man) and a shepherd's plaid draped across the stone on his right, evocative of his connections to the work and traditions of rural Scots and the outdoor life.

Miller offered many reflections on the attributes of labouring men of the day, differentiating between the 'workmen that pass sedentary lives within doors, such as weavers and tailors, and those who labour in the open air, such as masons and ploughmen'.[48] He thought the sedentary men least content with their lot than those who worked outside, because they worked in groups, could chat amongst themselves since their work was not physically taxing and 'are generally much better able to state their grievances, and much more fluent in speculating on their causes'. The different employments, according to Miller, generated different interests and dispositions. The barber had to entertain his customers, be courteous and avoid controversy. The tailor cultivated fine clothes and manners and 'hence [there is] more ridicule of tailors among working men than of any other class of mechanics'.[49] He reflected on the sagacity of the village smith, who heard as much gossip as the village barber, but did not need to please his customers by his talk and kept his counsel. And of his own trade,

> The professional character of the mason varies a good deal in the several provinces of Scotland, according to the various circumstances in which he is placed. He is in general a blunt, manly, taciturn fellow, who, without much of the Radical or Chartist about him, especially if wages be good and employment abundant, rarely touches his hat to a gentleman . . . The mason is almost always a silent man; the strain on his respiration is too great, when he is actively employed, to leave the necessary freedom to the organs of speech; and so at least the provincial builder or stone-cutter rarely or never becomes a democratic orator. I have met with exception cases in the larger towns; but they were the result of individual idiosyncrasies, developed in clubs and taverns, and were not professional.[50]

Blacksmiths, whom Miller admired, like masons or weavers, were found in rural areas throughout the country. A portrait by an unknown photographer, probably based in Galashiels or Hawick in the Scottish border county of Roxburghshire, taken in the 1890s, shows master blacksmith Robert Davidson, aged about 50 years, dressed in his working clothes of stripped, collarless, heavy cotton shirt and waistcoat, with flat peaked cap and leather blacksmith's apron over trousers and sturdy boots. His shirt sleeves are rolled to the elbows and he strikes a pose, not dissimilar to that adopted by Hugh Miller and typically seen among men involved in the physically demanding metal and building trades, with brawny arms crossed high on his chest and a penetrating stare. The full beard and walrus-styled moustache, fashionable at the time, add a patriarchal air. He is stood alongside his daughter Mary, who wears a walking skirt, matching jacket and flat straw hat – a style of dress adopted by the later nineteenth century 'new woman' and typically worn by lower-middle-class clerks or schoolteachers. Behind them is Woodfoot lodge house and the gates to the Stobs Castle estate near Hawick, which along with the house itself was designed by Robert Adam in 1793 for the Elliot family. To the left of the gate piers, which still survive today, was the cottage and blacksmith's shop then occupied by Robert Davidson and his family.

Robert was descended from a long line of Roxburghshire blacksmiths. His grandfather, father and elder brother, all named Walter, were the blacksmiths who occupied the Newmill-on-Teviot smithy a few miles south of Hawick for most of the nineteenth century. In 1861, when Robert began his apprenticeship, the father and elder son's business employed one man and an apprentice. Robert's aunt, a dressmaker, lived with the family and one of his sisters was a domestic servant.[51] As second son, there was little opportunity for Robert to go into business with his father, hence his first place as journeyman blacksmith was at the nearby hamlet of Appletreehall, which had a water-driven wool mill that provided employment for two blacksmiths, two masons and a master carpenter. He moved to Woodfoot in 1874 on becoming a master crafts-man. One of his sons, another Walter, also became a blacksmith and his second son John became a joiner at Overhall by Hawick. Joiners and blacksmiths commonly worked together, which accounts for this pattern of strategic family training and employment.

A country blacksmith like Robert Davidson could turn his hand to many activities, such as shoeing horses, mending and making farm or local workshop equipment and fashioning tools for use by other crafts-men such as hammers, knives, files and chisels. The Stobs Castle estate, from which he rented the cottage and workshop attached to the main gates, would have generated much work as would the passing traffic on

Figure 3.4 Robert Davidson, blacksmith, and his daughter Mary. Stobs Castle, Roxburghshire, c.1895. © National Museums Scotland.

the nearby road connecting Edinburgh to Carlisle, which opened in the 1820s (now the A7). The Border Union Railway, opened in the 1860s, had a station at Stobs. Robert was a respectable member of the artisan community; he advertised in the local commercial directories and men of his background participated in various aspects of institutional and church life. His older brother Walter, blacksmith at Newmill-on-Teviot, was one of the candidates for the Hawick School Board elections in 1888.[52] Though records have not survived, the Davidson brothers may well have exhibited their craft wares at the Handicraft and Industrial Exhibition that was held in Hawick in 1887 under the sponsorship of the Duke of Buccleuch.[53]

The blacksmith's trade was well rewarded, but Robert's life changed dramatically in 1903 when the Stobs Castle estate was sold to the War Office to become an army camp and most of the cottages and workshops, including the one he had occupied for 30 years, were demolished. The army employed its own tradesmen, who were serving soldiers, so Robert and his immediate neighbours, joiners John and Thomas Scott, moved to Whitlawhaugh just a few miles away where they continued in their respective crafts, though the upheaval along with growing old age would have taken its toll on Robert. Long retired and widowed, possibly now living with his daughter, Robert Davidson died at 10 Union Street, Hawick in 1921, an event that was marked in the local newspaper.[54] His later life was clouded by the death of a great-grandson in the war. This was Lance Corporal John J. Davidson, killed in the Dardanelles in 1915 aged 22. Before the war, John had served a joiner's apprenticeship with his grandfather, also called John, the second son of Robert the blacksmith, at Overhall in Hawick.[55]

As each of these life histories show, craft employment could change swiftly and migration in search of work was commonplace. For many this entailed modest movement within a locality, whilst for others it involved emigration, particularly amongst the young and ambitious, with some rural communities sending large numbers to distant places. In the later eighteenth century, for instance, many teenage boys who were apprenticed as wrights, joiners or cabinetmakers in the Borders counties migrated to the West Indies to work in the plantation system, with some making their fortunes there through land purchase and slave-based production.[56] Canada was the destination of choice for the mid nineteenth century Scottish migrant whose numbers included Andrew McIlwraith (1830–90) a patternmaker from Ayrshire. McIlwraith was born into a large family in Newton-on-Ayr, a small coastal burgh near the town of Ayr. His father was a handloom weaver at a time when the

town supported over 200 weavers, mostly working for Glasgow manufacturers.[57] His elder brother Thomas was an apprentice-trained cabinetmaker who became manager of a gas company before emigrating with
his new-married wife to Canada to run a similar business in Hamilton.
Andrew, whose life and thoughts we know from a detailed diary he kept
from the mid 1850s to early 1860s, was an apprentice patternmaker in
an engineering shop in Ayr who followed his brother to Canada in his
early twenties, to take up a job as draughtsman in a railway company.[58]
Over the next few years, before marriage in his thirties, he led an itinerant existence moving from one job to another in engineering shops and
foundries in both Canada and New York and he also made an extended
visit home to Ayrshire in 1857.

Andrew's working day, though starting early, was flexible and like
many craftsmen he was able to take time off on fine days to pursue
leisure activities, though he made up his hours in the evenings. Much
of his free time was directed towards self-improvement, with reading
and drawing at home in his lodgings recorded almost daily. He joined
mechanics' institutes, singing clubs and debating societies. He collected
butterflies and insects, which he mounted in display cases of his own
making and shot birds for his brother, who was an amateur ornithologist
and taxidermist. He played chess with his male friends and took genteel
teas with his female friends, the latter mostly connected to the churches
he attended or to family networks. He was teetotal. When he visited
home for several months at the end of 1857 to comfort his mother following the death of his elderly father, Andrew's social life was much the
same with family teas, church-going, walks and rambles to nearby beauty
spots and visits to former workmates. He also travelled to Edinburgh to
take architectural drawing lessons to extend his skills as a draughtsman
and see the tourist sites.

In these early years, Andrew McIlwraith moved jobs frequently, sometimes because the contracts were short and sometimes for better opportunities. He was in many respects a typical journeyman, but, though he
tried his luck in the US city of Detroit and took a job in New York for
a while, he rarely moved far from his base, the Scottish settlement in
Ontario, with its small towns with Scottish names, such as Hamilton
or Dundas. He lived comfortably and had money to spend on books or
exhibitions and fairs. He had a photographic portrait taken and sent
copies home to his mother and sister. But he also worried about the
future, hence the self-improvement and frequent movement. On taking
up a new job at a foundry and engineering shop in Dundas, where he
was engaged in drawing patterns for furnaces and pumping engines for

a nearby waterworks, he described what he took with him – his tools, books and clothing – and how, on arriving, he met up with the foreman, a Scot, and set about making the bench where he was to work. Fitting into a new place was relatively easy when he could join the local church and social clubs for respectable single men like himself. He saw North America as a place of opportunity and expressed his opinion in a long letter he wrote from New York, where he was working at the time, for publication in the *Ayrshire Times*. [59] It is titled 'Is the Working Man Better Off in America than in Britain' and the narrative answers with a decided 'yes'. There were different employment practices to those of the 'old country', with less protection for American workers, but wages were better and living costs lower. 'I have only to remark that a man who has learnt his trade well at home can find himself at no loss here.'[60]

Andrew ceased keeping a diary when he married in his early thirties. Through his wife's family, he became a bookkeeper and sometime pattern drawer in a foundry in the Scots-settled town of Galt. He soon became the manager, later set up a small branch of his own, then sold it and in middle age was an accountant in a fire insurance company. When he died aged 60 he was a modestly successful, well-respected family man and prominent figure in his community, worthy of an obituary in the local newspaper.

CRAFT PROFILES IN RURAL COMMUNITIES AND SMALL TOWNS

These four individuals – the weaver, stonemason, blacksmith and patternmaker – were part of the craft profile of rural areas. Some belonged to old and declining crafts, others were new and evolving, but in each case their family lives and work experience was connected in various ways to nearby small towns as well as the rural hinterlands. Over the course of the nineteenth century there was much change in the character and distribution of craftworkers and even the tiniest of urban settlements could be transformed.

The rural counties of Scotland varied considerably in their population characteristics and craft communities, though the bedrock of all, particularly in the first half of the century, was handloom weaving. In addition to its weavers, the county of Ayrshire in the south-west supported large numbers of craftworkers in villages and small towns in 1841, with 218 cabinetmakers, 613 blacksmiths, 1,302 men described as 'carpenters, joiners and wrights' and 999 masons and stone cutters. Additionally, Ayrshire boasted of large numbers of skilled craftswomen, dominated by the textile trades, with 140 described as embroiderers. The Highland county of Argyll, north-west of Glasgow, was home to 22 cabinetmakers in 1841, 322 blacksmiths, 553 carpenters, joiners and wrights and 445 masons and stone cutters. But further north the numbers dwindle. Ross and Cromarty in the far north-east – a prosperous farming county in many ways – had just 43 cabinetmakers in 1841, 250 blacksmiths, 480 carpenters, joiners and wrights and 378 masons and stone cutters.[61] And as the century progresses, the numbers of such highly skilled workers mostly decreased in the distant places, where population depletion was a usual experience and the skilled moved south or abroad. So, Ross and Cromarty in 1911 had only 11 cabinetmakers with an average work-force of just two per employee.[62] In contrast, the county of Ayrshire in 1911 had growing numbers of the traditional craftsmen in small towns and villages alike. There were 458 cabinetmakers and 47 cabinetmak-ing employers, making an average workplace unit of ten, which was not dissimilar in size to businesses found in Edinburgh at the same time. There was also a good representation of French polishers in Ayrshire, the majority women, and upholsterers and woodcarvers suggesting the production of comfortable and even fine furniture.[63]

Such figures, however, obscure significant local circumstances that shaped the artisan workforce. The Ross-shire royal burgh of Tain, for example, with a population of c.2,000 in 1901, was in a flourishing state with a remarkably large craft community, the product of being a retail hub in a prosperous rural area and well positioned on the railway line running from Inverness northwards to Wick and Thurso. It was a cen-tre of the tourist industry, attracting golfers and anglers and had fine churches and schools. According to the *Statistical Account* in 1792, the town was in an underdeveloped state, with agriculture and nearby fish-ing the main employments. But even at this early stage there were 12 merchants and shopkeepers in Tain and up to 80 'tradesmen and arti-ficers, besides 20 in the landward part of the parish.'[64] By 1845, urban improvements had widened and paved the streets and an iron foundry was operating on the edge of town. The burn powered sawing, carding and grinding mills, a dyeing mill and a brewery.[65] A *Gazetteer* account of the 1880s described the main businesses of Tain comprising four bank branches and 14 insurance agencies, along with three hotels, a gas com-pany, a fortnightly grain market and seasonal fairs. Nearby was a distill-ery and woollen mill, which may account for the dominance of women among the employed population.[66] What the *Gazetteer* failed to notice was the rich array of craftsmen. Yet someone who thought they were worth recording was local bookseller and photographer William Smith, who kept premises in Tain's High Street from the early 1850s to his

Figure 3.5   Danny Thompson's cabinetmaking workshop. Tain, *c.*1890. © Tain & District Museum.

death in 1906. He took many photographs of local scenes and people including 'characters of the town', mostly elderly men and tradesmen in their places of work and servants connected with some of the great houses nearby. He also published a series of colour-tinted photographic postcards for tourists showing notable buildings and street scenes.[67] He erected a special glasshouse to the rear of his shop for his studio portrait business. As a thriving town in a prosperous north-east farming district, Tain provided a constant flow of customers.

Danny Thompson, a cabinetmaker, was one of the craftsmen that William Smith recorded, in a portrait of the workshop interior in Upper King Street, Tain *c.*1890. The photograph shows six men and a teen-age apprentice, a typical workshop size in the sector, all wearing white aprons, with the proprietor stood in the centre. The firm was founded by Danny Thompson, a local man, in the 1880s, was sold to William Fraser, who appears on the left of the photograph, in the early twentieth century and continued to trade under the same name through succes-sive ownerships to 1994. Several part-finished objects can be identified in the photograph, including picture and mirror frames, a carved chair back and hall stand or mirror back.[68] Upholstered cushions and textiles are seen on the left. The proprietor, who was a master craftsman, is stood behind a ladies' Davenport writing desk, which was a complex and expensive piece of furniture. To the rear of the workshop, fixed to the roof, is a wheel with a mechanised belt-drive, for running a sawing or turning machine and there are numerous hand tools in racks on the wall. Wood is stored above in the rafters and prints and designs are pasted onto the walls. In common with most local workshops of this type, Danny Thompson also made coffins, though none are visible in the image, and he fitted out house interiors with wood panelling and chimney pieces. The workshop as photographed is arranged to show the range of products made and the different processes of manufacture. It is unlikely, however, that tasks like upholstery work were undertaken in such a dusty environment. A later outside photograph of the same premises *c.*1910 shows a range of windows at right angles to the workshop, which was probably the showroom.[69]

The situation in Tain was reproduced across rural Scotland, with thriving craft communities in small county towns where the hinterland supported a prosperous rural economy. These places were rarely the focus for extensive manufacture, though the early textile industry generated a wide array of workshop and putting-out arrangements in many. The town of Dumfries in south-west Scotland was bigger than Tain, but similar in character, and from the later eighteenth century had flourished as a centre of rural consumption for rich farmers and the local gentry, many of the latter keeping houses in the town. It also had its textile and leather processing industries, though these, with the exception of shoemaking, had largely disappeared by the mid nineteenth century.[70] A later survey suggests a thriving place with the usual array of cabinetmakers and fine jewellers alongside tailors, clothiers and retailers.[71] Several were regular exhibitors at international exhibitions, including John Fallas, saddle and harness maker in Dumfries, who won prizes in London in 1862.[72] Some small towns, drawing on local specialist trades and proximity to favourable transport linkages became unusual focal points for craft production. Foremost amongst them in rural Scotland was the town of Beith in Ayrshire, famed for furniture making.

Beith was unremarkable when described in the *Statistical Account* of 1845. About 20 miles south-west from Glasgow and well connected by road, it suffered from being bypassed by modern transport developments that included the abandoned Glasgow to Ardrossan canal project of 1805. The population grew steadily in the early nineteenth century from nearly 2,000 in 1792 to just over 5,000 by 1831, but it was mostly made up of rural labourers, with 400 handloom weavers the largest craft group and the usual array of other tradesmen dominated by masons employed in house building in the town and nearby on small gentry estates. There were 26 joiners but no cabinetmakers in 1845.[73] The largest industry after weaving was cheese making.[74] In the 1840s, a railway connection from Ayr to Glasgow was routed via Beith, but it was decades before the impact of swift access to Glasgow was felt.[75]

Textiles remained a feature of Beith with a linen thread factory and silk printing and dying works operating by the 1870s, though the numbers of handloom weavers had ebbed away. Processing leather saw growing employment, but more remarkable in the later century were the cabinetmaking works specialising particularly in chair making. By 1881, the population, though still typical of a small town, had risen to over 6,500.[76] It peaked in 1901 at 7,523, equally divided between men and women, before declining to 6,700 in 1911.[77] The town had four main furniture firms, the most important being the Caledonia Cabinet & Chair Works, founded by Matthew Pollock.[78] Pollock had served an apprenticeship in the 1840s with the first Beith cabinetmaker, James Dale, and established his own firm in partnership with a brother and subsequently a son in 1857. By the 1890s he employed 250 hands in a highly mechanised enterprise and was reputed to make 20,000 chairs annually. Accounts of the firm focused on technical innovation, the quality of the designers and the product lines.[79] But though an extensive and highly mechanised concern, it retained craft-based furniture production, apparent from newspaper reporting of a major fire in February 1895. Starting in the engine shed and quickly spreading to workshops and wood stores, with only the offices and showrooms saved, the fire caused over £20,000 of damage and had a traumatic impact on the workforce: 'There were 255 hands employed, and, with the exception of some half-dozen chests, all the tools were destroyed, but it is understood that the greater part of them are insured in the society of which the artisans are members.'[80] In short, and as typical of artisanal employment, the craftsmen's tools were their own and insured at their own expense through their trade club or union and not the possession of the employer.[81]

Other firms in Beith were smaller, such as J. & J. Gardiner of Reform Street, with a workforce of 46, 'personally directed by Mr Gardiner . . . a practical man and has had a lifelong experience of the business'.[82] The Janefield Cabinet and Chair Works started in the early 1880s by Stevenson and Higgins with just 16 hands, expanded rapidly with mechanisation to about 150 hands by the early 1890s, but maintained a strong craft dimension and was particularly well known for interior fittings for ocean-going liners.[83] The firm of Wilson and Galt, with about 60 hands in 1891, was 'particularly celebrated for their high-class chairs, artistically designed and carved and for their dining room suites'.[84] The firm of Robert Balfour had showrooms in Glasgow by the 1880s and exhibited at the 1888 Glasgow International Exhibition, where the stand comprised a 'Jacobean dining-room suite in one half . . . and in the other half shows bedroom furniture'.[85] Pollock & Co. had showrooms in Edinburgh.[86] Yet all was not well in the furniture trades, with employers in dispute with workers in 1898, largely due to attempts to reduce wages and impose systems of piecework payment, which was bitterly resisted by the United Furniture Trades Association and the Amalgamated Union of Cabinet Makers.[87] A strike ensued with some skilled cabinetmakers leaving Scotland for work in London, despite objections from the employers' federation.[88] A compromise was not agreed until the following year.[89] Further disputes followed and the industry declined in the interwar years.[90]

In addition to small-town cabinetmaking, the Ayrshire town of Cumnock supported earthenware and porcelain manufacture using craft techniques. The main output was 'motto ware' for the tourist market.[91] Shoemaking was concentrated in the small town of Maybole, where workshops evolved quickly in the last few decades of the century. One was the firm of John Lees & Co., founded in 1878 by a father and son partnership with a workforce of 15 artisans. By 1928, when they published an anniversary history, their Townend Works, which included a tannery, employed 350.[92] Elsewhere in Ayrshire and south-west Scotland, small towns and villages supported other specialist trades. Woven, reversible three-ply wool carpets, commonly called 'Scotch carpets', were made by the Sanquhar Carpet Co. in Crawick, a village on the outskirts on Sanquhar. Their designs combined richly coloured geometric, floral and seaweed forms. Carpet manufacture was also introduced to Kilmarnock in 1777 and was at its most prosperous in the 1830s, developing from small domestic hand-weaving concerns.[93] Increased mechanisation and competition from larger firms in Glasgow undermined the Ayrshire carpet trade and the Sanquhar Carpet Co. ceased production in 1858. But the Crawick Mill found a further lease of life in 1876 when taken up by John McQueen, who fitted a new waterwheel to power the large-scale production of wool blankets. Wool was always central to craft industries in and around Sanquhar. When the carpet works closed, Sanquhar's working women turned to home-based knitting of distinctive geometric patterned gloves that have been associated with the town ever since.[94] Another textile product long associated with south-west Scotland was whitework, a form of fine cotton or linen with cut-out and embroidered patterns in white thread, which was introduced in the 1820s.[95] The industry was largely operated by firms in Ayr or Glasgow via a 'putting-out system' amongst rural workers and employed thousands at its height, many producing whitework souvenirs for the tourist trade. The impact of tourism on the Scottish craft is economy is explored in the next chapter.

Notes

1. George Sturt, *The Wheelwright's Shop* (Cambridge, 1993), 17.
2. George Bourne [Sturt], *Change in the Village* (New York, 1912), 117–18.
3. Ibid., 304.
4. Ibid., 305.
5. The photographs are in the Scottish Life Collection at the National Museums Scotland. The private and business records of James Simpson, joiner in Fala *c.*1880s–1920s, along with some of the contents of his cottage and workshop are also housed in the National Museums Scotland.
6. Census of Scotland, 1911. Abstracts.
7. *Pigot and Co's National Commercial Directory of the Whole of Scotland* (1825), 411.
8. *Slater's Commercial Directory and Topography of Scotland* (Manchester, 1861), 701.
9. *Carment's 1889 Directory for Dalkeith and District* (Dalkeith, 1889), 23.
10. James Hunter, *Fala and Soutra* (Edinburgh, 1892), 121–2.
11. Ibid.,137.
12. Ibid., 142.
13. Ibid., 146.
14. Ibid., 28.
15. *Scotsman*, 9 April 1887.
16. NMS. Scottish Life Archive, W.MS. 1997. James Simpson, Joiner, Fala Dam, Business Papers, 1912–22.
17. James Simpson, joiner, is listed in *Directories* from *c.*1900. The NMS record describes the acquisition as 'furniture, furnishings etc from house at Fala Dam, Midlothian, mid to late nineteenth century'. Archaeology Data Service, Donations and Purchases for the Museum, 1969–70.
18. See Nenadic and Tuckett, 'Artisans and aristocrats'.
19. NRS. GD112/11/2/3/89. Papers of the Campbell Family, Earls of Breadalbane. Petition of Donal MacCallum, 4 November 1791.
20. NRS. GD112/18/24/15. Breadalbane Papers. Account due to John Sinclair, joiner, Easdale, 1815–16.
21. NRS. GD112/11/9/3/64; GD112/11/9/4/6. Breadalbane Papers. Petitions from Margaret McKay, Seamstress, n.d. and 1828.
22. NRS. GD112/11/9/6/11. Breadalbane Papers. Petition of John Robertson, Wright, 31 May 1830.
23. NRS. GD112/11/9/6/11. Breadalbane Papers. Petition from Four Blacksmiths, 3 February 1835.

24. NRS. GD112/11/10/5/20. Breadalbane Papers. Petition of Tenants in Aberfeldy, 1837.
25. NRS. GD1/1208. Invercreran Photograph Album, 'Our Glen', 1866.
26. Indicated on contemporary maps. NLS Argyll and Bute Sheet LVIII.SW, 1897.
27. Sinclair, *Statistical Account*, vol. 1, 496.
28. *New Statistical Account*, vol. 7, 249.
29. University College London, Legacies of British Slave Ownership, Alexander McCallum, d.1824, www.ucl.ac.uk (last accessed 15 February 2021).
30. Flora Annie Steel [nee Webster] (1847–1929), a noted educationalist and writer who also lived in India, was a member of the family.
31. NRS. GD1/1208. Invercreran Photograph Album.
32. NRS. GD112/14/13/4 22–3. Breadalbane Papers. Letter from Robert McGillewie, 20 August 1821.
33. William Thom, *Rhymes and Recollections of a Handloom Weaver* (London, 1845); *New Statistical Account*.
34. Sinclair, *Statistical Account*, vol. 7, 332.
35. Thom, *Rhymes and Recollections*, 47–8.
36. Ibid., 9.
37. Ibid., 21.
38. *Spectator*, 18 March 1848.
39. NRS. GD224/511. Papers of the Montague-Douglas-Scott Family, Dukes of Buccleuch. Correspondence relating to conditions of work on Buccleuch estates, 1842.
40. Helland, *British and Irish Home Arts and Industries*.
41. *Scotsman*, 23 September 1929. 'Crotal cloth' was woollen tweed dyed a reddish-brown with dye derived from lichen.
42. *Daily Mail*, 3 April 1931.
43. Hugh Miller, *My Schools and School Masters: Or the Story of My Education* (London, 1845).
44. Ibid., 51.
45. Ibid., 153.
46. Ibid., 272.
47. Edinburgh-quarried sandstone was especially damaging to health. Ken Donaldson, et al., 'Death in the New Town: Edinburgh's hidden story of stonemasons' silicosis', *Journal of the Royal College of Physicians of Edinburgh*, 47 (2017), 375–83.
48. Miller, *Schools and School Masters*, 188.
49. Ibid., 189.
50. Ibid., 190–1.
51. Census schedules.
52. *Scotsman*, 7 April 1888.
53. Detailed in Chapter 6.
54. *Southern Reporter*, 2 June 1921.
55. *Scotsman*, 21 July 1915.

56. Detailed in Chapter 5.
57. *New Statistical Account*, vol. 5.
58. Andrew C. Holman and Robert B. Kristofferson, eds, *More of a Man: Diaries of a Scottish Craftsman in Mid-Nineteenth-Century North America* (Toronto, 2013).
59. *Ayrshire Times*, 29 August 1860. Reproduced in *More of a Man*, 51–8.
60. Ibid., 54.
61. Census of Scotland, 1841. Abstracts.
62. Census of Scotland, 1911. Abstracts.
63. Ibid.
64. Sinclair, *Statistical Accounts*, vol. 3.
65. *New Statistical Account*, vol. 14.
66. Frances H. Groome, ed., *Ordnance Gazetteer of Scotland: A Survey of Scottish Topography, Statistical, Biographical and Historical* (Edinburgh, 1884–5). Census of Scotland, 1911. Abstracts.
67. 'Tain Through Time' Image Collection, Tain Museum.
68. Tain Museum has a similar carved chair attributed to Danny Thompson.
69. 'Tain through Time' Image Collection.
70. Groome, *Ordnance Gazetteer*; Bob Harris and Charles McKean, *The Scottish Town in the Age of Enlightenment, 1740–1820* (Edinburgh, 2014).
71. *Glasgow and Its Environs*, 278–98.
72. Ibid., 297.
73. Sinclair, *Statistical Account*, vol. 5; *New Statistical Account*, vol. 4.
74. Ibid.
75. *New Statistical Account*, vol. 5.
76. Groome, *Ordnance Gazetteer of Scotland*.
77. Census of Scotland, 1911. Abstracts.
78. *Glasgow and Its Environs*, 233.
79. Ibid., 236–7.
80. *Scotsman*, 4 February 1895.
81. The complex subdivisions of cabinetmaking craftsmen by this date is detailed in the Maria Ogilvie-Gordon, *Handbook of Employments Specially Prepared for the Use of Boys and Girls on Entering the Trades, Industries and Professions* (Aberdeen, 1908), 169–73.
82. *Glasgow and Its Environs*, 237.
83. Ibid., 234.
84. Ibid., 233.
85. *Scotsman*, 3 September 1888.
86. *Scotsman*, 22 July 1889.
87. Pat Kirkham, *The London Furniture Trade, 1700–1870* (London, 1989); Clive Edwards, 'Vernacular craft to machine assisted industry: The division of labour and the development in machine use in vernacular chair making in High Wycombe, 1870–1920', *Proceedings of the 9th International Symposium on Wood and Furniture Conservation*, Amsterdam, 2008.

88. *Scotsman*, 4 May, 4 June, 17 June 1898.
89. *Scotsman*, 7 January 1899.
90. *Scotsman*, 27 May 1919. For the later history, Glenn Hooper, 'Furnishing Scotland and the world. Morris & Co., Glasgow 1945–65', *Journal of Scottish Historical Studies*, 37:1 (2017), 52–72.
91. See Chapter 4.
92. John Lees & Co., 'From Tanyard to Wearer', unpublished brochure, 1928.
93. Groome, *Ordnance Gazetteer of Scotland*; James Brown, *History of Sanquhar* (Dumfries, 1891).
94. See Chapter 4.
95. See Sally Tuckett, '"Needle crusaders". The nineteenth-century Ayrshire whitework industry', *Journal of Scottish Historical Studies*, 36:1 (2016), 60–80.

4

Tourism and Craftwork

THE FIRST TOURISTS TO SCOTLAND were gentlemen travellers with scholarly interests in mind, antiquarian and literary for some and natural history for others. In the mid and later eighteenth century such men required time, money and connections, because travel was slow and expensive, with limited accommodation for visitors outside the cities other than in the private houses of those they knew or could meet through letters of introduction.[1] Travellers such as James Boswell and Samuel Johnson in 1773 acquired mementos of their journey around the Highlands and went to places that were later part of the standard tourist itinerary, but their souvenirs, including antiquities, were unique not commercially produced. Other pioneer visitors, particularly Thomas Pennant in 1769, wrote and published on their experience, thereby creating the first tour guides which could be enjoyed from the armchair as well as when travelling.[2]

Mass tourism in Scotland began with an early-nineteenth-century trickle of interest in places connected to two literary figures – mythical Ossian in the Highlands and Robert Burns in the Lowland south-west. With the publication in 1810 of Walter Scott's poem *Lady of the Lake* and the *Waverley* novels from 1814, various sites in the Trossachs and north-east garnered attention. Walter Scott's Abbotsford, his house near Melrose, was a tourist attraction by the 1820s.[3] Steamship services from the 1820s took travellers from Glasgow and along the scenic west Highland coast to places like Fingal's Cave on the Isle of Staffa, and railways from the 1840s turned the trickle into a flood.[4] Alongside new transport services, a network of affordable accommodation evolved, detailed in the press and in tourist guides along with the nearby sites of interest. A *Scotsman* advertisement of May 1850 was typical:

Bridge Inn, Galashiels. William Elliot respectfully solicits the patronage of Commercial Gentlemen, Families and Tourist etc to his INN . . . To

Tourists he begs to remind them that Galashiels is the nearest station on the North British Railway to Abbotsford, the renowned home of the late Sir Walter Scott; also the primitive but hallowed birth-place of Mungo Park [contemporary Africa explorer]; parentage of the Ettrick Shepherd; St Mary's Loch . . . [etc.][5]

Wealthy sporting tourists attracted to shooting and fishing became a notable phenomenon from the 1820s, bringing profits to rural estates and demand for fashionable clothing made from woollen tweeds.[6] The royal family at Balmoral made Deeside a flourishing sportsman's destination. Golfing or yachting attracted other wealthy holidaymakers. Highland games for a popular audience, building on earlier clan events, attracted growing numbers of summer visitors to easily accessible places with good transport connections. From mid century, seaside towns flourished and where there were seaside towns, there was also demand for tourist souvenirs.[7] By the end of the century, starting with Edinburgh in 1886, the summer-months-long international exhibitions drew visitors in their millions with money to spend on trinkets or postcards to mark the occasion.[8]

The relationship between mass tourism and evolving consumer cultures that gave rise to commercial souvenir production is well understood and can be seen in the nineteenth century in the developed West and in India.[9] Studies of modern tourist purchases reveal the types of objects favoured and the meanings attached to them, offering insights to motivations in the past. Five categories have been identified: images of a place, dominated by picture postcards, which became popular and easily available from the later nineteenth century and, as we shall see, often depicted 'traditional' craftworkers; a piece of the place, such as a pebble or shell, sometimes purchased but more often simply gathered from the ground; a small manufactured version of whatever has been seen, suitable for an ornament; an item with words or images on it that evoke a place or person linked to the place; and local food or craft-made objects that are distinctly identified with the place.[10] Some of these are purchased for the self to act as an aide-memoire, others intended as gifts. The placing of souvenirs in the home can have personal emotional resonance or be intended for display to others to give status to the owner. For many commonly acquired tourist souvenirs in the past, as the present, issues of authenticity help to form the value attributed to an object.[11]

Before they were commonly available in Scotland, tourist souvenirs were made and purchased elsewhere in Britain and Europe and brought to Scotland. The eighteenth-century 'grand tour' of Italy was marked by participants, mostly wealthy young men, with the purchase of paintings and antiquities, but also with commercially manufactured souvenirs such as statuettes of famous buildings or fans intended as gifts for sisters or mothers, which were decorated with images of Italian scenes including the Venice Carnival or landscape features such as Vesuvius.[12] English tourist destinations including Bath or the south-coast seaside resorts generated other sorts of souvenir. Small, enamelled boxes for pills, patches or snuff were particularly popular. Known as Bilston or Battersea wares, these were made in London and Staffordshire in the second half of the eighteenth century and decorated with famous English scenes or buildings, or with mottos and quotes, or with a simple statement such as 'A Present from Brighton'.[13] The manufacturers of these objects called on the technical skills and artistry of enamellers, many of them émigrés from continental Europe, including women, working at home or in small workshops. The output was vast and the best were expensive. Though there was no equivalent in eighteenth-century Scotland, the development from the early nineteenth century of a craft industry making small decorated wooden boxes, known as Mauchline wares or 'treen', had many similarities. And the wood itself, being a natural product of the land, was frequently valued as 'authentically' connected to places and people that tourists wanted to see.

HERITAGE WOOD AND MAUCHLINE WARES

In the second half of the nineteenth century, published tourist guides to Scotland included advertisements for hotels and transport services and also for businesses that sold tourist souvenirs. The tenth edition of *Black's Picturesque Tourist of Scotland*, published in Edinburgh in 1874, was a typical case. One of its featured advertisements was for the firm of R. S. Shearer of 6 King Street, Stirling, which offered 'souvenirs and presents from Scotland' in what was described as a 'depot for Scotch woodwork'. Alongside illustrated guides, photograph albums and books of poetry, Shearer advertised 'souvenirs made of Stirling Relic Wood, Bannockburn and Abbey Craig Wood' available to buy from his shop.[14] In short, local places with historical resonance, from the ancient castle that dominates the town, to the nearby Bannockburn battlefield or the National Wallace Monument, which opened in 1869, were made tangible and portable in the form of trinkets fashioned from wood grown nearby.

The popular interest in 'heritage wood', also known as 'relic wood', has a long genesis that included some Jacobite memorabilia of the eighteenth and early nineteenth century and the growing of Scots pine trees on English estates to signal Jacobite sympathies.[15] Walter Scott, who inspired many developments in Scottish tourism and doubtless was the

author of some of the books of poetry on sale at Shearer's Stirling emporium, provides an illustration of the use of such wood in the manufacture
of a unique piece of hand-carved furniture for Abbotsford. The object
in question is the 'William Wallace chair' that today sits in Sir Walter's
study, which was made from the oak rafters of a derelict ancient cottage
in Robroyston near Kirkintilloch, which had strong Wallace connections.
A gift of 1824 from Joseph Train, a fellow antiquarian, the chair was
modelled on one in Hamilton Palace and 'is nearly covered with carved
work, representing rocks, heather, and thistles, emblematic of Scotland,
and indented with brass, representing the Harp of the North, surrounded
with laurels, and supported by targes, claymores, Lochaber axes, war
horns, &c.'[16] Crowds lined the streets and the banks of the Union Canal
to see the celebrated chair transported to Abbotsford and visitors to the
house have admired it ever since. These same tourists sought souvenirs
of their visits to Abbotsford and heritage wood objects such as small
boxes or card cases made from trees grown on the Abbotsford estate, or
nearby on the banks of the Tweed, were made locally and further afield
to capitalise on the market. A *Scotsman* advertisement of 1869 indicates
the relationship between places and people, wood and tourist objects:
'Strangers now in Edinburgh should visit the Tourists' Emporium, 13,
15, 17 Hanover Street [for] elegant articles manufactured at Mauchline
from wood grown at Abbotsford and other places of Romantic Interest.'[17] One of the firms that made such items with Walter Scott connections and others of a similar character from timbers harvested in places
associated with Robert Burns or Bonnie Prince Charlie, was the Mauchline, in Ayrshire, firm of Andrew and William Smith, who pioneered the
production of decorated boxes and trinkets.

The origin of the Scottish decorative box ware industry is found in the
combining of particular materials with a mechanical invention. At the
end of the eighteenth century, James Sandy of Alyth near Perth invented
an ingenious hidden hinge, which was then manufactured by Charles
Stiven from Laurencekirk who produced pale-coloured, sycamore wood
snuff boxes. The new 'concealed-hinge' boxes arrived in Cumnock, near
Mauchline, in the early 1800s, triggering the establishment of a significant local industry, with boxes initially hand painted and later decorated
with transfer prints.[18] The Smith brothers, sons of a Mauchline mason,
began production in 1825, but with snuff-taking in decline, their product
range expanded to include tea caddies, ladies' embroidery work boxes,
needle cases and other sorts of trinket boxes. They made decorated rulers
and knife and umbrella handles adorned with numerous different fancy
motifs and scenes, often suggesting their purpose as tourist souvenirs.[19]

The firm was entrepreneurial and ever on the lookout for new markets. When Abbey Craig, a hillside overlooking Stirling, was cleared of woodland in the 1860s for the building of the Wallace Memorial, the firm acquired some of the timbers for making into relic wood trinkets decorated with images and text connected to the memorial, which was quickly established as a tourist attraction.[20] The main output of Mauchline ware was from a small factory employing local craftworkers, designers and artists, many of them young women with decorative skills equivalent to those found in the pottery industry. By mid century there were two other firms nearby making similar goods. One of them, Davidson, Wilson and Amphlet, had a partner in Birmingham from where much of the output was distributed in England.[21]

In the first half of the nineteenth century, the Smith brothers' company enjoyed support from the Board of Manufactures and also applied to the Board's school of design in Edinburgh to provide design training for a son of one of the firm's owners.[22] Though decorated treen was made elsewhere, including south-west England, in conjunction with a flourishing Victorian holiday market in Devon and Cornwell, it was the Ayrshire industry that secured celebrity and reputation for quality and originality. A particularly successful line of goods from the late 1820s comprised boxes and buttons, knife handles and bodkin cases decorated with Scottish tartans. To validate their tartans at a time of contested clan heritage using a strategy employed by several craft sectors that made goods with antiquarian associations, the Smiths published a catalogue titled *Authenticated Tartans of the Clans and Families of Scotland, Painted by Machinery*, which was printed in Ayr in 1850 and dedicated to the President of the Society of Antiquaries, the Marquis of Breadalbane. The Marquis was already a patron of the firm and they gave his name to a popular range of tartan buttons. Through this nobleman, the firm also enjoyed the patronage of Prince Albert, confirming a hierarchical relationship from locality to royalty that was reproduced in numerous instances of craft production.[23] The Smiths exhibited their wares at the 1851 Great Exhibition, winning several prizes.[24] All of these connections ensured a steady market amongst tourist visitors to Scotland, with objects, often quite small, made to suit every purse as indicated in a newspaper advertisement of 1859: 'Souvenirs of Scotland. Tourists will find clan tartan woodwork in great variety from 6d upwards at Soutter's Bazaar 93–97 Princes Street'.[25]

In addition to tartan-decorated Mauchline wares, another popular line was known as 'fern ware', characterised by naturalistic patterns based on Scottish ferns.[26] The Smith brothers' firm was famed for its fern ware, as was Archibald Brown's Caledonian Fancy Wood Works in nearby Lanark. Brown held several patents for applying decorative finishes to boxes, including one registered on 11 April 1870, which described a 'spatter' effect.[27] Demand for souvenirs decorated with fern motifs grew from a trend in botanical exploration that became widespread from the 1840s and reached fever pitch by the 1850s and 1860s, adding to the collecting delights of tourists visiting Scotland. Many popular books on the subject were written for experts and amateurs, including William Carruthers and Jeanie Couch Moffat, *A Collection of Ferns Found in the Neighbourhood of Moffat with Popular Descriptions and Locations of All Known Species*, which was published in 1863 and linked to a town that was itself a popular tourist destination, having a history as a spa resort going back to the eighteenth century.[28] Applying fern patterns to boxes was a skilled and complex process. Decorators used a reverse stencil method whereby dried fern leaves were arranged and pinned in place on a surface coated with resin before being sprayed or speckled with dyes and varnish. Repeating this process in layers gave fern ware its delicate, three-dimensional quality. Ferns were collected for the purpose from across Scotland and from the Isle of Arran in particular, though botanical experts have noted that not all of the wood-ware ferns were Scottish or even British and that many came from New Zealand, the Americas and West Indies or South-east Asia.[29] The process for decorating fern ware was sometimes carried out by small-scale producers as a subcontracted cottage industry with undecorated 'white-ware' bought direct from the manufacturers for final decoration. Thomas Morton (1859–1945) of Muirkirk, near Cumnock, specialised in applying fern patterns to small items of wood ware and furniture. He worked at home with the help of his daughter, Rachel, who remembered packing the finished items to be sent to customers in Canada.[30] Wood ware was not the only Scottish decorative art that featured representations of ferns. Manufacturers across Britain produced fern-decorated goods in other materials, from domestic pottery to exterior ironwork.[31] Catalogues for the Holyrood Glassworks in Edinburgh include illustrations of fern-decorated glass, the handiwork of engravers, which were also displayed at international exhibition. Fern patterns were woven into Scottish- and Irish-made damask linen tableware.[32] And, of course, at the peak of the fern's popularity between the 1850s and early 1900s, they were commonly found as houseplants in complex handmade glass cabinets and jars known as terrariums.

The production of decorated boxes in the small Ayrshire town of Mauchline and places nearby generated employment for skilled male and female workers for well over a century. Designers and decorators, some technical innovators, the carpenter-trained box makers as well as the other types of workers – in wood supply and processing or product packing for onward distribution – sustained thriving semi-rural small-town communities. In the 1840s, the population of the parish Mauchline was less than 2,000 and the area was dominated by agriculture, weaving and shoemaking for men and tambouring for women, but the report to the 1845 *Statistical Account* also highlighted the importance of an 'extensive manufactory of wooden snuff-boxes'.

> In this works about sixty persons are employed, who work ten hours a-day, and six days per week. The workmen are remunerated according to their knowledge of the art of box-making or painting. The stranger will be well rewarded by paying a visit to this works, as he will have an opportunity of seeing many elegant specimens of the art.[33]

Consistent with the preoccupations of the local clergyman who wrote the report, it was also remarked 'the works are so conducted as to be injurious neither to the health nor the morals of the individuals engaged in them'. What is particularly interesting in this description is the invitation to 'the stranger', a commonly used term for tourists, to visit the works, look at the items being made and presumably, also make a purchase. The reference to tourists is not surprising in an area associated with Robert Burns. Burns lived in Mauchline for a while, the town and its people featured in several of the poems and his farm of Mossgiel is a few miles to the north. The parish was crossed by the Glasgow to London turnpike road and the main Ayr to Glasgow and Ayr to Edinburgh roads, with frequent coach services running on all routes which further encouraged tourism.[34] Good railway connections followed in the 1840s. Burns tourism, which was actively cultivated by local organisations and town councils who hosted Burns celebratory events and monument building, brought large numbers of visitors to the county by the 1820s, with the growth in box-ware production expanding to match a rising demand for souvenirs.[35] The Burns-inspired tourist could view the nearby celebrated waterfalls on the upper reaches of the River Clyde and the iconic cotton factory at New Lanark. A visit to the Mauchline workshop was part of the same tourist itinerary for much of the nineteenth century, with souvenirs decorated with views of places associated with the poet or imagined scenes from the poems available for purchase. Quotes from Burns were inscribed on boxes or needle cases and the Burns monument, completed in 1823 and interior of the Burns cottage museum, opened in the 1880s, were also depicted.[36]

In addition to wood and ferns, other types of naturally occurring organic materials in Scotland were crafted into tourist souvenirs. In parts of the country, particularly the south-west, bog oak was found, which could be carved to give a fine effect. Bog oak, that is, ancient oak trunks or branches preserved in bogs, black in appearance, hard and easily polished like ebony or jet, was particularly associated with Ireland and generated a large craft industry in and around Dublin making trinkets, small boxes and jewellery with antique Irish or Celtic-inspired design.[37] As in Ireland, the Scottish bog oak carvers focused on designs taken from antique carvings on churches and gravestones, which heightened the appeal, but the association with trees taken from and preserved by the landscape was also important for the souvenir collector. Items of jewellery in bog oak were commonly sold alongside Whitby jet, as an advertisement for Houldon's Royal Fancy Bazaars in George Street and Nicholson Street, Edinburgh, announced in 1862.[38] Furniture was also made in bog oak with the provenance of the materials often noted by makers' labels, which added to value and appeal. Another land-connected material that lent itself to carving and polishing was a type of coal found in east-central Scotland, and particularly Fife, that is called cannel coal. Though neither practical (because it can easily shatter and is heavy) nor cheap to make and buy, there was a small but celebrated and frequently exhibited production of coal-carved objects in the second half of the century that included furniture items, snuff boxes and trinkets.[39] Unlike the box makers or bog oak carvers, however, the skills required for this type of work were more akin to those of the stonemason than the carpenter or cabinetmaker.

First-hand nineteenth-century tourist accounts of the acquisition of souvenirs or mementos are rare. Women were better chroniclers of such detail than men and one who gives some insights is the celebrated American writer and abolitionist campaigner Harriet Beecher Stowe (1811–96), whose extended European tour of 1853 included several weeks in April spent in Scotland, which she chronicled in letters to family at home. Her ostensible purpose was to attend and speak at public meetings to promote the anti-slavery cause, but she also visited numerous popular tourist destinations, inspired by the works of Burns and Scott and stories of ancient castles and clans. Her visit to Abbotsford and nearby Dryburgh Abbey, Scott's burial place, was eagerly anticipated, but marred by poor weather; she and her party were comfortably housed at a small inn in nearby Melrose. Having gathered pebbles from the Tweed to 'carry home to America' she shopped for souvenirs and gifts.

> Just on the verge of twilight I stepped out, to see what the town afforded in the way of relics. To say the truth, my eye had been caught by some cunning little tubs and pails in a window, which I thought might be valued in the

home department. I went into a shop, where an auld wife soon appeared, who, in reply to my inquiries, told me, that the said little tubs and pails were made of plum tree wood from Dryburgh Abbey, and, of course, partook of the sanctity of relics. She and her husband seemed to be driving a thriving trade in the article, and either plum trees must be very abundant at Dryburgh, or what there are must be gifted with that power of self-multiplication which inheres in the wood of the true Cross. I bought them in blind faith, however, suppressing all rationalistic doubts, as a good relic hunter should.[40]

In addition to these rustic-sounding woodware items, Mrs Stowe, the wife of a clergyman and a woman of faith, was also gifted an engraving of a popular painting titled *The Covenanters' Sacrament* by Edinburgh artist George Harvey, son of a Stirling watchmaker who was best known for his paintings of Scottish historical and religious subjects, 'which I shall keep as a memento of him and of Scotland'.[41]

PEBBLE JEWELLERY

There were other materials derived from the Scottish landscape, including semi-precious stones and pebbles such as garnets, agates and cairngorms, that generated craft production of ornaments and jewellery with tourists in mind, though such items also appealed to domestic consumers and were widely sold beyond Scotland. The richly varied geology of Scotland had attracted elite visitors with natural history interests from the later eighteenth century and polished examples of colourful stone and fossils were sought by amateurs and professionals for cabinet displays with many collections eventually gifted to public museums.[42] Popular publications with a geological focus, including those of Hugh Miller, a stonemason by training who 'made geology an integral part of the world as he saw it . . . merged with local history and folk law', enhanced the appeal of Scottish pebbles and rocks, fuelling the Victorian interest in collecting.[43]

Certain specially formed and beautiful Scottish pebble stones had long commanded a popular allure that preceded the interests of enlightenment or Victorian geologists and jewellers. Unusual specimens were valued as amulets to bring good luck and large, finely worked semi-precious stones were used in sword hilts, or for clasps and brooches, particularly in Highland Scotland.[44] These exceptional artefacts were possessed by elites and commonly passed through the generations as heirlooms. By the late eighteenth century, with Highland dress and Scottish cultural identity, real or assumed, increasingly fashionable, elite demand for large cairngorms or agates to be fashioned into jewellery was rising and what was fashionable amongst elites was soon adopted by the middle classes. Queen

Victoria and Prince Albert at Balmoral from the 1850s further stimulated the passion for decorative Scotch pebbles which remained popular throughout the nineteenth century and beyond. By the 1860s newspaper advertisements reflected the interest and suggested that pebble jewellery could be purchased directly from the jeweller or from fancy-goods warehouses along with other types of tourist souvenir, as in the following example of 1863, which was printed in English, French and German: 'Strangers now in Edinburgh should inspect the extensive stock of tartan woodwork, pebble jewellery, stereoscopic and other Scotch views to be seen at 16 Hanover Street [Edinburgh], suitable as souvenirs of Scotland.'[45] Or, from the same decade,

> George Laing, working jeweller, watchmaker and manufacturers of Scotch pebbles and Highland ornaments, 50 Leith Street Edinburgh . . . Tourists and visitors will find the stock of cairngorm and pebble jewellery exceedingly suitable for presents and souvenirs, being unsurpassed in variety and beauty of design, quality, workmanship.[46]

Much of what was made by jewellers for the tourist market involved relatively modest raw material costs – semi-precious stones were mostly mounted in silver – but high aesthetic and cultural appeal. Some entrepreneurs invested in design copyright to protect their interests, particularly when agates came to be incorporated into complex natural forms such as insect brooches or ferns and flower brooches, reflecting a parallel interest mid century in the flora and fauna of Scotland.[47] The 'moss agate', which is green-brown in colour with natural veins and marks that resemble Highland mosses, had particular appeal and looked well when worn on Scottish tweed and plaid. Not only jewellery for women, but also accoutrements for the decoration of male dress were made in large numbers, such as dirks with agate-studded silver handles, clasps for sporrans, clan badges and buttons for jackets, watch fobs and seals. Silverware incorporating local polished stones were made as boxes, bottles and vinaigrettes. Items for table decoration included snuff mills, sometimes fashioned from deer feet or horns and cowrie shells with silver mounts and agates. Statuettes of Scottish animals or Highland figures were also made, along with hip flasks for the sportsman and vesta cases for matches for the smoking man, all embellished with polished Scottish pebbles.[48]

The interest in pebble jewellery generated areas of concentrated production in some of the smaller northern towns, particularly Perth, Aberdeen and Inverness, which were important railway hubs with large numbers of tourists passing through. Jewellers in Aberdeen also produced a specialist output of polished granite brooches and bracelets fashioned from local

stone, which had a smoky pink colour, with the famous firm of Rettie &
Sons registering designs for their best work and exhibiting extensively in
the later nineteenth century.[49] At the Edinburgh International Exhibition of
1886, Rettie's granite wares were noted in press reports:

> The jewellery comprises a large collection of various and beautiful designs.
> Not the least noticeable in this class are some very neat initial brooches,
> inlaid with silver and fine gold. Essence bottles and match-boxes, artistically
> inlaid with silver, are entirely a new production by the firm. Amongst table
> ornaments, those specially commanding attention are napkin rings, candle-
> sticks, crumb-scoops and tobacco boxes – all quite novel in the manufactory
> of granite.[50]

The biggest centre for pebble jewellery production was, however, Edinburgh and this was where the largest number of lapidaries were found,
either working on their own account at cutting and polishing stones, or in
one of the big jewellery workshops. Artisans such as these were apprentice trained over six or seven years, commonly also took design school
classes and according to a contemporary observer were 'an intelligent
class of workmen'.[51] Such was the skill involved in making a good pebble
bracelet or brooch, the process was described in detail in an 1868 newspaper account of the manufacture of plate and jewellery in Scotland:

> Articles of an ornate character – such as brooches and bracelets – covered
> with designs in filigree work, or inlaid with pebbles, require great nicety of
> manipulation and the number of parts which go to compose some of them is
> immense. Pebble bracelets of a finely worked geometrical pattern are made
> in which there are no fewer than 160 pieces of stone.[52]

Most jewellers were urban, yet there was also a distinctive rural firm, a
husband-and-wife partnership, which was so connected with the evolution of Highland tourism and produced its output on such a large scale,
that it must be mentioned. This was the celebrated team of Alexander
and Euphemia Ritchie of Iona, who worked in the Arts and Crafts style
to produce decorative silver and copper items, sometime embellished
with coloured enamel or set with polished stones. Euphemia Ritchie
(1862–1941) and her husband Alexander Ritchie (1856–1941) met at
the Glasgow School of Art in the mid 1890s. They married in 1898 and
opened a shop and workshop in Alexander's native Iona in 1900, where
Alexander was also employed as guide to the abbey. Iona was popular
with tourists seeking escape from urban life through an immersive experience in a small island that resonated with ancient myths and legends of the
sixth-century Saint Columba and the origins of Christianity. The Ritchies
drew inspiration from the carved Celtic stones and crosses found on Iona

and elsewhere in the western Highlands. Illuminated manuscripts from early monasteries furnished design templates. They also made jewellery that harked back to Scotland's Viking age. Craftwork was combined with entrepreneurial flair and they ran a successful business through to the interwar years under the label Iona Celtic Art. As the business grew, they outsourced some aspects of production to manufacturers in Birmingham and Glasgow.[53] Though commercial in orientation, they enjoyed noble patronage and friendship, particularly from Lady Victoria Campbell, the pious younger daughter of the Duke of Argyll, who spent much of her adult years on Tiree undertaking good works to support the local people through employment schemes and craft training. She was strongly associated with the Celtic Christian revival that came to focus on Iona, which was part of the Argyll estates and which the Duke gave in trust to the Church of Scotland.[54] The religious revival and associated rise in Celtic Scottish nationalism further stimulated tourist interest.

The output from the Ritchie workshop was pitched at a middle market, though small silver brooches would have been price-accessible to most tourists who could afford the cost of a trip to Iona. There is a photograph of about 1910 of Euphemia Ritchie with her dog Kim on

Figure 4.1   Euphemia Ritchie, silversmith, outside her shop. Iona, *c.*1900.
© Private Collection.

the front step of the Iona shop just inside the southern gate of the nunnery grounds, surrounded by jewellery and silverware for sale.[55] Dressed well for the elements and because the shop was little more than a flimsy wooden booth, the small bag under her coat probably holds the proceeds from sales. On the back of the open door is a glass display case containing brooches, pendants and buckles in Scottish-Celtic revivalist designs. A shelf under the window displays objects in boxes and small pieces such as brooches and rings are pinned to board. A large brass metal plate hangs inside the window. Through the open door, objects and glass display cases glint in the light. The shop's prime position, framed by ancient buildings within a coastal landscape, made her goods popular with visitors to the island and the scale of the output is still evident today from the ease with which Iona Celtic Art items can be found in antique shops and auction catalogues.

TOURIST TEXTILES

The Ritchies were adept at marketing their jewellery and did so through newspaper advertisements and postcards for tourists. Another subject that appeared on numerous photographic postcards was the 'old handloom weaver' in a rural cottage, depicted working at the loom, usually with an artfully placed spinning wheel in the foreground. Indeed, several places used the same image, superimposed with the name of their town or village, for tourist postcards.[56] Tourist narratives detailing visits to isolated communities where the 'last of the handloom weavers' were to be found were popular in Scotland and northern England from the 1880s and the products made had romantic appeal.[57] A postcard image was a cheap alternative to buying what were often expensive handmade textiles whilst newspaper reports or obituaries speak to a wider nostalgic interest when they recorded the actual deaths of the 'last' handloom weaver in a town or district. The death in 1910 of John Sharp of Crieff in Perthshire aged 95, 'the last of the old race of handloom weavers in the town', described 'a remarkably cheery and intelligent old man . . . possess of excellent memory'. It went on to list the events of the past that he recalled, including the first visit of George IV to Scotland in 1822, the Catholic Emancipation Bill of 1829 and the Reform Bill agitation of the early 1830s. John Sharp was a member of the Volunteer Force and was present at the great reviews that took place in Edinburgh in 1860 and 1881. He was also a prominent figure in the local freemason's lodge.[58] His life lived in a scenic part of Scotland popular with visitors appeared to encompass almost the whole of the nineteenth century, an embodiment of times past and passing that resonated with popular romantic sensibilities and helped to shape tourist itineraries.

Tourists purchased tartan textiles as well as types of souvenirs that were decorated with tartan designs. Other handmade textiles were directed at tourists, though often sold through stores in the bigger urban centres, including whitework hand embroidery (with the cheaper souvenirs made by machine), knitwear and Harris tweed cloth for men's suits. Whitework embroidery dress items included ladies' collars and babies' christening gowns, but smaller objects for sale to tourists were also made such as lavender bags, pin cushions or table doilies. Knitwear for tourist sale embraced the distinctive black-and-white patterned Sanquhar gloves made in south-west Scotland and knitted lace shawls from the Shetland Isles which were so fine they could pass through a wedding ring and were often gifted as wedding presents. Harris tweed production was vigorously supported by the elite Highland Home Industries Association. Its appeal was in its haptic qualities and suitability for the Scottish climate, the colours that resonated with the landscape which were gained through naturally occurring dyestuffs, the materials that were grown locally and cottage-based manufacture in a distant place where peat smoke infused the cloth with its own unique smell. These ideas of touch, sight and smell – a romantic and culturally laden mix – were evoked in evidence given in a successful 1906 Board of Trade prosecution of copyright infringements of genuine Harris Tweed by a bogus London manufacturer:

> The real 'Harris' tweeds are to be distinguished from the imitations by the softness of texture, and length for length they are not so heavy [as the imitations]. At the same time, there is an oily feeling on the surface, and a smell of peat, which can easily be recognised by those who have lived in districts where peat is used as fuel. Their virtues are rain-resisting quality, beautifully blended colours, strength and elasticity in wear.[59]

In appealing to the later-nineteenth-century visitor and particularly the wealthy sporting tourist who could afford handmade tartan or tweed, the charitable dimensions of such purchases were stressed, since much of the manufacture was sponsored through make-work schemes designed to bring income to impoverished rural areas. Exhibition marketing in Edinburgh or London was thus deployed to attract potential purchasers. A case is illustrated with the 1911 Mansion House London exhibition of Harris tweeds and other Scottish home-made knitted and lace goods such as Shetland lace shawls. On opening the exhibition, the Earl of Rosebery gave a witty account of the 'claims of the cloth', which included it being 'so charmingly perfumed' with peat smoke. They had little need for tweed in London, where they had umbrellas and water-proofs, 'but when they went to Scotland in August they must remember what an advantage this cloth would be'. As he further remarked to the invited audience,

> The whole city of London – or the greater part of it – went to Scotland in August. They usually arrived in an unguarded moment in kilts which were put on in the train between Euston or King's Cross and their destination – (laughter) – and at Perth Station, which he thought was the rallying place of the Southern class, they were apt to appear in brilliant kilts with very white knees – (laughter) – except, perhaps, those more practised visitors to Scotland who stained them in walnut hues – (laughter) – and were therefore at once detected. Not being, like the Marquis of Tullibardine and Lord Dunmore, genuine products of the soil, he as a Lowlander did not don the kilt, but in this tweed, in the breeks of the Southerner, in the ordinary costume of daily life, they might pass into Perth Station, and might be taken, if not as Caledonians or Picts, as something uncommonly like them. (Laughter.) He pressed that consideration to the visitors to Scotland who brought such pleasure and money to their starving peasants.[60]

It was not only Scottish textile goods that wealthy tourists purchased, but also some of the quaint forms of technology for making textiles that attracted interest. Foremost was the domestic spinning wheel of a type employed in wool thread production across Scotland in the eighteenth century, which was largely superseded by factory spinning from the 1820s. Decorative spinning wheels for the lady amateur were made in Scotland throughout the nineteenth century. They were particularly popular from the 1860s when Queen Victoria took up hand spinning as a hobby and was photographed posed with a spinning wheel, as were several of her daughters, including Princess Louise who married the Duke of Argyll in 1871 and also fuelled the fashionable interest in Scottish pebble jewellery.[61] Many fine-made Scottish spinning wheels graced the drawing rooms of the Victorian middle and upper classes and for the tourist in search of a souvenir, spinning-wheel ornaments in wood, brass or pottery – or even a simple postcard image – were available.

ELITE PROMOTION OF THE SOUVENIR TRADE

Elite patronage was key to developing the relationship between the Scottish craft economy and the tourist industry and was seen particularly strongly in rural areas through the agency of the great estates and their owners. The reasons for this were complex, including the maintenance of employment and populations on estates in the face of changing agriculture. The great estates also encouraged tourism of various types because it generated estate income from hotels and inns and from the country sports they offered to rich visitors.[62] Though drawing on traditional skills, certain areas of iconic craft production with elite support were effectively 'invented traditions' for tourist consumption. The massive Buccleuch estates in southern Scotland employed numerous local craftsmen in country-house building works and supported communities of craftsmen producing souvenirs for the visitor market. In the 1840s, when structural shifts in the economy started to impact rural textile employment, estate factors sent the Duke of Buccleuch regular reports on the artisans in Hawick, where they were predominantly weavers, and in Sanquhar, close to the great Buccleuch house of Drumlanrig on the Queensberry estate, where there was a carpet-weaving workshop and a home knitting industry.[63] The lack of work for the Sanquhar carpet weavers was a cause for concern in the 1850s when production finally ceased.[64] But the knitters fared well, for in the second half of the century the Buccleuch family, with connections to royal patronage and intent on developing their commercial sporting interests, gave active support to the redevelopment of the 'traditional' Sanquhar knitting industry, making riding gloves from a wool and cotton mix, which were favoured by the genteel. Sanquhar knits adapted patterns from tweed, giving them names such as the 'Duke' pattern to secure elite associations. A 'Prince of Wales' pattern was launched in 1871 to mark a royal visit to Drumlanrig. One design was called 'Pheasant's Eye', connecting it with field sports. Another popular pattern was named the 'Cornet' in honour of one of the principal players in the Sanquhar Common Riding, an invented tradition of the later nineteenth century, which has long functioned here and in other Scottish Borders towns as a tourist attraction.[65]

There were numerous landed patrons for the Scottish craft economy with shifting interests and objectives, some personal and connected to the financial well-being of their estates, others part of a reputation-building articulation of a national public good.[66] The most famous endeavour, which was partly driven by the tourist and sporting visitor market, was the Highland Home Industries Association, created in the second half of the nineteenth century by a series of notable women. Though it sponsored many areas of domestic production largely from the hands of women, the focus was on support for and marketing of high-quality tweed and knitwear made in the Highlands and Islands. One of the founders of the movement was the Dowager Countess of Dunmore, owner of the Isle of Harris and estates in Stirlingshire, who stimulated hand weaving of woollen cloth as a source of peasant family income from the time of the Highland famines in the 1840s. The Dunmore input was seen initially in the production of Murray family tartan in Harris tweed and the manufacture of tweed suits for Dunmore estate workers. The Dowager Countess then used her elite connections to promote Harris tweed as a suitable cloth for outdoor wear for sporting gentlemen. She introduced mechanisms to improve the quality and consistency of home-made stuffs and some of the best weavers were taken to Alloa on the Dunmore Stirlingshire estate for further training in intricate patternmaking by skilled Lowland weavers and designers. Lady Dunmore's encouragement of Harris tweed marked a transition from estate-focused patronage for mostly local consumption to a more vigorously commercial approach directed at wider markets, including tourist visitors. Retail outlets were established in Edinburgh and central London in the 1860s and tweed and tweed makers were frequently displayed at the international exhibitions. By the late 1880s and the founding of the Scottish Home Industries Association under the patronage of Princess Louise, Marchioness of Lorne, Harris tweed was a well-known success story that others sought to emulate in different areas of handcrafted textiles such as lacemaking.[67]

Certain non-landed elites promoted textile manufactures in remote areas of Scotland. The wealthy Sheriff for Orkney and Shetland, George Thoms, who lived part of the year in Edinburgh, supported Fair Isle knitters and other Northern Isles female textile workers who made patterned jumpers, scarves, shawls and gloves. He promoted the marketing of their wares through the Home Industries Association and encouraged their exhibition activity, notably at the industrial exhibitions in Edinburgh in 1886 and Glasgow in 1888. Thoms funded the renovation of St Magnus Cathedral in Kirkwall, which employed many building craftsmen and attracted tourist interest.[68] He also promoted the business of David Kirkness of Kirkwall, the most famous maker of Orkney chairs, urging him to exhibit at the Edinburgh International Exhibition of 1890, where there was a stall for the 'local industries of Scotland', stating, 'I wish to advertise this as an Orkney native industry.'[69]

David Munro Kirkness (1855–1936), of the same generation as the Ritchies of Iona, was born in Westray and served an apprenticeship with Kirkwall joiner John P. Peace. He and his brother William set up as joiners and undertakers in 1880, a common combination, but he soon moved into full-time and lucrative chair production mainly for sale to wealthy visitors for shipment beyond the islands.[70] His first order for straw-backed chairs came in March 1888 from Miss Maud Balfour of Berstane House to be delivered to Lady Sinclair, Bara House, Caithness.

Elite female customers who had visited Orkney dominate his customer lists. He also received orders from naval officers stationed in nearby Stromness. He regularly supplied his stock to the Scottish Home Industries Association for sale in Edinburgh and London and to Liberty & Co. of Regent Street, London.[71] He exhibited at the Edinburgh International Exhibition of Science, Art and Industry in 1890, which generated orders that took years to fulfil.[72] Sheriff Thoms, his sponsor, was delighted at the success of the stand, though grew frustrated at the slow production from Kirkness's workshop, even suggesting that work be subcontracted to Holland – an idea that Kirkness chose to ignore.[73] The chairs found favour in Arts and Crafts circles. Architect Robert Lorimer and his sister purchased two in 1893 for the family home, Kellie Castle in Fife, which can still be seen *in situ* today.[74] The workshop in Palace Street in Kirkwall, just behind the Cathedral, was itself a tourist destination while Kirkness was alive.[75]

The Kirkness-made Orkney chair was a refined development, using wood sourced on the Scottish mainland and shipped from Aberdeen, of a local style of chair that was made in various shapes and sizes. They were traditionally fashioned at home, often using driftwood to compensate for the shortage of local timber, with seats and backs made of straw or reeds or other naturally growing plants that are found on the low-lying, windswept islands. Several examples of these home-made chairs, some of peculiar construction, along with recent versions, can be seen in Orkney's museums. Though of vernacular heritage, the Orkney chair was standardised by Kirkness to four advertised designs: the Hooded Chair, the Gentleman's Chair, the Lady's Chair and the Child's Chair. They were made in soft woods such as pine, stained either green or brown, or in solid oak, which was fumed and oiled, with brass and copper fixings and invisible castors. Rush seats featured on some chairs and under-seat drawers were an optional, costly extra.[76] Orkney chair making was labour intensive. Kirkness made and finished the frame himself with a few assistants, but the complex chair backs and sides were made by crofting outworkers, some living miles from Kirkwall. The latter, whose numbers were few and whose work was often seasonal, led to many apologies from Kirkness on the amount of time it took him to fulfil orders.[77]

Photographs of Orkney chairs were reproduced as commercial postcards from the later nineteenth century. One of these shows Robert Foubister and his daughter Lizzie making a straw-backed Orkney chair in Tankerness, Orkney, *c.*1910.[78] Foubister's name appears frequently in Kirkness order books for the 1890s. A typical entry for 1891 was for

Figure 4.2   Robert Foubister and his daughter Lizzie making Orkney chairs, *c.*1910. Postcard. © Orkney Islands Council.

two chairs, one mid-sized and one small, both backed by Foubister, who was paid 5s and 3s 6d respectively, which were ordered by a Miss Spead 'while on a visit at Berstane House', with the chairs and bills sent to Wm H. Longbottom, Cavendish Road, Nottingham, who Miss Spead was about to marry.[79] The carefully posed portrait postcard showing Foubister and his daughter was published in the Kent's Series and aimed at the tourist market. It is unusual for this genre of images that we know the names of the sitters, who are photographed in an artist's studio, probably in Kirkwall, and not their usual place of work on a croft about six miles away. The photographer was Tom Kent, locally born in 1863 but trained in America. He contributed to magazines such as *Country Life* and sold postcard images of Orkney views and traditional life, including fisher folk and some of the seemingly 'timeless' farming tasks performed on local crofts. One studio image shows a young woman seated on an Orkney chair knitting a shawl, with a decorative shawl around her shoulders. There is a wheel for spinning wool placed to one side of the chair and a straw basket on the other.[80]

Plaited or woven straw was made by ordinary people in their homes throughout the islands and rural mainland Scotland, to be used for many purposes, including mattresses for beds and also baskets.[81] The latter, known as 'cubbies' but with several other localised names, were fashioned in numerous sizes and structures, of varying degrees of strength, for farm work, fishing or domestic purposes. They were also purchased by tourists. Straw could be made into ropes for tethering animals, tying boats or fences and for straw-roof thatching. There was a commercially organised fine-plaited straw sector in Orkney in the later eighteenth and early nineteenth century, which used mainly female workers directed at home or in workshops in and around Kirkwall by local merchants, and which supplied the fashion industry in London, where there was demand for simple straw bonnets. Commercial production declined when European supplies were revived following the end of the wars in 1815 and ended altogether when fashions changed in the 1820s.[82] There were late-nineteenth-century attempts by the Home Industries Association to introduce commercial straw growing for basketmaking in the western Highlands and Islands, but with limited success due to poor growing conditions and cheaper output from Europe.[83]

SOUVENIR MAKING IN TOWNS AND CITIES

Tourism-focused craft-ware making was important for employment in many rural communities, but goods like Shetland shawls or Harris tweeds relied on urban facilities such as the great exhibitions or the Home Industries Association retail outlets in Edinburgh and London to reach their best markets. And though it is impossible to gauge where the bulk of sales of souvenirs such as Mauchline ware boxes and ornaments were transacted, the chances are it was also through shops in towns. Towns, with their transport connections and hotel accommodation, were important features of the tourist experience in Scotland, with all tourists from the south travelling through Edinburgh or Glasgow to reach the scenic north and often including both in their itinerary. Published tourist guides offered extensive description of the main sites of antiquity and interest in big cities and major retail streets like Princes Street in Edinburgh or the Argyll Arcade in Glasgow were tourist attractions in their own right. Edinburgh jewellers were the principal manufacturers of 'Scottish jewellery', as Marshall & Co. of Princes Street proudly advertised in *Black's Picturesque Tourist of Scotland* in the later nineteenth century.[84] City-based publishers and printers, with their engravers and later photographers, were also the dominant makers of tourist guides and books of images of scenes of tourist interest that included classic landscape views as well as sentimentalised depictions of vernacular buildings and peasant life.[85]

A robust craft economy in Edinburgh was mostly founded on local demand from a wealthy population, which sustained such areas as furniture making or silverware production. But the city was also a focus of production for the tourist market. Visitors could purchase from a large array of decorative and ingenious travelling boxes or leather-bound notebooks to record their visits. Wedding presents and gifts for honeymooners were advertised – indeed, Scotland became an important honeymoon destination as part of the tourist industry, with Gretna Green in the south-west a popular place to visit by visitors taking the standard Burns-related itinerary. Clothing for the sportsman or leisure traveller could be purchases ready-made in Edinburgh and Glasgow along with tartan wares, kilts and scarves. Tourists flocked to Scotland from across Europe as well as elsewhere in Britain. One business catering to this cosmopolitan market, the Tourists' Emporium in Hanover Street in Edinburgh, placed newspaper advertisements in English, French and German.[86]

Urban spectacles, starting with the 1822 royal visit to Edinburgh, drew huge numbers of leisure visitors to the cities and businesses responded with commemorative clothing and other mementos such as engravings or decorative wares.[87] The most remarkable events were the international exhibitions from the 1880s, which attracted vast visitor numbers to complex commercial sites with endless opportunities for souvenir purchase including photographs and postcards, guidebooks, pottery, woodwares and textiles.[88] Not all of these souvenirs were handmade nor were they necessarily made in Scotland. Scotland's textile factories made numerous goods for tourists, including colourful printed commemorative cotton handkerchiefs and linen tea towels. Yet the relationship between the craft economy and international exhibitions was as important as the better known ambition to showcase modern industry.[89] So powerful was the exhibition practice of viewing and appreciating items behind glass or items under construction by artisans as part of the display, that shops and businesses catering for tourists often created an exhibition experience in miniature in their retail premises, even in a small town like Inverness, which was an important tourist hub then as now. A flavour is given in the 1874 edition of *Black's Picturesque Tourist of Scotland*, where the 'great jewellery establishment' of P. G. Wilson of 44 High Street, Inverness, advertised its range of jewellery for all tastes, including 'Scottish jewellery' and invited visitors to view the shop and manufactory with no obligation to purchase. The shop interior, with its long counter and many glass cases, was described as having been 'fitted up in the style of an exhibition room or museum' allowing the viewer to better appreciate the quality of the wares and removing the act of viewing from mere commerce.[90]

The importance of tourism and the souvenir trade for Scottish crafts-men and craftswomen in the nineteenth century is impossible to quantify, but it can be gauged from contemporary reports and from later initia-tives. Following the Second World War and in the planning for the 1951 Festival of Britain celebrations, endeavours were made to revitalise the craft economy based on souvenir production. A touring exhibition was mounted in Scotland, starting in Edinburgh at the Aitkin Dott Galleries in Castle Street, to showcase 'continental examples' of tourist souvenirs for the 'inspiration of our own manufacturers and craftsmen'. Organised by the Scottish Committee of the Council of Industrial Design, the aim was to 'stimulate people in this country to revive old crafts and indus-tries and to produce new goods which our visitors would be glad to buy, and which we would be proud to sell'.[91] The exhibition sought to build on the success of a 1947 Scottish Tourist Board competition to stimu-late souvenir production of a character that was 'intrinsically Scottish [and] in its material, design or craftsmanship, was inherently national in character'.[92] This in turn was generated by an earlier concern about the cheap, foreign-made souvenirs that had flooded the Scottish market in the interwar years, displacing local production. In these mid-twentieth-century craft initiatives, as in the nineteenth century, elite patrons took a leading role. The importance of Scotland's wealthy few and particularly those possessed of landed estates is seen in other areas of craft produc-tion, particularly those associated with the building crafts. Many skilled artisans engaged in the great nineteenth-century enterprise of country-house building, decorating and furnishing. This forms the subject of the next chapter.

Notes

1. Rosemary Sweet, *Antiquaries: The Discovery of the Past in Eighteenth-Century Britain* (London, 2004).
2. Thomas Pennant, *A Tour in Scotland* (London, 1769).
3. Iain Gordon Brown, ed., *Abbotsford and Sir Walter Scott: The Image and the Influence* (Edinburgh, 2003).
4. Alastair J. Durie, *Scotland for the Holidays, c.1780–1939* (East Linton, 2013).
5. *Scotsman*, 29 May 1850.
6. Alastair J. Durie, 'Sporting tourism flowers – the development from c.1780 of grouse and golf as visitor attractions in Scotland and Ireland', *Journal of Tourism History* (2013), 1–15.
7. Susan Barton and Allan Brodie, eds, *Travel and Tourism in Britain, c.1780–1914* (London, 2014).

8. Christopher Smout, 'Tours in the Scottish Highlands from the eighteenth to the twentieth centuries', *Northern Scotland*, 1:1 (1982), 99–121. Also, see Chapter 6.

9. Michael Hitchcock and Ken Teague, eds, *Souvenirs: The Material Culture of Tourism* (Aldershot, 2000); Tina Young Choi, 'Producing the past: The native arts, mass tourism and souvenirs in Victorian India', *Lit: Literature Interpretation Theory*, 1 (2016), 50–70.

10. Beverly Gordon, 'The souvenir: Messenger of the extraordinary', *Journal of Popular Culture*, 20:3 (1986), 135–46.

11. J. Rickly-Boyd, 'Authenticity and aura. A Benjaminian approach to tourism', *Annals of Tourism Research*, 39:1 (2012), 269–89; R. Phillips, 'The collecting and display of souvenir arts: Authenticity and the strictly commercial', in H. Morphy and M. Perkins, eds, *The Anthropology of Art: A Reader* (Oxford, 2006), 431–53.

12. Metropolitan Museum, NY, 2011 Exhibition, Italy Observed: Views and Souvenirs, 1706–1899; Christina K. Lindeman, 'Gendered souvenirs: Anna Amalia's Grand Tourist *vedute* fans', in Jennifer G. Germann and Heidi A. Strobel, eds, *Materializing Gender in Eighteenth-Century Europe*, (London, 2016), 51–66.

13. Jessica Speed, 'English pictorial enamels. Battersea and Bilston enamels and their successors', *Magazine Antiques*, 6 (2007), 88–95.

14. *Black's Picturesque Tourist of Scotland* (Edinburgh, 1874), 75.

15. Neil Guthrie, *The Material Culture of the Jacobites* (Cambridge, 2013).

16. John Gibson Lockhart, *Memoirs of the Life of Walter Scott, Bart* (1827–8), vol. 5, chapter. 12.

17. *Scotsman*, 16 September 1869.

18. John Baker, *Mauchline Ware and Associated Scottish Souvenir Ware* (Princes Risborough, 1985), 6.

19. Various Smith-developed patents are described in the *Journal of the Society of Arts* from the 1850s to 1870s, such as one for 'improvements in strengthening umbrella and walking stick handles, and other articles or details wherein the cross or transverse grain of the wood or other material is subject to strains', *Journal of the Society of Arts*, 7 (October 1859), 720.

20. A treen souvenir egg timer and letter opener decorated with scenes of the National Wallace Memorial, *c.*1870 can be viewed on SCRAN, www.scran.ac.uk (last accessed 15 February 2021).

21. See www.ayrshirehistory.com (last accessed 15 February 2021).

22. NRS. NG1/3/26. Board of Manufactures. Minutes, 2 November 1841.

23. Nenadic and Tuckett, 'Artisans and aristocrats'.

24. David Trachtenberg and Thomas Keith, *Mauchline Ware. A Collector's Guide* (Woodbridge, 2002).

25. *Scotsman*, 11 July 1859.

26. Trachtenberg and Keith, *Mauchline Ware*, 93–5.

27. Ibid., 95. An 1880 advertisement lists the Caledonian Works as a manu-facturer of fern ware. Other firms associated with fern ware were Hayes & Howgarth and Jack Davidson & Son. See Future Museum: South-West Scotland. www.futuremuseum.co.uk (last accessed 15 February 2021).

28. Sinclair, *Statistical Account*, vol. 2.

29. Sarah Whittingham, *Fern Fever: The Story of Pteridomania. A Victorian Obsession* (London, 2012), 72.

30. Rachel Morton Gold, 'Thomas Morton of Muirkirk', *Mauchline Ware Collector's Club, Supplement*, no. 1 (August 2012), 1–4.

31. William and Ruth Hodges, 'Fern Ware tables', *Journal of the Mauchline Ware Collector's Club*, 55 (April 2004), 7.

32. *Scotsman*, 7 May 1890, 'The Edinburgh International Exhibition'.

33. *New Statistical Account*, vol. 5, 164.

34. Ibid, 165.

35. Murray Pittock and Christopher Whatley, 'Poems and festivals, art and artefact and the commemoration of Robert Burns, c.1844–1896', *Scottish Historical Review*, 93:1 (2014), 56–79.

36. For examples, see Future Museum: South-West Scotland.

37. Neville Irons, 'Irish bog oak carving', *Irish Arts Review*, 4:2 (1987), 54–63.

38. *Scotsman*, 28 March 1862.

39. David Jones, 'Coal furniture in Scotland', *Furniture History*, 23 (1987), 35–8.

40. Harriet Beecher Stowe, *Sunny Memories of Foreign Lands*, vol. 1 (Boston, 1854), Letter 8.

41. Ibid., Letter 9.

42. Montrose Museum and National Museums Scotland were both gifted nota-ble private collections in the nineteenth century. See Laurenson, 'Materials, making and meaning'.

43. Simon J. Knell and Michael A. Taylor, 'Hugh Miller: Fossils, landscape and lit-erary geology', *Proceedings of the Geologists' Association*, 117 (2006), 85–98.

44. Examples are discussed in Laurenson, 'Materials, making and meaning'.

45. *Scotsman*, 7 October 1863, advertisement for the firm of Knox, Samuel and Dickson.

46. *Scotsman*, 23 August 1861.

47. Edinburgh companies included Mackay and Chisholm, Goldsmiths of Princes Street in the 1880s and Peter Westren, Manufacturing Jeweller of Rose Street and later Frederick Street, who registered designs from the 1840s to 1890s. National Archives, Kew. BT42–51. Board of Trade Registers of Patents, Designs and Trade Marks, 1842–1908.

48. See Diana Scarisbrick, *Scottish Jewellery: A Victorian Passion* (Milan, 2009); Nick Crawford, *Scottish Pebble Jewellery: Its History and the Mate-rials from Which It Was Made* (Kingsdown, 2007).

49. Rettie was one of 68 firms from Aberdeenshire selected by local committee to exhibit at the 1851 Great Exhibition in London and the only jewellery firm.

Another was Charles Stiven and Sons of Laurencekirk, makers of ornamental boxes. *Aberdeen Journal*, 20 November 1850.
50. *Aberdeen Weekly Journal*, 5 May 1886.
51. Bremner, *Industries of Scotland*, 129.
52. Ibid., 28.
53. E. Mairi MacArthur, *Iona Celtic Art: The Work of Alexander and Euphemia Ritchie* (Iona, 2003).
54. Frances Balfour, *Lady Victoria Campbell. A Memoir* (London, *c*.1910).
55. Reproduced in MacArthur, *Iona Celtic Art*, 22.
56. George Washington Wilson Collection, University of Aberdeen, has examples.
57. Edmund W. Abram, 'The last Lancashire handloom-weavers', *The Leisure Hour* (September 1893), 737–41.
58. *Aberdeen Daily Journal*, 21 July 1910.
59. *Scotsman*, 18 August 1906.
60. *Scotsman*, 14 March 1911.
61. Royal Collections Trust. Photograph of 1865. www.rct.uk/collections (15 February 2021).
62. See Alasdair Durie, *Tourism and Scotland. The Long View, 1700–2015* (London, 2017), chapter 7.
63. NRS. GD224/511/2. Buccleuch Papers. Letter dated 14 February 1842.
64. NRS. GD224/492. Buccleuch Papers. Estate correspondence, 1858. Examples of Sanquhar woven double-sided carpets – called Crawick carpets – are in the Dumfries Museum. See also Brown, *History of Sanquhar*, 360–3.
65. Brown, *History of Sanquhar*, chapter 10. For examples and pattern histories see Future Museum: South-West Scotland.
66. Nenadic and Tuckett, 'Artisans and aristocrats'.
67. *Scotsman*, 28 August 1889.
68. Paul Sutherland, *Mirth, Madness and St Magnus and the Eccentric Sheriff Thoms* (Kirkwall, 2013).
69. Orkney Library and Archives [OLA]. D20/4/19/5 Letter from Sheriff Thoms to D. M. Kirkness, 7 April 1890.
70. Annette Carruthers, 'The social rise of the Orkney chair', *Journal of Design History*, 22:1 (2009), 27–45. V&A Exhibition Display. Furniture Rooms. Orkney Chair interpretation label. Author observation.
71. OLA. D1/33/4. Papers Relating to D. M. Kirkness, Chairmaker, 1909–14; D1/33/3 Order Book for David Kirkness 12 and 14 Palace Road Kirkwall, 1909–14. Private Collection. Kirkness Order Book 1880–1897.
72. OLA. D20/4/19. Letters from Sheriff Thoms to D. M. Kirkness, 3–27 March 1890. Private Collection. Kirkness Order Book 1880–1897. Order no 314. 10 May 1893.
73. Ibid., Letter 14 June 1890.
74. Kellie Castle personal observation; Private Collection. Kirkness Order Book 1880–1897. Order no 314. Paid on 10 May 1893.

75. Personal communication from family members.
76. OLA. D1/33/4. Miscellaneous Papers Relating to Kirkness, 1909–14. Advertising leaflet.
77. Ibid., Letter to unnamed recipient in response to receipt of 6 December 1912.
78. OLA. Tom Kent Photographic Collection.
79. Private Collection. Kirkness Order Book 1880–1897. Order no. 29 and 30. Paid on 13 March 1891.
80. OLA. Tom Kent Photographic Collection.
81. Woven Communities: Basketmaking Communities in Scotland. Project website has images, see https://wovencommunities.org (last accessed 15 February 2021); Stephanie J. Bunn, 'Who designs Scottish vernacular baskets?' *Journal of Design History*, 29:1 (2016), 24–42.
82. OLA. D9. Records of Frances Taylor, Straw Plait Manufacturer and Merchant in Orkney and Sandwick, *c*.1780–1850.
83. Parliamentary Papers. Report to the Board of Agriculture for Scotland on Home Industries in the Highlands and Islands. 1914 (Cd 7564).
84. *Black's Picturesque Tourist*, advertising supplement,79.
85. The leading photographers were George Washington Wilson of Aberdeen and James Valentine of Dundee, the latter an apprentice-trained engraver. Their firms published albums, stereoscopic views and postcards. 'The Dundee works of Messrs. Valentine and Sons, Dundee', *British Journal of Photography*, 51 (16 September 1904), 808–9.
86. *Scotsman*, 30 August 1869.
87. The NMS has various items of commemorative dress in tartan linked to the royal visit.
88. See Chapter 6.
89. Nenadic and Tuckett, *Colouring the Nation*, illustrates examples.
90. *Black's Picturesque Tourist*, advertising supplement,79.
91. *Scotsman*, 19 January 1949.
92. *Scotsman*, 13 January 1947.

5

Country-house Building and Furnishing

THE 'LONG' NINETEENTH CENTURY was a great age of Scottish country-house building and each new, extended or renovated house represented the building craftsman's work and world. Stonemasons and carvers, joiners and wrought-iron makers were trained according to the apprenticeship norms of their different trades. Each group was expert in the materials with which they worked as they formed building structures mainly in stone, fitted out the wooden elements for the doors, windows, joists and floors, and furnished ironwork for fireplaces, railings, gates or garden furniture. From early in the century, the new technologies of domestic comfort ensured that plumbers were important craftsmen in country-house projects, working with lead pipes for water and drainage and for gas for lighting. Once a structure was built, the internal fittings and furnishings called on the plasterers and glaziers, painters and decorators, carvers, gilders and cabinetmakers. Some of these workers could be found on country estates or living nearby and they engaged in everyday maintenance, but estate owners could rarely build a new house without bringing in craftsmen from elsewhere who travelled from project to project.

Overseeing the whole and carefully recording the complex deployment of personnel and costs was the project manager, who might be the owner or estate factor, but was increasingly a specialist builder acting as clerk-of-works, implementing a builders' pattern-book design or working alongside an architect. A project manager was essential for keeping a close eye on the building process, organising and paying the different craft groups in a timely manner, solving problems as they emerged and working within a budget. A good project manager could save considerable sums for his patron whilst also ensuring the highest quality work.[1] Country-house owners were always interested in their buildings under construction and liaised closely and frequently with their project managers, often making final decisions on decoration and choosing the fittings and furnishings. They also maintained close relationships with their architects, many with specialist country-house practices. An example is offered by Robert Weir Schultz, Scottish born and trained but London based for most of his career, who worked extensively over decades from the 1880s for the Marquis of Bute in Scotland, one of the great building patrons of the age, including on the extensive rebuilding at the House of Falkland in Fife.[2]

Rates of country-house building varied according to the different regional economies. Robust grain-producing areas, such as East Lothian, saw construction peaks following peaks in agricultural profits during the Napoleonic War years. New farm buildings, roads and churches were also built. The Biel estate near Stenton, owned by the Hamilton-Nisbet family, provides an illustration. Biel House, originally a tower, was extended between 1814 and 1818 to plans in the Gothic style by architect William Atkinson at a cost of nearly £40,000. In the eyes of one contemporary, 'in the interior there is a fine variety of marbles fitted up, as side tables, etc; also a good few pictures by the best masters. Altogether the mansion is one of the most splendid to be seen in any country.'[3] The same family spent £2,000 in the early 1820s on a new parish church.[4] William Atkinson, from County Durham, who originally trained as a carpenter, was a notable country-house builder and furniture designer. He held many commissions in Scotland, including contributions to Abbotsford and several Buccleuch and Breadalbane houses.[5] Most of his work at Biel House was demolished in 1952 at a high point of country-house destruction in Britain.[6] William Burn, who designed the Biel church, was the Edinburgh-born son of an architect, undertook numerous church projects and was also a prolific country-house designer with over 90 major commissions to his credit.[7] He was particularly adept at project management, being a 'man of the highest integrity and independence . . . he would demur at any expense beyond his employers' means'.[8] The main source of Hamilton-Nisbet wealth was arable farming. According to the *Statistical Account* report for Stenton in 1845, over two-thirds of the acreage of the parish was under tillage for wheat and 'the population is purely agricultural, with only its proportional accompaniment of carpenters, masons, blacksmiths etc'.[9]

In the parts of Scotland where trade and industry dominated, the rate of country-house building matched the prosperity of those business elites who invested in land purchase to mark their success. This was apparent in rural areas close to Glasgow in the later eighteenth and early nineteenth

century, which saw a spate of house building by merchants and manufacturers keen to unite a genteel country lifestyle for their families with
close attention to counting-house interests in the city. With later suburban
expansion, many of these properties were either demolished or engulfed,
giving rise to a notable publication, illustrated with photographs, dedicated to the *Old Country Houses of the Old Glasgow Gentry*, which was
as much an elegy on a lost generation of notable personalities as on the
loss of a swathe of local mansion houses.

> Whatever their faults, absenteeism was not one. If Glasgow chanced not
> to have been their birthplace, it certainly was their home. Even when they
> came to own their country house, it would be within an easy distance of
> the Cross, and the town house would still be kept on . . . Now-a-days, our
> leading merchant has too often ceased to be a citizen . . . he lives as far from
> it as he can.[10]

Industrial elites of the mid and later nineteenth century who chose to
live far from the source of their wealth, were drawn to estate purchase
in the Highlands, which after an initial boom in smaller country-house
building in the eighteenth century, as traditional lairds replaced primitive
castles and tower houses, flourished again in the nineteenth century as
sporting estates.[11] It is estimated that around 340 shooting estates were
created in Highland Scotland over the course of the nineteenth century
and all included the building (or remodelling) of a lodge house, usually
in the distinctive Scottish baronial style, along with investment in the
infrastructure of roads, paths and fencing.[12] The rate of country-house
building in this part of Scotland was driven less by local considerations
than by metropolitan fashions. The royal family purchase of Balmoral in
1852 further fuelled demand.

The repatriation of colonial wealth generated spikes in country-house
building in some areas, with clusters in the Lowland and Border counties in the later eighteenth and early nineteenth century. Indeed, this
period was one of high investment in many parts of Scotland as a contemporary listing of country houses in Ayrshire reveals.[13] The account
provides historical, ownership and building details on the 70 principal
occupied houses in Ayrshire at the time of publication in 1885. Of the
houses described, the largest number, 32 per cent, were built between
*c.*1780 and 1820. Mostly in the classical or faux-castle style with classical interiors, many were built by established families replacing earlier
castles or towers and sometimes using materials from the older structure.
The house of Dalquharran near Girvan was typical. The old castle was
described in 1686 as 'the best house in a district that is peculiarly rich

in noble mansions' but was replaced in the 1780s by a 'more splendid house', designed by Robert Adam for lawyer, landowner and local MP Thomas Kennedy of Dunure, thereby creating 'one of the most massive specimens of domestic architecture to be seen in the district of Carrick'.[14] The project management was local, though under close direction from Robert Adam in London. Some of the craftsmen were from Edinburgh but many were part of the Adam circle of favoured artisans, Scottish born but based in London.[15]

The middle decades of the nineteenth century saw another surge in country-house building in Ayrshire, now mainly in the baronial style and representing 15 per cent of great houses by 1885. These were sometimes commissioned by the original landowning families, but many estates had now passed into the hands of new commercial and industrial elites. The mansion house of Auchendrane near Maybole illustrates. It was built in 1856 on land acquired from a local gentry family by Sir Peter Coats of the Paisley thread manufacturers J. & P. Coats. According to contemporary description, 'the mansion-house is situated in a romantic spot near the brink of the River Doon and is well sheltered by the fine old trees which surround it. The style is an adaptation of the Scottish Baronial architecture to the requirements of modern life, and the effect is pleasing.'[16] The later nineteenth century saw further building in a county with a mix of landowner wealth sources, in contrast with the purely farming counties where agriculture depression saw building rates collapse. The baronial style remained popular and most of the architects and craftsmen who worked on these houses were Scottish-based, but other styles were apparent as in the Italianate villa called the New House of Auchans, constructed by the Earl of Eglinton for one of his estate commissioners in the 1870s, or the English Tudor-style mansion house of Holms near Galston, built by the Fairlie family with India wealth.[17]

EARLY NINETEENTH CENTURY: ABBOTSFORD AND HARMONY HOUSE

The Scottish Border counties saw a rich variety of domestic building projects in the early nineteenth century. There are several major aristocratic houses in the area, from the Duke of Roxburghe's Floors Castle in the east, which was built in 1721 and remodelled in the 1840s, to Drumlanrig, the seventeenth-century seat of the Duke of Buccleuch in the west. Smaller houses were also abundant, reflecting a vibrant gentry-farming economy and the role of such houses as status indicators and investment routes for Edinburgh's professionals and merchants, many originally from local families. Walter Scott (1771–1832) was such, an Edinburgh lawyer by residence and training from Borders farming stock who knew the region from childhood. His first country house, which he rented, was Ashiestiel near Selkirk, where he was Sheriff Depute from 1803. Reflecting his literary celebrity and growing wealth, he built a modern mansion from 1813.[18] Abbotsford, on the banks of the Tweed near Melrose, was constructed around an existing farmhouse and cost c.£25,000; far more than usually spent on houses of equivalent size due to the opulence of some of the materials and large numbers of craftsmen. Scott's fame as an author and his investment in the house went hand in hand and Abbotsford became a tourist attraction during his lifetime. Bankruptcy in the crash of 1826 meant that Scott had to sell his Edinburgh house at 39 North Castle Street and live full time at Abbotsford. He died there just a few years later.[19]

Abbotsford is in the Scottish baronial style and though modern it incorporates older and antiquarian structures, such as the doorway from the medieval Edinburgh Tolbooth, which was demolished in 1817. There were several architects and craftsmen involved in the project, which was completed in phases as funds allowed. The main architect was William Atkinson, who was notable for his Gothic house design and also worked on the restorations of Durham Cathedral and Scone Palace near Perth.[20] A second influence came from architect, engraver and antiquarian Edward Blore, a friend of Scott who also worked on Westminster Abbey. Scott contributed many ideas, as did some of his local builders:

> He desired to have about him, wherever he could manage it, rich, though not gaudy, hangings, or substantial, old-fashioned wainscot-work, with no ornament but that of carving; and where the wood was to be painted at all, it was done in strict imitation of oak or cedar. Except in the drawing-room, which he abandoned to Lady Scott's taste, all the roofs were in appearance of antique carved oak, relieved by coats of arms duly blazoned at the intersections of beams, and resting on cornices, to the eye of the same material, but really composed of casts in plaster of Paris after the foliage, the flowers, the grotesque monsters and dwarfs, and sometimes the beautiful heads of nuns and confessors, on which he had doated from infancy among the cloisters of Melrose and Roslin.[21]

Characteristic of this antiquarian interest is the large, carved, pink sandstone fireplace in the entrance hall, which was made by the Smith brothers of Darnick, a local building firm that was responsible for much of the work at the house along with other country-house projects and several Tweed bridges. The fireplace design is based on the so-called 'Abbot's Seat' at nearby Melrose Abbey, which also featured in an early Walter

Scott poem *The Lay of the Last Minstrel*. Set within the fireplace, the iron grate is modern and the tiles seventeenth-century Dutch delft. The wood panelling in the entrance hall comprises old panels taken from other buildings including Dunfermline Abbey and new panels carved and stained to match. In addition to the Smith brothers, several other Borders firms worked at Abbotsford, including Sanderson & Paterson of Buckholmside near Galashiels, who operated an extensive building firm and wood yard and worked on church projects.[22] Masons and carpenters were employed by these firms or by Scott directly, since he took a close interest and project-managed some of it himself. The elaborate plaster ceiling in the entrance hall and the painted shields and coats-of-arms celebrating Borders families, including Scott's own, were modelled to look antique. Craftsmen specialising in Gothic effects flourished in early-nineteenth-century Scotland. One of these was interior painter David Ramsay Hay (1798–1866) of Edinburgh, whose first patron was Scott and who subsequently dominated the decorators' world in mid-nineteenth-century Scotland.[23] Contributors to the house furnishings were identified by J. G. Lockhart, Scott's son-in-law, in the posthumous biography:

> The great table in the library, for example (a most complex and beautiful one), was done entirely in the room where it now stands, by Joseph Shillinglaw of Darnick – the Sheriff planning and studying every turn as zealously as ever an old lady pondered the development of an embroidered cushion. The hangings and curtains, too, were chiefly the work of a little hunchbacked tailor, byname *William* Goodfellow – (save at Abbotsford, where he answered to *Robin*) – who occupied a cottage on Scott's farm of the Broomielees – one of the race that creep from homestead to homestead, welcomed wherever they appear by housewife and handmaiden, the great gossips and newsmen of the parish, in Scottish nomenclature *cardooers*.[24]

The records and bills for work undertaken at Abbotsford demonstrate how a provincial building company like Sanderson & Paterson acted as general project manager and supplier of materials and services. In summer 1819, for instance, they sourced five bedframes with canvas bottoms costing £10 10s, also charging 18s for a wright for six days for 'putting up the beds [and] making a press in the cellar'. A mason was hired for three days to work on the fire grates. Lengths of wood and sheets of glass were supplied for doors and glasshouses. Frequent routine repairs were detailed along with the costs for nails and tacks. In the first half of 1819, the firm billed Scott for a total of £57 6s 8d.[25] An earlier account, probably for 1816, titled 'For Work Done at Abbotsford', records a bill of £2,545 that included polished hearths, pavements and steps as well as wages for wrights, plumbers and plasterers.[26] Atkinson, the architect, gave advice on finding specialised craftsmen, as in November 1821 when he wrote to Scott regarding bricks for work in the garden: 'I think you will easily find some steady brickmaker about Portobello [near Edinburgh] who will contract for making the bricks at a price per thousand – the brickmaker to find everything required so as you may have no trouble'. He sent a copy of an agreement with a brickmaker who worked on Taymouth Castle in Perthshire as a model for Scott's contract and advised that the bricks be fired with coal rather than wood as at Taymouth.[27] Inputs to the building process were blurred between the architects and builders. The latter supplied materials and skilled labour, but also furnished design ideas, often taken from nearby buildings, as in January 1822 when John Smith of Darnick sent Scott a 'plan of the larder at Haining', a country house near Selkirk, as solution for a pedestrian but necessary addition to the kitchen. The builder knew his client well, for after detailing the utility of the structure, with its cooling vents to the side, he suggested 'the dome roof would not answer at Abbotsford but it might be made, as you suggested yourself, to represent a flanking tower in a state of dilapidation'.[28]

Of the individual craftsmen, William Goodfellow, the tailor mentioned by Lockhart, who was employed for dress work, curtain making and upholstery, presented a bill for the period April to October 1822 for £2 6s 3d. The textiles came from Richardson of Selkirk. Joseph Shilllinglaw's accounts have also survived. He was the cabinetmaker, probably joinery trained, who made much of the fine carved furniture in the library and other public rooms. He employed his own skilled journeymen and charged for their time, as in August 1822 when he billed Scott for £22 10s for '12 weeks and 3 days of two making old carved work striking a cornish making 35 foot of carved cornish making 10 capitals and two new pieces above the side tables with three new circles for side tables carved etc'. For his own cabinet work he charged by the piece, as in October 1822 when he made a 'strong dining table' of the 'best wainscot' for £8 10s along with four carved black oak chairs at £7 12s. Shillinglaw's total bill for £52 4s was 'settled by check in Galashiels' on 24 November 1822.[29]

Some of the Abbotsford furniture was purchased in London, including mirrors from the London Plate Glass Warehouse at 44 Conduit Street where Scott spent a total of £120 11s in 1824. Furniture warehouses in Edinburgh were also used. Francis Allan's shop at 9 Hanover Street was the source of bell pulls, bamboo chairs, bedside stands, chair cushions and numerous other types of ready-made furniture and decorative goods. Allan offered a house removal service, arranging to pack and transport furniture from Scott's Castle Street town house in Edinburgh to Abbotsford and charging £46 13 4d for a long account at the end of 1824.[30] Francis Allan was a retailer more than a practical craftsman, though in his early career in Edinburgh he described himself as an 'upholsterer'. His credentials and aspirations were evident from advertising, as in November 1823 when he inserted a notice in the *Scotsman* stating,

> Paris, 25 October 1823, Francis Allan, Upholsterer of no. 9 South Hanover Street, Edinburgh, respectfully informs his friends he has been some time in Paris, after visiting London, to improve his style of Furnishing – on his return, which will be in a few days, he will endeavour to merit the support he has hitherto enjoyed: in the meantime, orders sent to his warehouse . . . will meet every attention.[31]

When Allan died young in 1827, his stock was sold by auction and comprised 'elegant sideboards, in various patterns. Dining tables, a great variety of oblong, octagon and circular loo tables in mahogany, rosewood, oak and zebra wood with tea and sofa tables to match . . .' There were easy chairs, sofas, worktables and dressing tables, beds and chintzes.[32] These were a ready-made resource for urban as well as country-house furnishing that Scott, like many others, employed.

Just a few miles from Abbotsford is Harmony House (called Hall in its early history), a small country house on the edge of Melrose, located on land to the north of the High Street that in the distant past had been part of the Abbey grounds. Built in 1807, it is a three-bay, rubble stone, typical Scottish neoclassical mansion, with a sunken service floor, two main floors, an attic and slate roof. Described in newspaper advertising when put on the market in 1842, it was a 'beautiful residence', with four and a half acres of 'pleasure ground' including an orchard, comprising a spacious dining room and drawing room along with 12 other apartments, most of them lit by gas from the Melrose Gas Works. There was a cottage of two floors, coach house, two stables, byre and another cottage in the flower garden. The property came with fishing rights on the nearby River Tweed.[33]

Harmony was built for Robert Waugh (c.1745–1832), a Melrose-born son of a shoemaker. Waugh trained as a joiner and wright in or near Melrose, but at an early age in 1761, along with younger brother John, was sent to Jamaica to make his way in life. The circumstances behind this move are unknown though it is possible the boys' father had died. A sister, Janet, remained in Melrose and married George Broomfield, a wright and small landowner of nearby Gattonside.[34]

John Waugh became a plantation overseer, working for the York Estate in the Clarendon District of Jamaica. He died there on 27 November 1794, 'snatched by a putrid fever in the course of a few days'.[35] The death announcement in the Kingston *Royal Gazette* told how he had left his native country aged just 13 and lived in Jamaica for 33 years. Unmarried, the bulk of his fortune went to nephew John Broomfield and four nieces, the children of sister Janet. Robert Waugh's early career in Jamaica is not recorded, though it seems likely he was involved in the building trade and his passage to Jamaica might have been connected with a scheme introduced in 1740 by Sir James Campbell of Auchinbreck to take Scottish craftsmen to the island. These craftsmen were important for building the infrastructure of the plantation economy and they designed and built many estate houses for Scottish owners. Both men and boys were described in the 1770s in glowing terms: 'The artificers, particularly stone-masons and mill-wrights, from that part of Britain, are remarkably expert, and in general are sober, frugal and civil; the good education which the poorest of them receive, having great influence on their morals and behaviour.'[36] Though starting as a joiner and wright, when he returned to Scotland in the early 1800s, aged in his late fifties, Robert Waugh was a rich plantation owner. He retained the Jamaica estates to his death in 1832 and had trading interests in Jamaican commodities such as sugar, timber and indigo. There is no account of how he acquired the Jamaica property, which was described as a pimento plantation called Harmony in the Parish of Clarendon, comprising 44 acres and 373 slaves in 1817, with later slave compensation records giving a value of £2,530 19s 3d.[37] Robert Waugh's wealth at death comprised Harmony House and nearby land in Melrose, various properties in Jamaica which were retained by the family for income and shares in the 'chainbridge' over the Tweed linking Melrose and Gattonside, built in 1825–6 as a toll bridge, which he left to the Poor Law authorities for the benefit of the Melrose poor.[38]

The Harmony builder is unknown, though Waugh, with his craft background and local connections, would have had no difficulties in supervising the project and finding skilled labour. The contractors may have been the Smith brothers of Darnick, who built the adjacent Abbey Manse in 1810 and contributed to Abbotsford. The outward appearance of Harmony House is mostly unremarkable, though there are two unusual features that can be inferred as having some relationship with Waugh's lengthy sojourn in Jamaica. The first is the high set of steps to the front door, of a sort typically seen in Jamaican houses of the period to keep out wild animals. The second is the high wall surrounding the

property, which echoes a security feature used in Jamaica against upris-
ings. According to Lockhart,

> Mr Waugh was a retired West Indian, of very dolorous aspect, who had
> settled at Melrose, built a large house there, surrounded it and his garden
> with a huge wall, and seldom emerged from his own precincts . . . The villag-
> ers called him 'the Melancholy Man' – and considered him as already 'dreein'
> his dole for doings amang the poor [slaves]'.[39]

Internally, Harmony had large dining and drawing rooms, but the other
chambers were relatively small. This focus on rooms for entertaining
is typical of the merchant classes and, since Waugh was a single man,
his limited socialising was probably dominated by men. The furnishings
were acquired in 1809–10 in Kelso and via his nephew John Broomfield, a clerk in the Leith timber trade. The main Kelso cabinetmaker was
James Mein of Roxburghe Street, whose family was in business from
1784 to 1855 and supplied fine furniture for many gentry and noble
house.[40] There are two surviving letters between Waugh and his nephew
for April and June 1810. The first describes furniture commissions, detailing Broomfield's visits to various warehouses in Edinburgh and enclosing
the prices his uncle might expect to pay for 'handsome chairs' at between
£1 6s and £1 15s, elegant carved sideboards costing £16, ornamented
canopy beds with merino wool covers costing up to £50 each and carpets
at all prices according to quality. Broomfield ordered chimney pieces for
his uncle from James Thomson, mason and marble cutter of Constitution Street in Leith.[41] In the same letter he commiserated with his uncle
on the rainy, cold weather which delayed work on the garden and made
Tweed salmon fishing impossible. By way of compensation, he sent his
uncle a 'cod fish' from Leith via the carrier Mr Martin. The second letter details Broomfield's plan to go to Jamaica for work and provided his
uncle with information on a Jamaica ship just in port with a ruined cargo
of sugar. He mentioned a duty on foreign timber which was impacting
the Leith trade, gave news of his sisters and arranged for the dispatch of
a box of indigo that his uncle had ordered.[42] John Broomfield, an attentive nephew, vanished from the family record shortly after and it seems
likely he died in Jamaica.

A striking internal feature of Harmony House was the drawing room
panelled with Jamaican cedar wood, which Walter Scott admired. Cedar,
which is pleasantly scented and has insecticidal properties, was used in
fine furniture construction, mainly as drawer linings, for cupboards for
storing clothing and for bookshelves. Having seen the 'very pretty apart-
ment', Scott decided to line his study and library at Abbotsford with

similar cedar. Waugh, his neighbour, sourced the wood. This is how Scott described the undertaking in a letter to friend Daniel Terry in London, who supplied him with much for the house in the way of antique furniture and armaments. Having spent some time writing about the storage of his books and fears for damp, he continued,

> . . . I have at present some doubt – namely, the capacity of my library to accommodate my books. Should it appear limited (I mean making allowance for future additions) I can perhaps, by Mr Atkinson's assistance, fit up this private room [the study] with a gallery . . . The cedar, I assure you, is quite beautiful. I have had it sawn out into planks, and everyone who looks at it agrees it will be more beautiful than oak. Indeed, what I have seen of it put to that use, bears no comparison unless with such heart of oak as Bullock employed, and that you know is veneered. I do not go on the cry in this, but practical knowledge, for Mr Waugh, my neighbour, a West Indian planter (but himself bred a joiner), has finished the prettiest apartment with it that I ever saw.[43]

Waugh was one of many country-house owners in the Borders, Berwickshire or East Lothian made wealthy through the slave economy. Others included the Maitland family of Lauder, owners of Thirlestane Castle; the Dalrymples in North Berwick, who built several houses; and the Homes at Paxton House. Walter Scott had family connections with slavery through younger brother Daniel, who trained for a merchant career in London and worked in Jamaica as an estate overseer, though he did not prosper. Scots in India could make fortunes and repatriated wealth from that part of the British empire was similarly invested in country houses.

MID NINETEENTH CENTURY: FALKLAND HOUSE

Country-house building in Highland Scotland mid century included large numbers of gentleman's mansions for use as summer homes. There were several in the Appin district of Argyllshire not far from Oban, such as Fasnacloich, high in Glen Creran, a simple house associated with the Stewart family that was transformed into a modern castellated Gothic hunting lodge in the 1840s.[44] Further down the glen was Invercreran House, owned by the McCallum Webster family and detailed in the 'Our Glen' photographic album (see Chapter 3). An advertisement of 1892, when it was offered for holiday rent, described it comprising four public rooms, ten bedrooms, stables and gardens, with salmon and sea fishing nearby and associated boats and equipment.[45] Perthshire saw much country-house building or house redesign by great aristocrats including the Earl of Breadalbane at Taymouth Castle near Loch Tay, which was

an Adam-designed house of the later eighteenth century that underwent alterations and Gothic-style redecoration in the 1840s.[46] Across
the county border in Fife, Falkland Palace, owned by the Marquis of
Bute, was redeveloped at vast cost in the 1880s, employing many craftsmen from beyond Scotland. Using the same workforce, nearby Falkland
House was also subject to Bute-instructed additions and redecoration.
The earlier history of the house, however, casts valuable light on the local
building craft economy.

Just outside the small burgh of Falkland in the shadow of the Lomond
Hills, Falkland House is a two-storey, six-bay house in a Jacobean style,
with an attached single storey and attic servants' wing. It was designed
by William Burn, the Edinburgh architect and built between 1839 and
1844, replacing an earlier mansion called Nuthill.[47] The latter and a
smaller Fife property called Grangehill, were owned by John Bruce, Professor of Logic at Edinburgh University, who extended his family estate
by purchase and retired to the life of a country gentleman. In a fulsome
Scotsman obituary of 1826, Bruce was described as

> carrying on improvements on a most extended and liberal scale, giving
> employment to great numbers of tradesmen and labourers of all descrip-
> tions. He also laid out a large sum in repairing what remains of the Palace
> of Falkland, so as to preserve, for centuries to come, that relic of royalty in
> Scotland.[48]

The mid-century owner of Falkland House was Margaret Steuart Hamilton
Bruce (1788–1869), illegitimate daughter of a military man in India by an
Indian lady, who was adopted when orphaned as a small child and raised
by her uncle, John Bruce, in Edinburgh. Margaret's husband, Onesiphorus Tyndall, who took his wife's surname upon marriage in 1828, was the
Bristol-born son of merchants, slave traders and bankers, who was educated in Edinburgh and trained as a barrister.[49] The couple devoted most of
their married life to improving and extending their Fife estates and engaging
in local charitable causes. They also instructed the new house.[50] The decision to improve Nuthill came shortly after John Bruce's death along with
a commission for a monument to be designed by English architect Charles
Robert Cockerell. Cockerell, a noted antiquarian, was also involved in
early discussions about Nuthill, but he wanted the Tyndall Bruces to focus
on conserving Falkland Palace and parted with his patrons. The house
project then passed to William Burn.[51]

The Tyndall Bruces, with their India wealth, were great consumers of
luxury goods. Shortly after marriage and long before they started work
on the house, they made extravagant orders for table silver as well as
jewellery from silversmiths in London, including Storr & Mortimer of

New Bond Street, who supplied richly chased wine coolers.[52] They spent lavishly on building and furnishing the house with multiple sources of supply – local, from Edinburgh, and further afield – with considerable correspondence on the issue with friends and paid advisors, including the architect and tradesmen. Though closely involved in the project, the day-to-day activities of craftsmen, materials ordering and payments were supervised and recorded by an attentive clerk-of-works, William Spottiswoode, who also supervised the later building of Falkland Parish Church. At the outset of the project the aim, according to old Edinburgh friend the Rev. John Sandford, should be to have a comfortable house: 'banish magnificence but not good taste – be not over housed but satisfy every possible demand for comfort'.[53] In the event, luxury and magnificence seemed to shape the agenda with furniture ordered from Paris and Italy and many pedestrian fittings from London. One of the main furnishers was Ringuet-Leprince of Paris, who supplied an ebony armoire, a bedroom suite, bookcases, mirrors and Buhl cabinets of distinctly glamorous character.[54] These commissions were undertaken through a friend in Paris, who also sent pattern swatches for silk furnishing fabrics. Other furniture items, including a zebrawood writing desk and bookcases for the library, were made in Edinburgh by the prestigious firm of Charles Trotter of Princes Street. Trotter corresponded on the room painting and advised on the use of silk decorative papers for the walls.[55] In essence, in common with many of the bigger cabinetmaking firms, he offered an interior design service.

Fire surrounds were sourced in Edinburgh and London, with the former favoured over the latter according to Burn:

> You have done quite right as to the chimney pieces, which will not only cost less at first here, but they are in fact ten times better and more substantial than any I ever saw in the south and you have only to look at those sent the other day to Balbirnie to satisfy yourself to this fact – as I have never seen more inferior work, or such trashy articles.[56]

Several carved marble fireplaces were made by David Ness of Leith Walk, described as 'sculptor, marble cutter and marble merchant'.[57] He was born in Edinburgh in 1786 and owned a marble-cutting business from 1821 until his death in 1852.[58] But despite the advice quoted above, other chimneypieces along with statuary were supplied from London, mainly by Joseph Browne & Co., who had a 'marble and scagliola works' in University Street. The latter, like David Ness, also specialised in funerary monuments. The fire grates came from W. & M. Feelham of Clifford Street in London, who advertised as stove makers to the Crown.[59] Damask wallpaper was supplied by Williams, Coopers, Boyle & Co.

of Ludgate Hill in London, a long-established firm that began as block printers in the eighteenth century and continued in business to the 1860s, exhibiting wall coverings at the 1851 Great Exhibition.[60]

Several local craftsmen of repute were involved in building Falkland House, such as Andrew Symington of Kingskettle in Fife, a clock- and watchmaker who made the clocks for the clock tower and entrance hall. Symington, active from 1834–45, was noted for mechanical inventions and patents.[61] The Falkland clock was so innovative that it yielded a newspaper notice which described Symington's work as of 'elegant appearance' and 'beautifully adapted for gentlemen's houses and public buildings'.[62] Other craftsmen were Edinburgh based, such as the famous decorator David Ramsay Hay of George Street, who had worked on Abbotsford decades before and undertook much of the interior painting and gilding. Another Edinburgh firm was ornamental plasterers James Annan & Son, who also had a branch in Perth and did the plasterwork for Falkland Parish Church.[63] Annan's work at Falkland House for the years 1840–3 cost £1,375 16s 9d and is indicative of the vast sums laid out on the project.[64] Most of the local rural or small-town craftsmen worked on pedestrian parts of the building, though these often involved extensive contracts, where knowledge of local supplies and materials, as well as command of a local, mainly semi-skilled workforce, was important. John Black of Kirkcaldy was the primary builder and mason and David Miller of Auchterarder and Falkland was the principal joiner and glazier providing structural timberworks, doors and windows, and some internal panelling. Robert Clark, a local painter and decorator, undertook the outdoor paintwork.

Falkland House took four years to complete and whilst the interiors were extensively remodelled later in the century, it proved to be a comfortable home and survives to the present. Yet, as detailed records show, the project was not without problems, which, despite the employment of an effective clerk-of-works, added to the costs. Some difficulties were born out of clashes of personality and questions of taste, some were down to managerial ineptitude and others were the product of fraudulent charging. Keeping key craftsmen on-site and usefully employed when other parts of the project were delayed was a challenge for clerk-of-works William Spottiswoode. This proved a critical issue with workers engaged in outdoor, seasonal work who might easily find employment elsewhere at peak times. To keep his stonecarvers busy and on the payroll when work on the house was delayed by problems with the builder, Spottiswoode brought forward some of the stonework in the garden, though this was usually undertaken after the house was completed.[65]

Clashes of personality and taste focused on decoration and involved the owners and architect in a sometimes-strained correspondence. One contentious issue was the employment of David Ramsay Hay. Hay was a celebrated art decorator with a distinctive aesthetic who could pick and choose his projects. Tyndall Bruce selected him for the ornamental painting against the recommendations of architect William Burn. Hay's estimates were acceptable, though his opinion on wall coverings soon conflicted with those offered by Charles Trotter the furniture maker, who suggested silk over paint for some of the main rooms. Several painters were deployed at Falkland as part of Hay's team, but the man himself was mostly absent and in May 1843 when working at Dumbleton Hall in Gloucestershire, he wrote a peevish letter to Tyndall Bruce complaining of changes imposed by Burn on his painting of the dining-room ceiling and appealing for the owner to intervene.[66] Though completed as planned, William Burn disliked Hay's work and he was not employed for the decorative scheme at Falkland Parish Church a few years later.[67] The painting contract for this related project went to the rising firm of Bonnar & Carfrae of Castle Street, Edinburgh, whose ambition was signalled when they exhibited in the Great Exhibition of 1851 with a display including 'design in imitation of fresco painting and of inlaid wood. Designs in imitation of inlaid marble'.[68] Bonnar & Carfrae were successful over several generations in Edinburgh. By the 1880s they were based in prestigious George Street, where they had retail premises and were described as painters, gilders and carvers, and decorative art designers for curtains, carpets, textiles and ornamental metalwork.[69] They undertook some of the interior work for the later refurbishment of Falkland Palace.

If matters of taste were a cause for conflict, matters of money were a greater concern. At least one supplier submitted misleading invoices, identified by William Burn in a letter to Tyndall Bruce concerning the London maker of marble fireplaces, Joseph Browne & Co. 'He cannot make anything of Mr Browne's account so he has sent it to Lord Stair [legal advisor] to arrange as he thinks fit. Mr Browne is not easily dealt with and if I can help it, I shall not readily engage with him again.'[70] The bill was amended. Far more serious was the impact of chaotic estimates, poor labour management and the eventual bankruptcy and death of the main builder and mason for the project, John Black of Kirkcaldy. At the outset, Black was a suitable choice for the role. A respected Fife tradesman of long standing, he was admitted a burgess of the burgh of Kirkcaldy in 1812 when probably in his late twenties.[71] Like all country builders, he had his own workforce and was familiar with nearby quarries, which was necessary given the high cost of transporting stone. Yet this experienced master craftsman ran into problems, with delays in the mason's work at Falkland House explained by him as a product of his own mistakes in the initial estimates, along with difficulties with stone supply, compounded by ill health and mounting debts. By May 1842 he was unable to pay his masons, the business entered the first stages of bankruptcy and John Black died a few months later.[72] The clerk-of-works took over the management of the building side of the project, paid the workforce directly and sought to rescue the situation. But problems with masons' work had consequences for the other main contractor for the building structure, David Miller of Auchterarder, who was hired in September 1839 as joiner, smith and glazier for a fee of £5,980.[73] Miller and his team found themselves unable to work to the initial contract. He complained to William Burn in July 1841 about delays caused by failure of the masons to keep to schedule and the difficulties he suffered from non-payment of his instalments.[74] He made a claim for compensation for 'financial loss caused by the slow progress of the mason's work', which was eventually settled in November 1844 at £100 after discussion between the architect, clerk-of-works and owners.[75] Problems such as these were not unusual in country-house building projects, though they are unusually well documented for Falkland House.

Though local builders commonly undertook country-house projects in the eighteenth century and first half of the nineteenth century, the complexity entailed as houses got bigger and more exacting in their decorative stonework or heating and plumbing arrangements was increasingly beyond them and the second half of the century saw growing reliance on city firms. Indeed, the next significant Tyndall Bruce building project, the Falkland village church, completed in 1850, saw most contracts go to Edinburgh craftsmen including the building and joinery firm of Charles and John MacGibbon of Great King Street, who were paid £1,818 9s 0d. A local mason, George Page, was subcontractor, but only for smaller projects on the Falkland estate, such as a garden folly in the later 1840s.[76]

LATER NINETEENTH AND EARLY TWENTIETH CENTURY: KINLOCH CASTLE, HILL HOUSE AND MAR LODGE

In the later nineteenth century rates of country-house building shifted again. Incomes from agriculture were under pressure, but wealth from industry and trade was rising, with the latter driving building, often in far-flung places and on a grand scale by second- or third-generation entrepreneurs with inherited wealth. Kinloch Castle on the Isle of Rum, a sporting estate, offers an example. Built in the late 1890s for Lancashire industrialist Sir George Bullough, the scion of a textile-machine-making dynasty, everything about the castle spoke of luxury and leisure. It was designed by the London firm of Leeming & Leeming as a square-turreted mansion in quasi-baronial style on a bay allowing easy access from the sea. Fashionable rose sandstone was transported great distances from Dumfriesshire by steamer whilst soil for the greenhouses and gardens came from Ayrshire. Most of the nearly 300 craftsmen who worked on the house came from way beyond the Highlands, with many from Lancashire or London. They dressed in Bullough-tweed kilts for an extra shilling payment a week. The internal fittings were in the highest style and included elaborate woodcarving, glazing and plasterwork along with state-of-the-art plumbing and lighting. The furnishings came from far afield, including Africa, India, China and Japan which Bullough had visited on an extended tour just a few years before he built the castle.[77] Almost nothing was made in Scotland, though some of the contents, such as the dining-room suite, were first commissioned for George Bullough's Clyde-made steam yacht *Rhouma*, a mobile country house of sorts. Furniture, curtains and carpets were supplied by the departmental store of James Shoolbred & Co. of Tottenham Court Road in London, holders of a royal warrant, whose modern and antique furnishings, many in a style associated with the Aesthetic movement but also embracing other historic styles such as 'Old English' or 'Adam' neoclassical, were advertised annually by catalogue.[78] Costly specialist furniture included a billiards table for the games and smoking room, supplied with cues, balls, lighting and related equipment by the London firm of Burroughes & Watts of Soho Square, whose catalogue for 1889 shows the finest full-scale tables costing up to 250 guineas. Kinloch Castle was built over ten years and cost its owner *c.*£250,000, a remarkable sum for the day and more remarkable still given its purpose as a short-stay sporting mansion used for a few weeks each year.[79]

At the other end of the size and style spectrum, another iconic mansion, built between 1902 and 1904 for publisher Walter Blackie, was Hill House on the outskirts of Helensburgh in Dunbartonshire. Designed by Charles Rennie Mackintosh both inside and out, the house, a testament to a distinctively Scottish modernist style, made extensive use of Scottish suppliers and craftsmen and craftswomen. Several were Helensburgh residents, a town famous for its numerous large mansion houses, many in the English Arts and Crafts style, owned as weekend or summerhouses by Glasgow's commercial elite.[80] Local mason and builder Anthony Trail and slater William Thom & Son both worked on Hill House, though the principal contractor was Aikenhead & Sons of Greenock. Furniture, much of it made to Mackintosh's designs specific for the house, was crafted by Alex Martin or Francis Smith, cabinetmakers and upholsterers in Glasgow. The Glasgow department store, house furnisher and decorators, Wylie & Lochhead, supplied more standard items, particularly for bedrooms, as well as wallpaper, curtains and light fixtures. William Kemp & Co. of Glasgow, house-furnishing ironmongers, made many of the customised metal fittings for doors, windows and fireplaces.[81] Several of these craft businesses and individuals worked with Mackintosh on other projects, domestic and commercial.[82] An illustration is provided by Francis Smith, the second generation of a Glasgow firm of cabinetmakers and upholsterers, who in 1881 employed 60 craftsmen and their apprentices and 30 women upholsterers. Smith supplied furniture for commercial buildings in Glasgow, including the famous Mrs Cranston's Tea Rooms, which Mackintosh designed and in the 1890s advertised their specialist lines in 'library and office furniture, revolving bookcases, consulting tables, club chairs, office desks'.[83]

With a practice mainly in eastern Scotland, the career and connections of architect and designer Robert Lorimer offers further insights to networks of craft communities engaged in country-house building. As a boy growing up in Fife, Lorimer established relationships with local craftworkers that were sustained into adulthood. These included the Wheeler family of Arncroach, who were furniture makers, wrights and undertakers.[84] When William Wheeler, famous for chairs, died in 1914, at which point in his lengthy career he was described as an 'art furniture maker', his list of payments due from customers included Mrs Lorimer at Kellie Castle, J. H. Lorimer of Drummond Place in Edinburgh and Sir R. Lorimer of Melville Street in Edinburgh along with numerous Fife gentry.[85] Lorimer's country-house projects embraced a range of styles, including the neoclassical Hill of Tarvit in Fife, completed in 1907 for a wealthy collector as showcase for his antiques and Scottish baronial Ardkinglas in Argyll, built in 1906 for industrialist Sir Andrew Noble. He undertook remodelling or restoration projects in an Arts and Crafts style, several in Fife. He worked in Scotland and England and his celebrity, rewarded with a knighthood, was marked in September 1913 when *Country Life* magazine published an 'architectural supplement' dedicated to Lorimer's work, which included features on his key commissions and advertisements from over 50 craftworkers and firms, mostly Scottish and many highlighting their relationships with his projects.[86]

The 'Directory of Scottish Craftsmen and Builders' that was appended to the 1913 *Country Life* supplement included photographs of the products they made, mostly in situ in a Lorimer house. The Edinburgh firm of Scott Morton & Co., noted for carved wood and interior panelling, emphasised 'recent contracts carried out for' Lorimer including 'carpentry & finishings' at Ardkinglas along with nine other major projects. They illustrated the page with a photograph of a fully fitted wood panelled interior made in British oak for the dining room of the New Club in Edinburgh, an elite gentleman's club.[87] A photograph of the front elevation of Hill of Tarvit was used to embellish an advertisement for Neil McLeod & Sons, builders in Edinburgh. Thomas Beattie, an architectural sculptor and plaster modeller based at the Dean Studio in Edinburgh, listed 11 Scottish and English houses designed by Lorimer on which he had worked, whilst James M. Inglis, plumber in Edinburgh, listed 16 Lorimer projects, including an illustration of Monzie Castle near Crieff, a notable restoration of 1908 following a fire.[88] There were cabinetmakers, painters and decorators, stained-glass makers and decorative iron workers, mostly Edinburgh based, who were all part of the Lorimer circle on whom he called time and again over decades to produce the finest of work for his country house clients. Some survived well into the twentieth century, including furniture makers Whytock & Reid and architectural wrought-iron makers Thomas Hadden.

The architect with his own circle of trusted craftsmen was a phenomenon that could be seen amongst more provincial men such as Aberdeen-based A. Marshal Mackenzie. The banks of the River Dee in Highland Aberdeenshire are dotted with mansion houses mostly built as shooting lodges. They include Queen Victoria's Balmoral and Mar Lodge, owned by the Duke of Fife and his Duchess, Princess Louise, which was destroyed by a fire in June 1895 and subsequently rebuilt by Marshal Mackenzie. Descriptions of the fire and its aftermath give an indication of the tradesmen and communities that a great country house supported. The fire began during routine upgrading work when a group of Aberdeen plumbers were fitting a ventilation pipe into a closet near the Duke's rooms and carried a pot of molten lead into the house. A draught from the windows blew a spark onto wood shavings used to protect pipes from frosting and fire took hold, spreading rapidly through the building. The plumbers were joined in their efforts to extinguish the fire by estate workers summoned by the overseer and by a team of masons who were also on site, led by a builder, Mr MacDonald.[89] The contents were saved, but not the lodge, which was rebuilt shortly after, with the Queen laying the foundation stone.[90]

Alexander Marshall Mackenzie, who had recently completed Crathie Church at Balmoral, designed the new Mar Lodge. Born in Elgin,

Mackenzie had an established team of skilled Aberdeen craftsmen to draw on for his north-east Scotland work, who lived in bothies on-site for the duration of projects.[91] The Mar Lodge construction was famed for its use of local-grown wood in the building structure and for interior panelling and some of furniture, though other furniture came from Maples of London, a fashionable store.[92] The stone came from the Duke of Fife's quarry at Braemar and the house design incorporated a 'beautiful verandah of rustic woodwork'. It was planned from the outset to include electric lighting and the projected costs were between £15,000 and £20,000.[93] A photograph survives of the men who worked on Mar Lodge, formally seated together as the building neared completion. It reveals pride in craft and community, showing 35 individuals, with their trades and professions indicated by clothing and tools, posed in front of the house. The men seated on the ground at the front are plumbers, with one of them holding an impressive U-bend pipe and another displaying the soles of his hobnailed boots. A man on the far left holds tinsmith scissors. A suited young man with watch chain on the right is probably the clerk. An older man on the middle left with rolled plans under his arm is the builder overseeing the works. Men dressed in white are painters or plasterers. The second-to-back row has the carpenters, with their saws

Figure 5.1   Craftsmen working on Mar Lodge, Aberdeenshire, c.1910. © National Museums Scotland.

and planes displayed. An illustrated account of the building, décor and furnishings at Mar Lodge was featured in *Country Life* in June 1937.[94]

Of course, the owner of Mar Lodge was a great aristocrat married into the royal family and though this house was a fairly modest construction, at the highest level of society country-house building could be on a spectacular scale, with great patrons capable of supporting whole communities of craftsmen of their own. The most remarkable was the Marquis of Bute, who commanded a vast income of *c.*£300,000 per year derived mainly from Welsh coalfields and railways and docks in south Wales.[95] John Patrick Crichton-Stuart, the 3rd Marquis, had strong links with Cardiff and twice served as mayor in the 1890s. He was interested in architecture and restoration, and in collaboration with architect William Burges invested vast sums in rebuilding Cardiff Castle for which he brought together a group of Welsh craftsmen skilled in stonework and woodcarving.[96] These craftsmen, known collectively as the 'Cardiff Workshops', were dispatched to Scotland when he set about rebuilding Mount Stuart, the family seat on the Isle of Bute, which was destroyed by fire in 1877. The same individuals worked on other restoration and building projects for Bute including Falkland Palace and Falkland House.[97] Scottish craftsmen worked for Bute, including local builders and Glasgow furnishers Wylie & Lochhead.[98] Specialist London firms were also employed, such as decorators Campbell Smith & Co. But the distinctive presence of the Cardiff craftsmen, who lived in their own temporary village constructed on the lawns in front of Mount Stuart, is testament to the wealth and patronage of a great aristocrat.[99]

Country-house building flourished with the wealth of their owners and offered significant demand for certain types of craft businesses, particularly those based in Edinburgh. Some of these craftsmen made fortunes of their own and a few even invested in country-house building. This was particularly true of the cabinetmakers that constructed fine furnishings to commission and managed and supplied whole-house decorative schemes. In the early decades of the century, William Trotter, whose distinctive neoclassical designs exemplified the highest level of cabinet work in Scotland, had a distinguished career in local politics as well as trade, becoming Provost of Edinburgh in the 1820s and establishing himself and his family as small landowners with an estate and house at Ballindean in Perthshire, which remained in Trotter ownership to the 1930s.[100] Another Edinburgh furnisher, William Reid, son of a cabinetmaker, married to the daughter of a wealthy plumber, who owned the cabinetmaking and retail furniture firm of Morison & Co. of George Street, Edinburgh in the later nineteenth century, spent a fortune on the purchase and restoration of Lauriston Castle to the west of Edinburgh where he lived into the 1920s and amassed a famous collection of pictures, antiques and books.[101]

Country-house and estate owners, providing much employment to generations of Scottish craftsmen and craftswomen in the building and furnishing trades as well as supporting the rural craft economy in areas like tourist souvenir making, were notable patrons elsewhere. They played important roles in promoting the exhibition movement, a popular showcase for craftsmen and craftswomen, acting as patrons and committee members for major and local events and were also lenders of antiques and pictures for public display, as we see in the next chapter.

Notes

1. Richard Wilson and Alex Mackley, *Creating Paradise. The Building of the English Country House, 1660–1880* (London, 2000), gives the best account of the process. See also Megan Leyland, 'Patronage and the Architecture Profession. The Country House in Nineteenth-Century Northamptonshire', PhD thesis, University of Leicester, 2016.
2. *DSA*, Robert Weir Schultz, 1860–1951; David Ottewill, 'Robert Weir Schultz (1860–1951). An Arts and Crafts Architect', *Architectural History* 22 (1979), 87–115.
3. *New Statistical Account of Scotland*, vol. 2, 57.
4. Ibid.
5. *DSA*, William Atkinson, 1775–1839.
6. Sonia Baker, *The Country Houses, Castles and Mansions of East Lothian* (Catrine, 2009).
7. *DSA*, William Burn, 1789–1870.
8. Thomas Leverton Donaldson, 'Memoir of the Late William Burn, Fellow', *RIBA Transactions*, 1869–70.
9. *New Statistical Account of Scotland*, vol. 2, 58.
10. John Smith and John Mitchell, *The Old Country Houses of the Old Glasgow Gentry* (Glasgow, 1870), Preface.
11. See Nenadic, *Lairds and Luxury* on eighteenth-century country-house building.
12. Andy Wightman et al., 'The cultural politics of hunting: Sporting estates and recreational land use in the Highlands and Islands of Scotland', *Culture, Sport, Society*, 5:1 (2002), 53–70.
13. A. H. Millar, *Historical and Descriptive Accounts of the Castles and Mansions of Ayrshire* (Edinburgh, 1885). Millar (1847–1927) was City Librarian for Dundee and wrote a series of 'shire' illustrated histories. *Times*, 1 March 1927.
14. Millar, *Castles and Mansions of Ayrshire*, 72.

15. NRS. GD27/7/323. Papers relative to building Dalquharran House to designs by Robert Adam, 1787–90.
16. Millar, *Castles and Mansions of Ayrshire*, 24.
17. Millar, *Castles and Mansions of Ayrshire*, 20, 96.
18. Abbotsford House Building Work Ledger and Letter Book.
19. Brown, *Abbotsford and Sir Walter Scott*.
20. *DSA*, William Atkinson; Abbotsford Building Work Ledger.
21. Lockhart, *Life of Sir Walter Scott*, vol. 5, 323.
22. NLS. MS Collection, Acc 4006. Sanderson and Paterson, Builders and Timber Merchants. Galashiels. Ledger 1806–35. Other records relating to the firm are in the Borders Regional Archive at Hawick.
23. Edinburgh University Library Special Collections [EULSC]. GB237-Coll329. Papers of David Ramsay Hay (1798–1866), Decorative Artist and Author.
24. Lockhart, *Life of Sir Walter Scott*, vol. 5, 322.
25. Abbotsford House Building Work. Sanderson and Paterson Accounts, March to July 1819.
26. Ibid., Sanderson and Paterson Accounts, *c*.1816.
27. Ibid., Letter from William Atkinson, St Marys le Bone, 17 November 1821.
28. Ibid., Letter from John Smith, Darnick, 9 January 1822.
29. Ibid., Accounts various.
30. Ibid., Accounts various.
31. *Scotsman*, 8 November 1823.
32. *Scotsman*, 22 April 1829.
33. *Scotsman*, 3 December 1842, 30 August 1843.
34. UCL, Legacies of British Slave Ownership. Robert Waugh of Melrose, Profile and Legacies Summary. Genealogy.
35. *Royal Gazette*, 29 November 1794.
36. Sophie Drinkall, 'The Jamaican plantation house: Scottish influence', *Architectural Heritage*, 2:1 (1991), 56–68. Quote from the diary of Edward Long, 1770s, 58.
37. UCL, Legacies of British Slave Ownership. Robert Waugh.
38. National Archives. PROB 11/1886. Will of Robert Waugh.
39. Lockhard, *Life of Sir Walter Scott*, vol. 5, 145 – 'dreein his dole' means 'doing penance'.
40. Borders Regional Archive, Hawick. SBA/183/1. James Mein Papers.
41. EULSC. Gen 1070 (204). Letter from John Broomfield to Robert Waugh, Edinburgh, 8 April 1810.
42. Ibid., Letter from John Broomfield to Robert Waugh, Edinburgh, 10 June 1810.
43. Herbert Grierson, ed., *The Letters of Sir Walter Scott* (1932–7), vol. 7, 299–300, Letter to Daniel Terry, 9 January 1823; Lockhart, *Life of Sir Walter Scott*, vol. 5, 239.
44. Frank Arneil Walker, *The Buildings of Scotland: Argyll and Bute* (London, 2000), 261.

45. *Scotsman*, 7 May 1892.
46. NRS. GD112/20/1/45. Breadalbane Papers. Work at Taymouth and Ard-mady, 1834–1840.
47. *DSA*, William Burn (1789–1870).
48. *Scotsman*, 3 May 1826.
49. Monument to Onesiphorus Tyndall Bruce, Falkland. Inscription.
50. Ownership subsequently passed to Lieutenant-Colonel Hamilton Tyndall in 1870. *Scotsman*, 9 June 1875. It was sold to the Marquis of Bute in 1887.
51. NRS. GD152/53. Papers of the Hamilton Bruce Family. Correspondence and discharge accounts, mainly of Onesiphorus Tyndall Bruce.
52. NRS. GD152/52/1/21. Hamilton Bruce Papers. Letters and accounts concerning jewellery and silver for Onesiphous Tyndall Bruce, 1829–34.
53. NRS. GD152/53/1. Hamilton Bruce Papers. Bundle 16/2. John Sandford to O. Tyndall Bruce 12 January 1831. The Rev. John Sandford, raised in Edinburgh, was son of the famous Episcopalian preacher Daniel Sandford, founder of the fashionable Charlotte Square Chapel. He enjoyed a leisurely career in England, spending much time travelling in Italy, and was a notable collector of Italian pictures. See also NRS. GD152/53/1/18. Hamilton Bruce Papers. Papers Relating to Art and Architecture.
54. NRS. GD152/217/3. Hamilton Bruce Papers. Bundle 9/4 and Bundle 15/3–4. Correspondence with G. Irvine and Mrs Joy, 1840–41. The firm moved to New York following the revolution of 1848.
55. NRS. GD152/53/3/15. Hamilton Bruce Papers. Account from the heirs of William Trotter, 1836–38.
56. NRS. GD152/58/3/1. Hamilton Bruce Papers. William Burn to O. Tyndall Bruce 28 January 1842. Balbirnie, a country house nearby, was undergoing renovations.
57. *Pigot's Directory*, 1837, 62.
58. 'David Ness', Mapping the Practice and Profession of Sculpture in Britain and Ireland, 1851–1951, University of Glasgow and HATII, 2011, www.sculpture.gla.ac.uk (last accessed 15 February 2021).
59. *London Morning Post*, 16 September 1837.
60. Alan Sugden and John Edmondson, *A History of English Wallpaper, 1509–1914* (London, 1925), 237.
61. John Smith, *Old Scottish Clockmakers from 1453 to 1850* (Edinburgh, 1921), 377–8. Symington also invented machinery for the textile industry. He made a similar clock for Markinch Town Hall in 1840.
62. *Edinburgh Evening Courant*, 20 December 1845.
63. *The Gazette*, 5 November 1852.
64. NRS. GD152/58/8. Hamilton Bruce Papers. Letters, estimates, measurements, accounts and receipts for tradesmen's work.
65. NRS. GD152/53. Hamilton Bruce Papers. Bundle 29/3. Report from William Spottiswoode, 7 June 1843.

66. NRS. GD152/8/5/5. Hamilton Bruce Papers. Letter from D. R. Hay, 23 May 1843.

67. NRS. GD152/53/4/27. Hamilton Bruce Papers. Letter from Alexander Roos, landscape architect, 22 January 1844.

68. *Official Catalogue of the Great Exhibition of the Works of Industry of All Nations 1851* (1851), 154.

69. *Edinburgh Post Office Directory*, 1883.

70. NRS. GD152/53/3. Hamilton Bruce Papers. Bundle 14. Letters and accounts June to September 1842. The bill was lowered from £620 to £584.

71. Fife Council Archive Centre, Carleton House, Markinch. Kirkcaldy Burgess Admissions. I am grateful of Mariella Crichton Stuart for this information.

72. NRS. CS280/42. Sequestration of John Black, Builder, Kirkcaldy. Black was sequestered for bankruptcy in September 1843 with the process only finally concluded in 1856 long after his death.

73. NRS. GD152/53/3. Hamilton Bruce Papers. Bundle 14/2. Contract 7 September 1839.

74. NRS. GD152/53/3. Hamilton Bruce Papers. Bundle 15/5. Letter 23 July 1841.

75. NRS. GD152/53/4. Hamilton Bruce Papers. Bundle 26/18. Accounts, 29 October, 1 and 4 November 1844.

76. Centre for Stewardship at Falkland. Temple of Decision.

77. *Accrington Division Gazette*, 18 July 1896, 'Mr George Bullough's three years tour'. Further details on the house, its contents and owner, see website for Kinloch Castle Friends Association, www.kinlochcastlefriends.org (last accessed 15 February 2021).

78. *Designs of Furniture Illustrative of Cabinet Furniture and Interior Decoration Specially Designed for James Shoolbred & Compy, Tottenham House, Tottenham Court Road. Cabinet Furniture and Upholstery, Carpets, Curtains, French and English Paper Hangings, Interior Decoration, etc* (1874).

79. *Kinloch Castle*, RCAHMS publication *c*.2010; Clive Aslet, 'Kinloch Castle, Isle of Rhum', *Country Life*, 9, 16 August 1984; HES Kinloch Castle. Inventory, Garden and Designed Landscape.

80. List of houses, their date of construction, architect and style appended to *An Appraisal of the Conservation Areas in Helensburgh*, Argyll and Bute Council, 2008.

81. Unpublished 'list of tradesmen' supplied by Lorna Hepburn, National Trust for Scotland Curator, Hill House.

82. University of Glasgow. Mackintosh Architecture: Context, Making and Meaning. List of artisans and their projects.

83. Ibid, *Glasgow Herald*, 25 July 1893.

84. Lindsay Macbeth, 'The Wheelers of Arncroach: A family of furniture makers in Fife', *Regional Furniture*, 5 (1991), 69–78; David M. Walker, 'Lorimer, Sir Robert Stodart (1864–1929)', *ODNB*, 2004.

85. NRS. SC20/50/96. Cupar Sheriff Court Inventories. William Wheeler, 1914.

86. *Country Life*, 1 September 1905.

87. *Country Life*, 27 September 1913, xii.

88. Ibid., x, vii, v.

89. *Scotsman*, 17 June 1895. This was probably George Macdonald of Aberdeen.

90. *Scotsman*, 16 October 1895.

91. *DSA*, Alexander Marshall Mackenzie (1848–1933).

92. National Trust for Scotland. Mar Lodge Estate.

93. *Scotsman*, 16 October 1895.

94. *Country Life*, 17 July 1937.

95. Martin Daunton, *Coal Metropolis. Cardiff, 1870–1914* (Leicester, 1977).

96. Rosemary Hannah, *The Grand Designer: Third Marquess of Bute* (Edinburgh, 2013).

97. Communications and unpublished papers from Mariella Crichton Stuart.

98. Mount Stuart Archives, Bute. BU/88. William Frame, Architect. Letter Book, 1880s. List of firms.

99. Bute also founded the Dovecot Studio in Edinburgh in 1912 to make tapestries for his country houses.

100. Jackson, 'William Trotter'.

101. See Chapter 1.

6

Exhibiting Craftwork

THE NINETEENTH CENTURY WAS an age of exhibitions, small and large, which, with innovations in public museums and shop displays, gave prominence to handmade goods and craft skills. The popularity of craft displays, which were widely described in the press, speaks to the social values attributed to handmade goods in an age better known for celebrations of the machine-made. Exhibition culture is famously associated with the 1851 Great Exhibition at the Crystal Palace in London, where there were many Scottish makers on display. It spawned numerous regional international exhibitions in the following decades, the first of these in Scotland taking place in Edinburgh in 1886 and two years later, on a more spectacular scale, in Glasgow. International exhibitions had multiple and complex purposes fsor the organisers and the exhibitors. They were intended to promote modern business and secure customers. They were competitive, with prizes awarded for the best goods displayed. They encouraged apprentice training and manufacturer awareness of innovative design or production techniques. They showcased artefacts and ideas from the past as well as the present and from different countries and places. They were a celebration of the people who made things in the industrial regions of the country and through their well-publicised committees of trustees, spectacular opening ceremonies and extensive loan collections of art and antiquities, were also a celebration of British aristocrats and elite patronage. For paying visitors, who attended in vast numbers, they were entertaining, educational and a source of civic and national pride.

EXHIBITION GENESIS

Before the great exhibition movement took off from 1851, there was a long history of small-scale craft displays. In Scotland, much of this activity took place in Edinburgh and was organised through the Board of Manufactures with a focus on the textile industry, though there were other bodies that also sought to promote high-quality manufactures, be they handmade or machine goods. In the run up to the first of the international exhibitions in Edinburgh in 1886, the *Scotsman* newspaper furnished an account of some of these early efforts to 'stimulate different branches of industry and art'.[1] They started, according to this account, with a 1755 initiative by the Select Society – a debating club whose members included Allan Ramsay and David Hume – to encourage the art of papermaking by offering prizes for new techniques along with premiums for 'printed cotton and linen, with a view to stimulating a taste for elegant patterns, good colouring, and strength of cloth'. The competition categories included designs submitted by boys and girls less than 15 years old. There were prizes for 'worked ruffles and bone-lace and edging' and for stocking, blanket and carpet making. Whisky and ale making were also showcased in an exhibition whose character was informed by the agricultural economy. The winners included Miss Jenny Dalrymple, awarded a gold medal for the best imitation of Dresden-work, a popular form of whitework embroidery, on a pair of ruffles, whilst a premium of £21 for the 'best invention in arts' was awarded to Peter Brotherston, weaver of Dirleton in East Lothian, for a 'piece of linen made like Marseilles work, but in a loom'.[2] A second exhibition was held the following year, attracting a greater range of contributors, with the prize for the 'whitest, best and finest Honiton lace' awarded to Jean Forrest, an orphan educated by the Duchess of Hamilton and Miss Jean Thompson of Edinburgh gaining the highest premium for Dresden-work on men's ruffles. Many of the goods exhibited were illustrative of the clothing and household fashions of the day in a world where handwork still predominated and where artisans offered useful public service, as in the final case detailed below.

> The industries embraced by the Society's premium list were of the most varied description, and included . . . the dyeing of worsted in different shades, the making of Turkey, Wilton and Scots carpets, livery lace, blankets, fustian, linen, felt and straw hats, baked hair for upholsterers, mohair buttons, soap, glue, kid gloves, bread-baskets and cradles made from Scottish willows and a prize was given to an Edinburgh mason named Carmichael for 'curing the greatest number of smokey chimneys'.[3]

The location and opening times of the two early exhibitions are not recorded. The Select Society met in various places including the Advocates Library and Masons Hall and probably hired space in one of these. The main later-eighteenth-century exhibiting body, the Board of

Manufactures, sometimes mounted displays in their own rooms in the Royal Exchange on the High Street, or in nearby commercial premises such as shops. From the 1820s, they rented space in the new Royal Institution building on Princes Street, which was purpose designed for exhibitions and public meetings.[4] Board exhibitions were normally held during the Christmas holiday period, lasted only a few weeks and whilst intended to stimulate public interest and promote the national good, they were worthy rather than spectacular or entertaining. The shift to summer exhibitions lasting many months began with the Great Exhibition in London, which was organised in the wake of the 1840s railway boom and designed for a mass audience able to travel for pleasure. And as exhibitions grew in scale and scope, requiring better transport for the large attendance along with facilities for purchasing food and drink, they moved from existing buildings in city centres to purpose-built temporary sites in suburbs.

The role of craft displays in exhibitions is complex. Early exhibitions were focused on the individual artisan and his or her goods, normally represented by a single object and requiring little by way of glass cases or display facilities beyond tables arranged for convenient public viewing. Similar displays were retained throughout the history of the exhibition movement, with the 'artisan courts', usually divided into female and male sections, a prominent feature of international exhibitions, attracting large numbers of submissions, including from amateurs. At the Edinburgh exhibition of 1886, for instance, which was held in temporary buildings on the Meadows, a park to the south of the city centre, and was themed around the celebration of electricity as a new technology, the Artisans' Court attracted over 100 individual entries and there was a separate section titled 'Ladies Industries Court'. The display area was 118 × 50 feet and exhibiting was free, though elsewhere exhibitors paid rental for their space. As observed when the exhibition was in the setting-up phase, 'it has been a very difficult task indeed . . . to reduce the heterogeneous mass of articles to order and regularity with some sort of classification'.[5] This suggests that the idea of the exhibition was connected to notions of classified knowledge and codified economic endeavour. The range of objects displayed by artisans in Edinburgh in 1886 embraced models of ships and buildings, cabinet work and smaller articles of furniture such as ladies' workboxes or bookracks. There were aquaria and birdcages, fountains and fern stands, textile hangings and patterns, clocks and musical instruments, paper goods and decorative articles in glass and crystal, scientific instruments, silverware and jewellery. The section also included 'a display of the regalia of the trades and other corporate bodies'

belonging to Edinburgh. These were the institutions that had once represented craft interests in burgh affairs and though no longer possessed of
political power, still participated in civic rituals and charitable functions.
Such artisan courts always attracted strong interest and newspaper commentary because exhibitors were mainly locals.[6]

The Ladies' Industries section of the Edinburgh exhibition of 1886
had features in common with the Artisans' Court and the work of
numerous women with Edinburgh addresses was displayed, though
more of them were amateurs than amongst the artisans and the geographical reach was wider. A typical example of the amateur was Mrs A.
F. Imlach of Ravelston Park in Edinburgh, wife of a society artist, who
displayed 'embroidery'.[7] There were several aristocratic exhibitors, some
with work of their own making, others acting as patrons of charities that
supported women's employment, such as the Duchess of Abercorn, of
Baronscourt, County Tyrone, who held titles in Scotland and Ireland and
sponsored a display of 'knitting and embroideries by Irish Peasants'.[8]
Mrs Thomas of Rose Park, Trinity, in Edinburgh – famed as one of the
early pioneers of the Highland Home Industries movement – sponsored
a display of 'cloth – spun, woven and dyed by the women of Harris'.[9]
School groups and genteel crafting societies, many in the Arts and Crafts
tradition, were represented from across the country with the range of
exhibits, though dominated by textiles, lace and embroidery, including woodcarving, ceramics, painted glass, Christmas cards, straw plait
and basket work and even a display comprising 'Flowers made of Fish
Bones'.[10] The largest subsection was the 'Irish Women's Industry Stall',
which had textiles, clothing and fancy needlework, food goods such as
mustard and cakes, fly-tying, fishing lines, matches and soap.[11] With 173
separate displays, the Ladies' Industries section was almost twice the
size of the Artisans' Court and embraced a greater variety of agendas,
commercial and charitable, alongside individual and collective creativity.
Male as well as female-owned businesses where the product was made
by or aimed at women were included.

The Glasgow International Exhibition of 1888 also showcased wom-
en's industries and artisans' sections along with displays of 'foreign'
exhibits that included the famous India Court.[12] It was bigger than the
equivalent event in Edinburgh two years before, and attracted a vast
attendance from across the country with over two-thirds of participants
local to the area.[13] The women's art and industry section, though extensive, was conservative in character and focused entirely on sewing skills,
mostly plain work supplied by schools and female friendly society groups
and what were termed 'servants and mill girls'.[14] Preliminary regional

exhibitions had been held to select the entries for display, including one in Haddington, East Lothian. But the handwork of women was also evident in other parts of the event, including a stand mounted by Mr T. Coombs of Bedford, a lace manufacturer who,

> besides showing a large variety of Bedford and Buckingham laces, has three girls (from the Bedford district) constantly at work in illustrating the manufacture of Bedford lace. The youngest of these workers is quite a little girl, who attracted the attention of Her Majesty on the occasion of the State visit to the Exhibition. Her Majesty, while admiring Mr Coombs's exhibits, addressed a few kindly words to the juvenile lacemaker.[15]

As well as the Artisans' Court, which was dominated by models of ships and industrial machines, commercial craftwork was exhibited in the glass cabinets and stands of larger firms, such as John Shields & Co. of the Wallace Linen Works in Perth, whose specialist hand-woven, monogrammed table and bath linens 'chiefly for hotels, steamers etc' included 'some fine specimens of this work'. There was another firm from Perth, jeweller David Macgregor of George Street, who occupied 'a large stall in the centre of the Transverse Avenue, in which will be a display of fine art engraved work on gold and silver plate – of which Mr Macgregor is the personal designer'. The stall was fitted up with workbenches where workmen demonstrated the different processes of manufacturing and it also included 'an exquisite show of Scotch pearl and cairngorm jewellery'.[16]

Even as such large exhibitions with their mass summer attendance were mounted, smaller local events still took place such as the Dundee Exhibition of Industry of 1887, which was held in the Drill Hall, organised by the Dundee and District United Trades Council and ran for just a few weeks over the Christmas holidays. The published 'rules for the guidance of exhibitors' gave a clear indication of the purpose of the event. This included, 'the work entered for the competition must be the actual handiwork or production of the exhibitor' and 'special prizes and certificates will be given for work done by scholars and apprentices'. Scholars were required to state which school they attended and apprentices had to give the name of their firm. 'Employers may send objects for exhibition executed by their workmen, and in cases where the judges consider superiority of skill or originality of design displayed, certificates will be awarded.' There was also provision for 'heirlooms and other articles of the nature of art or handicraft, which may have passed from the original producer' to be exhibited, 'but parties wishing to do so should, if possible, supply the names of the person who did produce them'.[17]

Consistent with the spirit of the age, the Dundee exhibition had areas given over to women's work, as well as 'trades and manufactures', art and natural history. The former, which was listed first in the catalogue, comprised 'industrial or domestic work, hand done' which in Class 1 consisted of 'plain needlework, darning, patching etc' and in Class 2, 'crochetwork: fancy knitting: netting, meshing and tatting: lacework: macramework: embroidery: fancy needlework and crewelwork'.[18] Many of the 109 exhibitors were school groups and their teachers, the largest collection on display supplied by the pupils and teachers of Newport Public School. The 'trades and manufactures' section was organised according to the conventional industrial classification seen elsewhere. The exhibitors were entirely male and frequently commercial, though there were many examples of artisans' work and amateur or schoolboy craft. There were numerous ship, engineering and workshop models displayed alongside models of workmen's dwellings, which was a frequent theme in an age of debate about the housing of the poor. One of the latter was described as 'Model of a Kitchen of a Working Man, made in leisure hours with a pocket knife, John Grant, Weaver, 1 Wolsey Street'.[19] Woodworked items were popular among the amateur exhibitors, whose occupations, which included large numbers of shipwrights, were recorded. There were architectural drawings and pattern designs and several apprentices submitted work, including a 'Miniature Drawing Room' made jointly by 'Matthew Stewart, Apprentice Upholsterer and James Scott, Apprentice Cabinetmaker, Queen Street Cottage, Broughty Ferry'.[20]

EDUCATE AND INSPIRE

As the Dundee event reveals, encouraging apprentices, showcasing good design and offering opportunities for education and inspiration were primary considerations of the nineteenth-century exhibition movement. The Board of Manufactures exhibitions in Scotland from the later eighteenth century had similar agendas, though on a smaller scale and focused on a few trades thought crucial to the development of the Scottish economy. The Board also ran a design school in Edinburgh and promoted design education for full-time students and industry apprentices elsewhere in Scotland from the 1840s. Edinburgh had another claim to importance in design education in Britain with the appointment of William Dyce, an Aberdeen-born artist and designer, as the Master of the School of Design in 1837. Dyce was only in Edinburgh for a short period, but during that time he visited progressive schools in Europe and published plans for reform in design training in Britain, which included exhibition. Propelled to national celebrity, he moved to London to run the main art education establishment there and inspired the founding of a network of provincial schools.[21]

The schools of design mounted regular competitions and exhibitions which were reported in the local press. In Edinburgh in July 1857 the *Scotsman* detailed the state of the Board's School of Design, noting the numbers of students attending and their classes as well as the end-of-year exhibition prizewinners.

> For the '*Artist*' group there were 8 painters; 1 draftsman; 16 architects/engineers. For the '*Artisans*' group there were 3 housepainters; 2 ornamental painter; 1 picture engraver; 4 engravers on wood; 1 seal engraver; 9 lithographers; 4 die, stamp and punch cutters; 4 woodcarvers; 1 brassfounder; 2 coach painters; 3 upholsterers; 4 silversmiths and jewellers; 2 stone carvers and marble cutters; 6 mechanical engineers; 8 joiners and cabinet makers; 8 pupil teachers; 23 miscellaneous.[22]

These Edinburgh students, dominated by decorative artists and trainees in the luxury trades, reflected the local craft economy which in turn stimulated the creation of the Art Manufacture Association, founded in 1856 on similar lines to an equivalent body in London, whose aim was to educate the public in good design and workmanship as well as encouraging young practitioners.

> After these Pupils leave the Schools, they are thrown adrift without guide or compass; some of them attempt to reach the highest walk of the Fine Arts, and after long and arduous struggles succeed; others waste, on abortive attempt, talents which . . . might yet qualify them to aid in the supply of Works of Utility and Ornament, and thereby to attain both fame and emolument.[23]

The Art Manufacture Association organised annual winter exhibitions in the National Galleries in Edinburgh, comprising student work, loan collections and retail stalls mounted by Edinburgh and London craft-goods producers such as cabinetmakers, glass engravers and jewellers. Prices were high, reflecting the intended exhibition audience. In the second exhibition in 1857 there was, for instance, a display mounted by John Ford, glassmaker of Edinburgh, that included a cut-crystal dessert service priced at £50. William and Andrew Smith, the famed makers of Mauchline wares, were regular exhibitor-retailers of their quality hand-decorated goods, which included cigar cases painted with famous scenes such as 'Death of the Stag', Loch Katrine or the Scott Monument, priced at 17s.[24] According to a later account given at the mounting of the 'exhibition of decorative handiwork' in Edinburgh in 1888, the first Art

Manufacture Association event in 1856, though only open for six weeks, had an attendance of 37,030.[25]

Museum displays were similarly directed at craftworkers and designers for their education and inspiration. The Great Exhibition of 1851 was, famously, able to use its considerable operating profits to purchase some of the exhibits for a national collection of manufactured goods called the South Kensington Museum which came later to be known as the Victoria and Albert Museum.[26] The Board of Manufactures in Edinburgh mounted an exhibition in 1861 based on 'specimens of decorative art of former epochs' with the nucleus comprising 'the circulating collection of works of art selected from the Museum at South Kensington'.[27] Museums in Scotland purchased exhibition goods at the end of an event to form local collections of contemporary artefacts to sit alongside the antique. Indeed, the Kelvingrove Museum and Gallery in Glasgow was built on the site of the 1901 international exhibition.[28] Observing fine artefacts manufactured in the past in order to better understand the techniques employed in their making was one of the rationales for the loan collections of antiquities that featured so prominently in most public exhibitions. And it was one of the reasons why individuals and businesses sought access to private collections. The Society of Antiquaries, with its many noble members and large museum, offered endorsements and support for craft products with a distinctive Scottish identity and also provided antiquarian models for inspiration or reproduction. The Society commissioned copies of its own artefacts—as casts in plaster or metal – either for display in museums elsewhere or for presenting to donors or sellers of important items gifted to its collection. The Society also purchased copies of objects in other museums or in prominent Scottish buildings, as in 1850 when they acquired a set of casts of medieval sculpture at Roslin Chapel, made by local craftsmen for what was described as a reasonable 27s.[29] The appeal of ancient Celtic and Roman precious metal wares led to many requests to the Society of Antiquaries for permission to study and copy for commercial sale. The Society usually resisted these requests, but to ensure the highest quality output allowed authorised copies by the best craftsmen. One of those chosen was the Edinburgh firm of Marshall & Sons, long established and prominent in Edinburgh's elite Goldsmiths Company. Marshall & Sons was known for its Scottish-themed wares and exhibition stands, including those at the 1851 Great Exhibition. In the 1890s, Thomas Marshall, the owner, wrote to the Society regarding the famous ancient Hunterston Brooch, setting out his credentials for seeking access to the piece for his workmen:

This firm has for many years fostered a public taste for Celtic art in personal ornament. Last year we published a short historical account of Scottish and Celtic art illustrated which I believe in its way helped to educate the public taste to the beautiful and characteristic art displayed in the penannular brooches.

He asked for private access to the brooch to make a cast, to give 'a fine example to put before our craftsmen. It would not only be an education for them, but for the public also'. This was refused on the grounds that the original would be damaged, but the Secretary assured Marshall of his willingness to make the collection available for the craftsmen to view and thereby study and sketch.[30]

As owners of handcrafted antiquities, organisations such as the Society of Antiquaries or elite individuals gave conspicuous support to the educational and competitive aspects of exhibitions. Aristocratic patronage was important for all forms of public display in the nineteenth century, though the extent of support could vary from the 'ornamental' to the active. Aristocrats lent their names for advertising a 'supporters list' when an event was being planned and they also offered paintings and objects. Attendance at an exhibition opening was particularly crucial for attracting public interest. Exhibitions of modern craftwork, often run as competitions, were normally paralleled with exhibitions of historic craftworks on loan from country-house collections. The purpose of the latter was twofold. They provided models of style and design to be emulated in historicised goods of contemporary manufacture. They also provided examples of fine workmanship. For the viewing public, the loan collections were a celebration of Scottish pride in manufacture for and ownership by great families and they were invariably showy and attractive. One of the greatest of the aristocratic patrons was the Duke of Buccleuch who through several generations supported Scottish public life and progress on their extensive estates and beyond. Buccleuch's support for the local craft economy was exemplified in 1887 with the opening of the Buccleuch Memorial Hall in Hawick, launched with a Handicraft and Industrial Exhibition that ran for several months and was designed to showcase and inspire local production. The opening event and speeches were widely reported in the press. The exhibition, which included elaborate displays of antiquities on loan from the Buccleuch family and other local elites, along with objects loaned by the British Museum and Victoria and Albert Museum in London, offered four competitive classes open to craftsmen from the Borders area, with cash prizes presented by the Duchess. Class 1 was for cabinetmakers and joiners and the exhibits included inlaid tables, 'elegant' doors, mantles and over-mantles, dressing tables and workboxes, desks and clock cases. Class 2, consistent with the rural character of the region, was for mill-wrights and agricultural instrument makers, whilst Class 3, for engineers and smiths, also included decorative iron work. The final class, Class 4, was for draftsmen and decorators producing ornamental panels, archi-tectural drawings and etchings on glass, the latter mostly showing local scenes of tourist interest.[31]

The Duke of Buccleuch was approached to make loans for an Edin-burgh craft exhibition the following year. Held in the Royal Scottish Academy during the winter of 1888–9, this was a bigger affair, involving a series of printed pre-exhibition prospectuses to drum up support and advertise the classes and prizes. The aim of the event, whose organising committee included notable Edinburgh craft-based business owners, such as Hugh Reid of Whytock & Reid, furniture makers, was to give 'an opportunity for those skilled in any of the forms of handiwork com-prised within the scheme, both professional workers and amateurs, to exhibit specimens of their craft, and prizes will be offered for excellence of design and workmanship'.[32] The parallel aim was to exhibit a loan collection of historical items, with special prominence given to Scot-tish work. The extensive list of Buccleuch loans, which involved com-plex negotiation and concern over security and insurance, came from nearby Dalkeith House and included furniture, pictures, rare books and objects linked to Mary Queen of Scots. As exhibition plans progressed, more craft-business owners joined the organising and judging commit-tees and offered prizes. They included cabinetmakers John Macrae of John Taylor & Son; the interior designer William Scott Morton; several goldsmiths, such as Thomas Marshall; decorators, including Thomas Bonnar; carvers and gilders, glass stainers and brass founders. The final list of patrons, headed by Buccleuch, included the Marquis of Lothian, the Earls of Haddington, Stair, Rosebery and Hopetoun and several gentry landowners. There were five classes for professional craftwork-ers, with each class including prizes for apprentices and three classes for amateurs. Unlike the Hawick exhibition, some of the exhibitors were women. The cost of entry was 1s for professionals and 2s 6d for amateurs, with entries available for sale at the end. Class 1 was for woodcarving, with a top prize of £3 for a wooden panel in the style of Louis XVI. Other classes included carving in stone or marble, modelling and carving in clay, *repusse* metalwork, wood inlay, turnery, picture frames, painted decoration and book ornament. Class IV was for gold and silver work and included an apprentice prize of £1 for a bracelet of Celtic design and another of £3 3s, which was offered by the

Goldsmiths Incorporation of Edinburgh, for a brooch and bracelet to match in Celtic design.[33]

ADVERTISING AND INCOME

One of the purposes of international exhibitions was to provide a venue to demonstrate economic achievement through displays mounted by firms and individuals. These were a celebration, but also an opportunity to make sales, sometimes at the exhibition itself – though most had strict rules on commercial activity within the event other than at those stands set up for retail which usually focused on food and drink or small souvenirs – or afterwards through using a display for advertising and to take orders. Newspaper reports of events and the exhibitors were another marketing device. Though the costs of exhibition attendance were high for travel, accommodation and space rental, the financial benefit was significant and one of the reasons why Scottish craft businesses as well as larger industrial concerns mounted display stands in London and sometimes even abroad. The London International Exhibition of 1862, for instance, though dominated in the Scottish contingent by textile and engineering displays also included extensive Scotch jewellery exhibits, glass wares, fine furnishings and ceramics, with some of the firms represented, such as Rettie, Middleton & Sons of Aberdeen, makers of granite jewellery and silver brooches, regular participants in international exhibitions.[34] The 'Scotch pebble, amber and granite work' produced by the latter also featured in lavishly illustrated publications produced to accompany prestigious London exhibitions.[35]

A Scottish craftsman who was particularly adept at exploiting the business opportunities that exhibitions represented was Peter Gardener of the Dunmore Pottery near Airth in rural Stirlingshire. The firm was established in the late eighteenth century to take advantage of a seam of local clay that could be fashioned into domestic wares and tiles. Peter Gardener (1834–1919), who took over his father's business in 1866, was a gifted designer and clever entrepreneur who exploited international exhibitions and aristocratic patronage to forward his reputation and sales. The firm was a small concern with only 15 skilled potters at its peak in 1881 but attracted much attention. The *Scotsman* in 1886 highlighted Gardener's 'vases of artistic design, flowerpots of various shapes and colours, garden seats and pedestals of lovely appearance, mantelpiece, table, and other useful and ornamental goods of excellent finish'.[36] Dunmore ceramics were sold in high-end shops throughout Britain and abroad. The company also had a specialist line in commemorative wares, mostly commissioned to mark marriages or anniversaries. The Dunmore Pottery was well known for its vivid glazes and made numerous animal-shaped vases and ornaments to suit Victorian taste. Some were of naturalistic design, such as the much-reproduced seated pig, which in more highly decorated form was also made at the Wemyss factory in Fife by the firm of Robert Heron & Son, another regular exhibitor. The owl was a popular subject and both pig and owl designs were produced in large numbers as money boxes for children. Oriental design featured prominently in the later nineteenth century as trade with the East expanded and the international exhibition movement exposed imports from China or Japan to a wider audience. Some of the best-selling Dunmore Pottery lines were Far East inspired crackled red-and-turquoise glaze vases. These caught the attention of Queen Victoria when first exhibited in Edinburgh in 1886 and were subsequently named 'Queen's Vases'. Peter Gardener exhibited abroad, including the Philadelphia Exhibition of 1876, but it was the Glasgow Exhibition of 1888 that saw the biggest and most spectacular of his displays, with the 'Lady Dunmore Bowl', named to honour his Stirlingshire patron and sometime design collaborator, garnering praise and prizes.[37]

Exhibition prizes were a source of pride and prestige, and details were commonly deployed in business advertising. A Certificate of Merit awarded for 'Excellence in the Manufacture of Linoleum' to the Kirkcaldy Linoleum Company at the Edinburgh Exhibition of 1886 was used to promote the firm.[38] The company, which employed hand blocks for printing and had many innovative designs, mounted an unusual display that was described in detail in newspaper reports.

> A prominent object in the Central Court is the Grecian Temple designed by Mr Sydney Mitchell for the Kirkcaldy Linoleum Company (Limited). It was erected as the best means of showing a number of patterns and the various uses to which 'lino' may be put in the coverings of walls and ceilings as well as floors. Inside the temple may be seen samples of linoleum of different widths and quality for different purposes. For lobbies and stairs it is made in narrower widths – from half a yard broad with a printed or plain centre and border. For this use a specially pliable quality is manufactured.[39]

The Holyrood Glass Company, with factory premises off the Canongate, was one of several celebrated glassmakers in Edinburgh that also made extensive use of exhibitions for business promotion. The firm's success was based on a product image developed around elite associations and conspicuous display of its handcrafted output. Notable in this context was a celebrated cut-glass epergne (table centrepiece) in 40 separate pieces, about a metre in height, constructed between 1840 and 1842 to mark the accession of Queen Victoria.[40] Richard Hunter, the firm's foreman glass cutter made and probably also designed the epergne, taking two years to complete it and bringing prestige and publicity for his employers in the process. It represents an ingenious design with numerous cut-glass elements in the eight separate bowls and on the upper section, which is topped with a glass replica of a crown and a Maltese cross. It served as a royal table setting for use on state occasions at Holyrood Palace and was regularly displayed at international exhibitions for many years, as in Edinburgh in 1886.[41]

A striking exhibition stand that attracted plaudits two years later in Glasgow was that mounted by the London ceramics firm of Doulton & Co. Famed for its domestic sanitary wares, but also engaged in decorative 'art pottery' production, the company supplied a large ornate terracotta fountain for the event, which it later donated to the City of Glasgow and can still be seen on Glasgow Green. The firm's exhibition stand took the form of a great Indian-themed pavilion and was notable for the numbers of craftsmen and craftswomen that were there to demonstrate the different elements of decorative pottery making. There were up to 20 men engaged in throwing, turning and moulding, and half a dozen women doing the painting and carved design work to 'supply the artistic decoration for which Doulton ware is justly celebrated'. Demonstration stands like this attracted massive public interest. 'The ease and grace with which these pretty artists perform the tasks assigned to them never fail to excite admiration.'[42] One of the decorators was painted by artist John Lavery, employed by the city council to make a record of the exhibition. In a portrait, titled 'Woman Painting a Pot', we see Alice Groom, ceramics artist, working at a bench, painting or incising a large jardinière, with pots in various stages of completion displayed in the background. She wears a tight-corseted dress with gold bangles and rings. Though the craft she demonstrates was typical of her daily employment, the fashionable clothing and jewellery were not. Alice Groom (1863–1952) described as an 'artist, painter' born in Pimlico in London, was living in Lambeth at the census of 1881 in a household headed by her widowed mother, a 'wardrobe dealer' and two brothers, one a tailor. She was probably trained at the Lambeth School of Art, which had been founded in 1854 to teach applied art and design to working artisans. The school formed a close relationship with the nearby Doulton pottery works and from the 1870s had a curriculum for training young men and women for the pottery trade. Though there were more famous women associated with the pottery, in particular sisters Hannah and Florence Barlow, Groom-signed pots can be found in antique sales today. Alice was married not long after the Glasgow exhibition and left the pottery business.[43] John Lavery (1856–1941), the Belfast-born artist who painted the portrait, was also of an artisan family background and was initially apprenticed as a photographer in Glasgow before becoming a painter. Whilst still a young man, he was employed by the municipal committee that organised the Glasgow 1888 exhibition as the 'official artist', charged with creating a record in a series of paintings and sketches of the buildings and people that caught his eye and were typical of what became a popular and profitable event. He also painted the grand opening ceremony.[44]

HAND SKILLS DISPLAYED

As in the glass or ceramic company displays described above, illustrating industrial processes and hand skills from raw materials to the end product was a common practice in public exhibitions and museums. Early exhibition bodies such as the Society of Antiquaries, the Highland Society or the universities, whilst largely devoted to natural history or archaeology collections, also acquired specimens of rock or plant material used in manufacturing, as did bodies with commercial interests at heart such as the East India Company. The latter employed many Scottish-trained botanists and doctors in India who were charged with collecting natural materials for potential medical or industrial uses. They sent samples to the company museum in London and to provincial museums.[45] There was complex reasoning behind this, including scholarly classification of natural materials in an age of scientific enquiry and exploiting the economic potential of materials that were not found in Britain or Europe. The combined desire to seek out new manufacturing opportunities and improve the goods that were made gave rise to a form of exhibition categorisation that was codified for the 1851 Great Exhibition and used extensively thereafter in broad groups going from raw materials to machinery and manufactures to fine arts.[46] The Industrial Museum of Scotland, founded in Edinburgh in 1854, which was later renamed the Edinburgh Museum of Science and Art, exemplified these ambitions and took in many gifts of the 'raw materials of manufacture' intended to 'form an admirable introduction to its finished products'.[47]

Certain exhibitions were focused on raw materials, including the first International Forestry Exhibition which was held in Edinburgh in the summer months of 1884, was modelled on the forestry section of the Paris Universal Exhibition of 1878 and was intended to inspire commercial forestry developments and manufactures. Though it did not have the mass appeal of the later general exhibitions, the displays still indicated the complex relationship between craft and industry, materials, tools and finished products, the present and the past. The loan collections included ancient objects with historical associations and relic wood items such as 'a stool made from the thorn tree planted at Loch Leven Castle by Mary Queen of Scots'.[48] Peter Westren of Edinburgh, a jeweller who was mostly associated with carved and polished Scotch pebble work, exhibited 'a collection of very old Wainscot and other Woods, procured from Old Edinburgh Buildings, Turned and Carved into useful and Ornamental Articles, with names and dates, historical of Old Edinburgh'.[49] Stand 16, which was one of the larger displays measuring 40 ×10 feet, mounted by W. S. Brown's Artistic Furnishing Warehouse in Edinburgh, included a Scottish oak dining-room set in 'Stuart Style', 'Jacobean Style' furniture as well as a range of imported woods and modern styles of furnishings.[50] There were carved picture frames and decorated Mauchline wares. Wood from famous forests or estates and from overseas were displayed in raw and manufactured form, with particular emphasis on the woods and carved work of Indian craftsmen along with Indian basket weaving.[51] A Mr R. Weir exhibited an 'old Carved, Scotch-grown Oak and Laburnum two-doored Wardrobe, with projecting Cornices and Base with two Drawers over 200 years old, bought in London 70 years ago at a cost of 180 guineas'.[52] Though there were no working craftsmen, there was a 'model of joiner's bench with two men at bench that can be moved backward and forward. Also Models of Joiner's Tools, all within a Glass Case.'[53]

The Forestry Exhibition was held in Scotland because the woodland industries formed an important part of the Scottish economy. All exhibitions to some degree celebrated their localities and this was achieved in a particularly powerful manner through regionally distinct craft goods and craftworkers. Scottish exhibitions of the later nineteenth century always included displays of what contemporaries regarded as typical Scottish craft goods such as Mauchline ware boxes and trinkets embellished with Scottish scenes, tartans or ferns.[54] Ceramic 'motto wares' from the Cumnock pottery, embellished with homely phrases in broad Scots, many taken from the poetry of Burns, were displayed. Orkney chairs made celebrated exhibition appearances from the late nineteenth century, as did handmade tweeds and knits. Craft objects were sometimes exhibited alongside the people that made them. The use of working exhibits was not unique to the world of craft, since demonstration displays of industrial processes were also routine. Nor were craft-working displays always composed of local people. Indeed, the India exhibits that featured so prominently included Indian craftsmen engaged in handwork, which drew extensive newspaper comment and popular interest.[55] But before the first-time exhibition of Indian craftsmen in Glasgow in 1888, the Edinburgh 1886 exhibition had displayed the eye-catching 'Jaw Bone' stand in the Women's Industries section comprising a group of six women presented as a community of knitters from mainland Shetland and nearby Fair Isle. The women were there to raise awareness of their skills and sell hand-knitted goods made on the islands. The unusual shape of the stand, which is illustrated in contemporary photographs, reflected its construction from whale jawbones, signalling the role of whaling as another important Shetland industry. Shetland flags were displayed on either side of the Shetland coat-of-arms with its distinctive longboat motif and a horizontal banner reading 'Zetland and Fair Isle Knitters'. The display incorporated a spinning wheel, a woven kishie (basket) perhaps to hold skeins of wool and tables on either side of the stand draped with knitted fine-lace squares. A large shawl was one of many items pinned and draped above the knitters. Some of photographs of the exhibit included an older standing woman, Barbara Muir, who chaperoned the young knitters. She was the sister of

Figure 6.1 Shetland and Fair Isle knitters at the 'Jaw Bone' stand. Edinburgh International Exhibition, 1886, Women's Industries Section. © Shetland Museum and Archives.

Margaret Currie who ran Currie & Co., a truck-free shop buying and selling Shetland knitting from premises in Lerwick.

The Shetland stand was co-organised by Sheriff Thoms of Orkney and Shetland, the firm of Currie & Co. and Mr Laurence of Fair Isle, as an educational spectacle where visitors could see the processes of the industry – carding, spinning, dyeing and knitting – 'practically shown' by the deft fingers of six young women dressed in national costume.[56] It offered an opportunity to bring makers and purchasers together, though prices had to be clearly tagged and items could not be removed by purchasers until the end of exhibition. A *Scotsman* newspaper report highlighted the display as one especially 'worthy of notice and proving of great interest to visitors'.[57] The women, with their rustic costumes and traditional hand skills harkened to a romanticised earlier age that held great attraction. Another cohort of women in picturesque dress who appeared frequently at international exhibitions had similar appeal, though they were not craftworkers as such. These were the Newhaven fishwives from the small fishing town near Edinburgh, who wore colourful costumes, with striped 'kilted' petticoats, floral blouses, knitted shawls and fish baskets (or creels) on their backs. Groups of these women toured and performed as choirs in numerous exhibitions where there were sea-based themes, including the London Fisheries Exhibition in 1881, the Edinburgh International Fisheries Exhibition of 1882 and several Scandinavian exhibitions.[58] More spectacular still were the displays of traditional craftworkers in constructed village settings designed to show whole communities in their day-to-day lives, including men, women and children, though in reality they were heavily biased towards attractive younger women. The earliest of these were the Irish village exhibits mounted from the 1860s to promote Irish lace and crochet making along with various social and reforming agendas. They were hugely successful spectacles in Britain and abroad. The Irish village at the 1908 Franco-British exhibition in London comprised over 150 'colleens' selected for looks, charm and craft abilities who remained in their exhibition village for the 1909 Imperial International Exhibition and the 1910 Japan-British Exhibition.[59] Several Irish village displays were organised by Scottish aristocrat Lady Aberdeen, wife of the Viceroy of Ireland in the later nineteenth century and an advocate of the Irish home industries.[60] The elite-sponsored Scottish Home Industries movement was similar. Indeed, when the organisation was formally constituted as a limited company, exhibition work was included in its formal objectives.

Highland craft-village working displays were mounted and commonly represented on souvenir postcards showing picturesque groups in traditional Scottish dress. The most famous was 'An Clachan', created for the Scottish Exhibition of National History, Art and Industry in Glasgow in 1911. Glasgow had hosted several major exhibitions since 1888 but this final event before the First World War embraced Scotland's growing nationalist spirit. The organisers sought to heighten public awareness of Scottish history by turning a reflective eye on the nation's past and achievements. An Clachan offered a romanticised reconstruction of bygone Scottish life intended to show a 'typical' Highland village and educate the public on the crafts carried out in crofting communities. It included a tableau of villagers engaged in wool washing, carding and spinning, all traditional female tasks. It was as much a commercial concern as educational, setting the scene for displays of Home Industries' products in the 'village store', where tweeds, plaids and basket work were sold by Gaelic-speaking salesgirls.[61]

Part of the narrative appeal of all craft villages is that they were constructed around an idealised past of rural simplicity and communal harmony linked to handwork. The notion that craftwork represented a link between present and past and that its practice had higher moral value than industrial work was not new, but it was given a new impetus in the later nineteenth century through popular and high culture, including the Arts and Crafts movement. These cultural tropes could be seen in displays of real, high-value craftworks from the past in the elite-owned loan collection displays. They were also exhibited through historic reconstructions like the 'Old Edinburgh' court in 1886. This comprised a wood-and-plaster scaled-down representation of Edinburgh's medieval High Street with its once notable buildings. It contained shop booths selling sweets and souvenirs and sheet music for old Edinburgh tunes, with shopgirls dressed as characters from history or fiction, such as Walter Scott's Jeanie and Effie Deans.[62] The Glasgow Exhibition of 1888 featured a reconstruction of the Bishop's Palace, containing relics of Mary Queen of Scots, Bonnie Prince Charlie and the Covenanters along with stained-glass windows and other antiquities.[63] It included,

> an admirable selection of varied articles which will help to illustrate the growth of the Scottish people, starting with the rude implements of prehistoric times, proceeding with many striking indications of rapid advancement . . . intended to demonstrate in this way the progress made in the north country in the arts and sciences.[64]

Craftwork and hand tools were combined into these narratives.

An area of craft exhibition that evoked a nostalgic sense of handwork possessed of high moral value and national spirit was seen in those displays given over to Paisley shawls and the 'gold age' of handloom weavers. The royal family and Scottish aristocrats were conspicuously associated with

Paisley shawls, as were many Scottish celebrities. In 1925, for instance, the *Scotsman* reported the sale of Burns relics that had belonged to the late Mr McKissock of the Plough Tavern, Ayr, who was 'well-known as an ardent admirer of the poet and a keen collector of relics'. One of the items was a Paisley shawl reputedly once the property of Burns' mother.[65] The opening of the David Livingstone memorial in Blantyre included an exhibition of relics linked to the great man and his family, including 'a beautiful Paisley shawl in which Livingstone was christened'.[66] Paisley shawls were exhibited on royal and aristocratic bodies on public occasions to dramatic effect and also in display cabinets, building on a tradition that had been set in the eighteenth century when displays of luxurious Kashmir shawls were mounted by specialist retailers and by the East India Company at their museum in London. The Great Exhibition of 1851 and subsequent industrial exhibitions, international and local, mounted regular displays of Paisley-made shawls while the industry was still alive and historical exhibitions began within a few years of its demise. The first major historical display was in Paisley in June 1905 in the Free Public Library and Museum, which included 650 specimens of Paisley, Oriental, French and other shawls. The museum, opened in 1870, was funded by Sir Peter Coats of the thread-manufacturing firm and was based on the collections of the Paisley Philosophical Society. The purpose of the 1905 exhibition was to 'instruct their young folk and their visitors at the Co-operative Congress on the basis of Paisley's greatness' and also to attract further specimen shawls to the museum to make the collection complete. The Co-operative Congress was a major international event with many hundreds of delegates and wide newspaper coverage. The exhibition was open for three weeks with an attendance of *c*.16,000.[67] Much of the organisation, along with the writing of a commemorative volume, was undertaken by Matthew Blair, former weaver and local historian, who also wrote about the Paisley thread industry.[68] There were regular exhibitions thereafter in Scotland, as in May 1915 in the club rooms of the Glasgow Society of Lady Artists in Blythswood Square, which was reported by the *Scotsman* in elegiac terms: 'Though the Paisley shawl was at one time familiar throughout the land, it has now passed into the region of historic things. The real article is neither made nor worn now: it is kept in lavender by families as an heirloom.'[69]

CREATING IDENTITY

Individual craftsmen and craftswomen visited exhibitions on their own account as interested specialists and for leisure. Few committed their views on such events to writing, though there was a later-nineteenth-century initiative designed to elicit opinions. In the run-up to the 1878 Paris exhibition – the Exposition Universelle – civic institutions in several major cities in Europe and Britain, including Edinburgh, sponsored what were termed 'artisan reporters' to visit, observe and report on the exhibition and their respective crafts as practised in Paris. The artisan reports were published in the *Scotsman*, generating a lively correspondence and where the editor subsequently observed,

> To the reporters themselves the task assigned them has evidently been one of much interest . . . they have brought intelligence, impartiality and discrimination . . . showing they were not less capable of examining with practical eye the products of the respective branches of industry in which they are engaged than of describing in a clear, intelligible way the impressions they have received.[70]

The sponsored artisans, with support from the Edinburgh Town Council, Chamber of Commerce, Merchants House and Scottish Society of Arts, included cabinetmakers John Cubie, William Aitken and Alexander Forrester.[71] Glassworkers and engravers were represented by Franz Beutlich, John Carter and James Brown, the first almost certainly one of the Bohemian glassworkers who had emigrated to Edinburgh mid century.[72] There was a brass worker, Charles White and also painter and decorator John Hamilton, who had premises in George Street.[73] The latter's published account gives a flavour of the undertaking.[74] Hamilton spent eight days in Paris, visiting and reporting on the exhibition with a view to comparing the quality of French and European artisanal work with that of Britain. He offered observations on manufacturing processes and design as displayed and he also visited several business premises to see craftsmen at work and employment practices. Details were given on rates of pay and hours at work, which he concluded were similar to Edinburgh and he also reflected on housing conditions and leisure activities. Craftsman education and design training was another theme, seen particularly in the several reports from cabinetmakers, who admired the French system and highlighted the role of museums in Paris as a source of design inspiration. In his report of 16 January 1880, William Aitken wrote,

> I regret that our own Industrial Museum, which we hope to see soon finished, should have so very few specimens of ancient art furniture . . . I would strongly urge upon the Commissioners of the Industrial Museum to apply a vigorous search for such rare articles . . . [to] enable our workmen to study and profit by those examples.[75]

The artisan reporters offer one perspective on the importance of exhibitions and individual craft exhibitors give another. An artisan who clearly valued his successful participation in exhibitions when a young man was

Figure 6.2 T. M. Ross, plumber of Haddington. Exhibition display of pipework, *c*.1886. © East Lothian Council Archives – Jack Tully Jackson Collection.

plumber and ornamental lead worker T. M. (Tommy) Ross of Haddington (1860–1937). Ross was a notable figure in local politics, elected to the Haddington Town Council in 1903 and appointed Provost in 1918. He founded a major East Lothian firm that undertook a range of public projects including the sanitary wares in new schools and some of his glazed bathroom fittings, decorated with his name, are found in museum collections.[76] A photographic portrait of the young Ross survives. It shows him as a dapper man of about 25 in a blazer and straw boater, seated by a display of elaborate pipework. The centre knot of his large, twisted lead construction 'was made up of a 12 feet length of 2 inch lead waste pipe'. Ross's ability to maintain a uniform hollow within its contortions required considerable talent. The portrait was taken in the studio of a professional photographer to commemorate Ross's successful involvement in several key exhibitions. The handwritten note beneath the photograph connects him to a London firm, John Smeaton Sanitary Engineers, where he was employed and probably also trained. Smeaton occupied stand number 938 at the International Health Exhibition in South Kensington in London in 1884 and in addition to Ross's bravura arrangement of decorative lead pipework, the firm's display included a range of ingenious domestic sanitary fittings, including a 'Tip-up Lavatory Apparatus' and a 'Bachelor's Bath and Lavatory combined with wardrobe'.[77] The note on Tommy Ross's portrait further explains that his pipework display was also exhibited at the Industrial Exhibition in Edinburgh in 1886 and awarded an 'honourable mention'. He was proud of his achievement and probably used it to advance his career. In later life, Tommy Ross provided exhibits for the 1896 'Plumbers' Exhibition' held at the Queen's Brigade Hall in London in connection with the Plumbers' Congress, a trade convention. This event featured loan collections of antique pipework, displays mounted by the major British firms such as Doulton of London and Shanks of Barrhead and competition exhibits including apprentice and students' work showing jointing and bending much in the manner of the pipes shown in the celebratory portrait. Ross's contribution to the 1896 event comprised 'old traps and pipes . . . showing effect on these of carbonate of lime, sewage gas etc'. According to an *Edinburgh Evening News* editorial, 'the exhibition is well worthy of a visit, more especially to those interested in sanitary matters'.[78] The first Plumbers' Congress was held at the International Health Exhibition in London in 1884. Its purpose was education and information on best practice in the plumbing trade, along with regulation of apprentices and journeyman registration.[79]

The late-nineteenth-century exhibition activity of Tommy Ross was largely conducted through events organised by national trade bodies or international organising committees. But there were many smaller, localised exhibitions, some calling on the organisational input of a working-class membership, that reveal the importance of craft activity and associated display for the creative identity of individual exhibitors. One of the earliest Scottish examples to show this was the Industrial Exhibition in Glasgow in December 1865, which was mounted by the Central Working Men's Club and Institute. The organisers advertised all the usual elite support that such events required, embracing royal patronage, honorary trustees that included the Lord Provost and local MPs and a grand opening led by the Duke of Argyll. It was held in exhibition rooms in Argyle Street, described as an exhibition of 'works of skill and art' and offered £100 in prizes to exhibitors.[80] The event allowed for the selling of exhibits. As a gesture to the 1851 Crystal Palace Exhibition, the organisers successfully petitioned the Queen to allow a bust of Prince Albert to be displayed.[81] The opening was widely reported in the Scottish and north-of-England press. The *Dundee Courier & Argus* detailed how it came to be developed and the significant financial contributions from the town council towards furnishing the exhibition space. The ground floor comprised 'upwards of one hundred models of stationary and locomotive engines . . . ingenious mechanical apparatus, extensive collections of coloured and photographic mechanical illustrations' as part of a usual gesture to the high technology of the age. There was an exhibition on an upper floor of foreign ornaments and curiosities, another gallery given over to natural science specimens and extensive displays of paintings. Most important of all, and the basic rationale for the event, were the artisan displays that included 'drawings and designs by working men' and a series of rooms given over to the work of 'operatives engaged in the manufacture of needles, glass ornaments, brushes, weaving of plaids, etc'. In all, the number of articles exhibited by 'working people' numbered c.1,200 and there were over 400 'exhibitors belonging to the industrious classes'. To accommodate the high level of interest, the opening ceremony took place in the evening at the end of the working day.[82]

The event was Smilesean in its cultural framing, indeed the work of Samuel Smiles on industrial 'rags-to-riches' successful lives, recently published, was referenced by the Duke of Argyll in his opening speech and its purpose embraced a conspicuous display of working class industry, ingenuity and peaceful civic participation.[83] At the exhibition end, some displays were taken into public ownership and kept open as the Glasgow Museum and Polytechnic Exhibition with the intention to 'provide a place of profitable resort for the working classes'.[84] This sustained interest, coupled with the large participation by working men and women who submitted exhibition items, speaks to popular haptic creativity and the tenacity of craftwork as a form of personal expression as well as paid employment. The exhibition catalogue is unusual in giving the addresses and occupations of the exhibitors. They included work by skilled craftsmen, such as the 'model of a French Wardrobe' by John Stupart, cabinetmaker of 2 Canning Street, Anderston, on sale for £12. There were also highly crafted items by individuals employed in lower-skilled occupations, such as the 'Miniature Chest of Drawers' by Thomas Brown, packing-box maker of 52 Tobago Street, priced at £4 10s. Some items were made by individuals with no obvious connection to hand trades, such as the 'Lady's Work-Box' by James Marshall, clerk of 73 John Street, which was not for sale.[85] William Temple, a railway servant of Provan Mill, exhibited a 'Set of Drawing-room Curtains in netted thread-work'.[86] Amongst the women exhibitors there were 'Two Window Curtains' made by Elizabeth McEwan, powerloom weaver of 12 Landressey Street and two anti-macassars made by Isabella Watt, a milliner of 34 Brown Street, which were on sale for £1 10s. Maggie Miller, a shopkeeper from Mauchline, exhibited a sofa-pillow in Berlin wool and bead embroidery and

Ellen Hudson, a domestic servant of 84 Charles Street exhibited a 'Bed Quilt, richly embroidered'. Mary Stewart of 6 Elmbank Street, who contributed 'Three Tea Infusers, in bead work', priced from £1 5s to 14s, was described as 'aged 14 years'. There were many examples of conspicuous ingenuity, such as the 'Lady's Work-Box, built and inlaid with about 4,000 pieces of variegated glass, by Robert Gray, flint-glass maker' of 40 Albert Street.[87] Indeed, the complex character of some of the artefacts was described at length, including a patchwork bedcover of 3,200 pieces made by regimental drill instructor Alexander McDonald, on sale for £10.[88]

Some of the historical and Scottish national themes that came to be so dominant in later international exhibitions were represented in the artisans' work at this 1865 Glasgow event. They included a 'Desk, made of part of the old door of the Glasgow Cathedral, by James Napier, block-cutter of 404 St Vincent Street', on sale for £2.[89] An 'Ornamental Glass Table-Top, with Portraits of Eminent Scotchmen, by John Stewart, glass stainer, 29 Turner's Court' was priced at £21 and further described as 'eminently Scottish' with an account in the catalogue of the individuals portrayed, which included Watt, Wilkie, Burns and Scott, also Livingstone, Wallace and Hugh Miller.[90] The circumstances in which work was produced was indicated in some instances, as with 'Two Columns, Imitations of Marble, Sienna and Galway Green' by William Smith, a house painter of 29 Cowcaddens Street, offered for sale at £1 5s each and described as having been 'painted after work hours by gas light'.[91] The latter gives poignant insight into the role of craft creativity in private lives and leisure. Indeed, the inclusion of so many individuals making beautiful handcrafted things as amateurs is telling, revealing handwork as personal expression, a desire to keep hand skills alive in the face of mechanised or unskilled employment and perhaps, for some, nostalgic gestures to the past.

Small-scale exhibitions such as this in Glasgow in 1865 took place throughout the second half of the nineteenth century. They inspired the artisans' courts that later featured in the larger international exhibition. They also signal the role of amateur craftwork in nineteenth-century cultural experience, for men and women, wealthy and poor. This topic is explored in the next chapter.

Notes

1. *Scotsman*, 13 May 1886, 'Past Exhibitions in Edinburgh'.
2. Ibid.
3. Ibid.

4. NRS. NG1/3. Board of Manufactures. Trustees Report of 1830. Appendix, 38.

5. *Scotsman*, 19 February 1886, 'The International Industrial Exhibition. Artisan Section'.

6. Ibid.

7. *International Exhibition of Industry, Science & Art, Edinburgh 1886. The Official Catalogue* (Edinburgh, 1886), 283. See also George Wilson Smith, 'Displaying Edinburgh in 1886: The International Exhibition of Industry, Science and Art', PhD thesis, University of Edinburgh, 2015.

8. *International Exhibition, Edinburgh 1886*, 280.

9. Ibid., 282.

10. Ibid., 287.

11. Ibid., 281.

12. Stana Nenadic, 'Exhibiting India in nineteenth-century Scotland and the impact on commerce, industry and popular culture', *Journal of Scottish Historical Studies*, 34:1 (2014), 67–89.

13. Kinchin and Kinchin, *Glasgow's Great Exhibitions*.

14. *Glasgow Herald*, 24 March 1888.

15. *Glasgow Herald*, 10 November 1888.

16. *Glasgow Herald*, 7 April 1888.

17. *Dundee Exhibition of Industry* (Dundee, 1887), Preface, 'Rules for the Guidance of Exhibitors'.

18. *Dundee Exhibition of Industry*, 'Prospectus'.

19. Ibid., 22.

20. Ibid., 24.

21. Tim Barringer, 'William Dyce, 1806–64', *ODNB*, 2004.

22. *Scotsman*, 1 July 1857.

23. *Catalogue of the First Exhibition of the Art-Manufacture Association in the National Galleries, Edinburgh 1856* (Edinburgh, 1856).

24. *Report of the Committee of Management of the Art Manufacture Association for Encouraging the Application of High Art to Works of Utility and Ornament for the Year 1857-8* (Edinburgh, 1858), 51, 84.

25. *Exhibition of Decorative Handiwork, Edinburgh* (Edinburgh, 1888), Prefatory Note.

26. Anthony Burton, *Vision and Accident. The Story of the Victoria and Albert Museum* (London, 1999).

27. *Official Catalogue of the Exhibition of Industrial and Decorative Art, 1861* (Edinburgh, 1861), Introductory Notice.

28. Kinchin and Kinchin, *Glasgow's Great Exhibitions*.

29. Further details in Nenadic and Tuckett, 'Artisans and aristocrats'.

30. NMS. UC17/467. Society of Antiquaries Correspondence. Letters from Thomas R. Marshall concerning the Hunterston Brooch, 1893.

31. NRS. GD224/184/6. Handicraft and Industrial Exhibition. Hawick, 1887. News cuttings.

32. NRS. GD224/1001/14. Edinburgh Exhibition of Decorative Handiwork, 1888. Advertising handbill.
33. *Exhibition of Decorative Handiwork, Edinburgh* (Edinburgh, 1888).
34. *International Exhibition, 1862. Official Catalogue of the Industrial Department* (London, 1862), 102.
35. Such as G. W. Yapp, *Art Industry. Metal Work Illustrating the Chief Processes of Art-Work Applied by the Goldsmith, Silversmith etc* (1878).
36. *Scotsman*, 25 May 1886.
37. *Glasgow Herald*, 26 July 1888. See also Kristin Jurgens, 'Dunmore Pottery: The Art of the Art Pottery Business', PhD thesis, University of Glasgow, 2007.
38. Kirkcaldy Museum and Gallery, Fife. Stores.
39. *Scotsman*, 29 July 1886, 'The International Exhibition'.
40. Museum of Edinburgh, Huntley House. Display.
41. See Chapter 2 for further details on the Holyrood Glass Company.
42. *Supplement to the North British Daily Mail*, 24 May 1888; *Glasgow Herald*, 23 August 1888.
43. Biographical details from a family descendant.
44. Kenneth McConkey, *Sir John Lavery* (Edinburgh, 1993).
45. Nenadic, 'Exhibiting India'.
46. Jeffrey A. Auerbach, *The Great Exhibition of 1851: A Nation on Display* (1999), 83.
47. *Scotsman*, 28 February 1855.
48. Cited in Jane Bowen 'The Edinburgh International Forestry Exhibition of 1884', *Journal of the Mauchline Ware Collectors Club* (1998).
49. *Official Catalogue of the International Forestry Exhibition* (Edinburgh, 1884), 20.
50. Ibid., 2.
51. *Scotsman*, 7 July 1884.
52. *Catalogue of the International Forestry Exhibition*, 10.
53. Ibid. 21.
54. Baker, *Mauchline Ware*.
55. Nenadic, 'Exhibiting India'.
56. *International Exhibition, Edinburgh 1886*, 280.
57. *Scotsman*, 7 May 1886, 7 June 1886.
58. Stana Nenadic, 'Gender, craftwork and the exotic in international exhibitions c.1880–1910', in Deborah Simonton, et al., eds, *Luxury and Gender in European Towns, 1700–1914* (Abingdon, 2015), 150–67.
59. Ibid., 163.
60. Helland, *British and Irish Home Arts and Industries*.
61. Neil G. W. Curtis, 'The place of history, literature and politics in the 1911 Scottish Exhibition', *Scottish Literary Review*, 7:1 (2015), 43–74.
62. Nenadic, 'Gender, craftwork and the exotic', 155.
63. *Scotsman*, 23 April 1888.

64. *Scotsman*, 3 March 1888.
65. *Scotsman*, 29 August 1925.
66. *Scotsman*, 24 April 1929.
67. *Scotsman*, 12, 13 June, 3 July 1905.
68. Blair, *Paisley Shawl*.
69. *Scotsman*, 8 May 1915.
70. *Scotsman*, 23 January 1880.
71. *Scotsman*, 12 January 1880.
72. *Scotsman*, 20 January 1880.
73. *Scotsman*, 27 December 1879.
74. *Scotsman*, 8 January 1880.
75. *Scotsman*, 16 January 1880.
76. Lillian Main, *The Closes of Haddington. A Walking Tour through the Backstreets of History* (Edinburgh, 2014), 28–9; *Haddingtonshire Courier*, 15 December 1899.
77. *International Health Exhibition, 1884. Official Catalogue* (1884).
78. *Edinburgh Evening News*, 25 June 1896.
79. *Liverpool Mercury*, 16 October 1884.
80. *Paisley Herald and Renfrewshire Advertiser*, 18 November 1865.
81. *Newcastle Daily Journal*, 8 November 1865.
82. *Dundee Courier & Argus*, 13 December 1865, 'Opening of the Glasgow Working Men's Industrial Exhibition'.
83. *Paisley Herald & Renfrewshire Advertiser*, 16 December 1865.
84. *Scotsman*, 11 July 1866.
85. *The Industrial Exhibition Catalogue* (Glasgow, 1865), 17.
86. Ibid., 20.
87. Ibid., 28.
88. Ibid., 27.
89. Ibid., 28–9.
90. Ibid., 25.
91. Ibid., 21.

7

Amateur Craft

Pᴜʙʟɪᴄ ᴇxʜɪʙɪᴛɪᴏɴs ᴛʜᴀᴛ sʜᴏᴡᴄᴀsᴇᴅ artisans and traditional skills alongside modern industry were remarkable because exhibits from men or women who made a living from craftwork were often displayed alongside the work of amateurs who made things for their leisure. Though commonly dismissed because of the variable quality of the output, amateur craft was complex, it changed through the century and was underpinned by its own sets of values that were distinct from those of professional craftworkers. This chapter explores the amateur craft phenomenon as practised by men and women, rich and poor, and considers the meaning of such activity for the individual and more widely.[1] It starts with some reflections on the concept of 'craft' as a socially constructed idea in the early nineteenth century with appeal to new types of worker and the new middle classes and elites. It considers the equipment and materials that amateurs could purchase, often through specialist shops, and the publications and magazines that were produced for the amateur and craft training. Exhibiting was a feature of training institutions, and amateurs of varying levels of competence had numerous opportunities, particularly from mid century, to display their work. Yet the relationship between the commercial craft practitioner and the amateur was not always comfortable and the emergence of the Arts and Crafts movement in Scotland, discussed in the final section, highlighted some of the tensions and contradictions.

So why did craftwork appeal so strongly to the nineteenth-century amateur when in the eighteenth century, other than amongst elite women engaged in fancy needlework or interior decoration of their own homes, it was largely unknown as a form of recreation with strong social or moral value?[2] Historically, of course, most commercially produced craft was domestic before the later eighteenth century or made in workshops attached to homes. At a basic level, it was the separation of the home and handwork through the mediation of new business organisations, including the factory and new technologies, that yielded opportunities for the handmaking of attractive 'things' to be appropriated as leisure. Such activity was and remains a form of creative expression when adopted through personal inclination and to see the construction of something 'beautiful' from start to finish, using attractive materials with haptic appeal, is intrinsically satisfying. Hence most amateur craft was in the sphere of the decorative arts or personal adornment. Such craftwork could be practical but was not utilitarian. There were no amateur plumbers or slaters, but there were amateur wood- and stonecarvers. What we now call 'do-it-yourself' or DIY and household repairs were a separate entity, more connected with working- and lower-middle-class householders than elites and whilst sometimes undertaken for leisure, usually motivated by cost saving.[3]

Much amateur craft for women was driven by traditional ideals and feminine roles linked to family and nurturing, seen in working with textiles to make clothing or soft furnishing, or creating decorations for the home or food preparation. Its purpose was to 'signify womanhood'.[4] Another area of active craft participation for women was linked to the church and charity fundraising, which included embroidery projects for church furnishings or objects made for sale through church bazaars. Yet these idealised attributes of craft practice for the female amateur are seen by some to have darker parallel meanings, connected to anxieties about modernity and change and a need to exercise control over consumption.[5] Likewise amateur craft for men was linked to traditional ideas regarding rationality and science, as exhibited through natural history-based craft projects or model making.[6] Some areas of amateur craft were considered to be healthy because of the physical effort required for those with sedentary lifestyles. Or, for those who engaged in physical employments as working men and women, they were healthy because they were a form of leisure undertaken in the home rather than the pub – alcohol-free and tending to confirm morally wholesome family relationships. Indeed, in the middle decades of the nineteenth century, amateur craft for working men was commonly advocated by the temperance movement and some exhibited craftworks, such as quilts, included complex iconography that declared teetotal connections.[7] For the working-class population with socialist inclinations in the second half of the century, amateur craft training and practice was a form of empowerment linked to collective behaviour and the Arts and Crafts movement.

The practice of amateur craft for women and men was frequently connected with gift giving and the emotional resonance that an item could hold for the maker/giver and the recipient. Gifts secured personal relationships and had value irrespective of the quality of the item that was made.[8] Another area of emotional expression that inspired amateur craftwork was connected to the act of mourning the death of a loved one, giving rise to commemorative embroidery or carving and the popularity of 'hair work' involving the hair of the departed incorporated into items of jewellery or used in embroidery.[9] The passing of time, romantic notions of continuity with the past and idealised backward-looking rural lifestyles and relationships were all articulated, overtly or otherwise, in amateur craft. For the amateur practitioner, their craftworking was emotional and layered with complex significance.

CREATIVE EXPRESSION

Amateur craft was mostly the preserve of the middle and upper classes with leisure time and money to spend on pastimes. The textile crafts had the clearest cultural meaning for leisured women, representing both a traditional contribution to the household economy as well as a passive female skill with an end product that could be used for a variety of demonstrative effects through finely wrought stitch detail, harmonious colour or design creativity. Some amateur textile craft practitioners were men, as contributors to public exhibitions reveal and this was particularly true of men whose routine employment entailed lengthy hours spent alone and away from family and home, as with seafarers or some soldiers.[10] These men often used of scrap materials that were readily to hand. One case is unusually well documented. It comprises a large and spectacular patchwork quilt which was made while at sea by Nicholas White of Dundee, a steward on a whaling ship in the late nineteenth century. The quilt was constructed from over a hundred differently designed textile samples, mostly in Turkey red printed cotton intended for the India market, which were probably taken from manufacturers' pattern books. The quilt design is one that was common in Scotland and Ireland at the time. How Nicholas White acquired the pattern books is unknown, but perhaps, like fabric that was purchased by female home dressmakers and quilters on land, they were part of a sale of salvaged stock.[11]

Display of decorative textile work held close to the body of the producer was a frequent device for articulating coded information. Elite women were commonly represented in words or images with embroidery in their laps or seated at a fancy worktable containing the paraphernalia of embroidery, crochet or knitting. Such accessories signalled female industry divorced from intellectual engagement and reflected a reality in which women of the higher classes spent much time in their formative years being taught to perfect such skills. Women novelists were particularly adept at using textile details to suggest the personalities and social position of their characters, most notably George Eliot in *The Mill on the Floss* (1860) where outspoken and unconventional Maggie Tulliver's plain but exquisite needlework for family linens is contrasted with rich cousin Lucy Deane's showy fancywork for a church bazaar. A demonstration of a different type, but still related to amateur textiles and female virtue, was reported in the *Scotsman* in 1843 as an exhibition in the Royal Hotel in Princes Street, Edinburgh, of a 'splendid Berlin wool carpet'. From the hands of 'nearly one hundred Presbyterian ladies of Ulster', the carpet was produced under the patronage of the Countess of Breadalbane for gifting to the Earl in recognition of his efforts in support of the Free Church of Scotland. The entry money raised by the exhibition was to be used 'in the erection of one or more of the Free Churches in the Highlands'.[12]

It was not just the actual practice of textile craftwork that garnered meaning, but also the equipment that held symbolic value. A ladies'

Figure 7.1   Mrs and Miss Ross. 'Household Industry in Tain Previous to 1850'. Tain, *c*.1865. © Tain & District Museum.

worktable was a fine piece of furniture, often incorporating intricate drawers and inlaid decorative details and intended for display in a drawing room. And there were other furnishing items, in particular the spinning wheel, which, when its use as a practical piece of machinery was in decline, was made as fine household furniture by firms such as John Jameson of the Toy and Turnery Manufactory in York. The latter sold fashionable wheels 'elegantly proportioned and crisply finished to meet the high decorative standards of the boudoir or drawing room in which they were used'.[13] Inspired by the Arts and Crafts movement, ornate antique spinning wheels were particularly popular as drawing-room furniture in the later nineteenth and early twentieth century, as revealed in contemporary photographs and newspaper 'wanted' advertisements.[14] In some instances, these wheels were merely for display, in others they were deployed by leisured women to spin the linen or woollen thread that they used in their own textile work. Wheels held symbolic cultural potency as is shown in numerous portrait photographs of elite women posed seated at a spinning wheel. A striking example is a photograph of Mrs and Miss Ross of Tain in north-east Scotland, taken c.1865 by amateur photographer John Ross, an accountant in Tain and son of Mrs Ross. Titled 'Household Industry in Tain Previous to 1850', it shows two women engaged in traditional female domestic crafts – spinning wool and knitting socks or stockings – which were also practised commercially to supplement household incomes among the rural poor. Mrs Ross is dressed in the simple clothing of an elderly Highland cottager in decades past, with a frilled and starched linen 'mutch' or cap on her head and a practical cotton skirt and shawl. She may have dressed like this on an everyday basis, though as the mother of an accountant her middle-class status suggests otherwise. Miss Ross, with knitting needles in hand, is fashionably dressed in a tartan silk gown. Despite the drapery in the background, the foliage on the ground reveals that the carefully composed photograph was taken outdoors. Mrs Ross sits by a Saxony wheel, which was widely introduced to Scotland from the mid eighteenth century as the linen industry evolved, replacing the portable but primitive distaff system of spinning. The wheel is powered with a foot treadle. Alongside her is a jack reel for winding yarn. There is a basket on the ground containing balls of wool and finished socks, the latter doubtless intended as gifts or for charity bazaar sale.

Nineteenth-century middle-class and elite women were commonly represented in paintings and photographs with spinning wheels. Processing textiles at home like this, though it was a technology long replaced by factories and machines, expressed an ideal of feminine industriousness –

called *eydence* in Scots – and evoked romanticised images of cottage life in the past and in the Highlands in particular that held special charm for Victorians. Tourist photographs of Highland Scotland, Ireland or Wales commonly focused on women in traditional costume seated with wheels outside cottages and they were displayed in the popular Highland and Irish villages that featured in international exhibitions. The emotional meaning attached to such wheels was nicely captured in a mid-nineteenth-century newspaper account, titled 'Notes of a ramble on Deeside', describing a visit to a family of cottagers.

> This interesting family are all of a most ingenious caste, and the older brother works principally at the getting up and repairing of the small spinning wheel, now so much superseded by the large manufacturing machinery of the low country, but the agreeable sound of which may still be heard in the homes of the mountains, acting so enchantingly in concert with the sweet strains of a buxom, bonnie, and healthful-looking highland maiden.[15]

Queen Victoria was photographed on a number of occasions posed with a spinning wheel, as were several of her daughters.[16] The elderly Victoria was also photographed with crochet in her hands, as were many aristocratic women, who were often represented with craft textiles that were made in the area where their estates were found. The Queen's relationship with the spinning wheel embraced its practical use, which she learned in Scotland and it was reported with approval in 1865 that she had taken a wheel south to Windsor Castle – 'how characteristic of her simple, homely and virtuous tastes!' The same newspaper account further advocated that other 'useful and honoured implements of womanly craft and skill' be once more made fashionable, including the knitting needle. The virtue of the spinning wheel, it claimed, included physical exercise that 'gives fullness to the chest, freedom and grace to the step, and general elasticity to the body'. The knitting needle, moreover, is the 'most social of all domestic employments'.[17] Whether women adopted the crafts to cultivate these attributes is unclear, yet the exercise and social benefits attached to traditional domestic handwork for women were articulated elsewhere. A late-nineteenth-century antiquarian account of 'old Sussex farmhouses and their furniture' declared that 'the spinning wheel which used to ornament every drawing room, and is still occasionally met with in Sussex houses, afforded a healthful recreation and not only was it a country occupation, but ladies in cities spun'.[18]

Amongst elite men also there is evidence that amateur craft played an important part in their emotional lives and creative expression. Sometimes this was connected to scientific interests, seen, for instance, in collecting and polishing semi-precious stones using the tools of the lapidary. Lord Francis Gray of Kilfauns Castle in Perthshire, a career politician who managed the early-nineteenth-century Scottish postal service from offices in Edinburgh, was an amateur naturalist and member of the Edinburgh Bannatyne Club and Society of Antiquaries of Scotland. His country house was in an area notable for its colourful agates and other stones such as garnets and he collected and polished many hundreds, which were purchased from his estate following his death in 1842 and gifted to the recently founded Montrose Museum.[19] The auction sale of Lord Gray's personal effects, which took place in Edinburgh, included 'a first rate turning lathe with excellent chucks and tools, a splendid engine, rose lathe, which cost above £300 . . .' There was a telescope, a small steam engine, two printing presses with type along with barometers and thermometers, all providing testament to a man of many scientific interests and creative abilities.[20] A near contemporary with similar interests and practical masculine skills was the Duke of Gordon, described by a contemporary as,

> a man of taste and talent, and of superior mechanical acquirements. He wrote some good characteristic Scotch songs in the minute style of paining local manners, and he wrought diligently at a turning-lathe! He was lavish of snuff-boxes of his own manufacture, which he presented liberally to all his friends and neighbours.[21]

The Duke also made jewellery as gifts for family and friends, and personal papers confirm his interests since they include for 1811 the cost of a turning lathe supplied by Alexander Abernethie of Aberdeen and in 1814 an account due for a '5 inch centre screw mandrill lathe . . . with extra chucks and other bits of machinery' costing £120. In 1819 the Duke paid an account due to Bonsall, Marsh and Guy of Mary-le-Bond Street, Piccadilly, London, who were engine lathe and tool manufacturers, for 'an eccentric tool with adjusting screw to carry sundry tools for ornamental purposes'.[22] W. C. Cunninghame Graham of Gartmore also purchased a lathe from London for his country house in Dunbartonshire in 1823 and two years later he had a specialist lathe made to order for personal use.[23] There was clearly a fashion for such activity in this generation of practical men, many having served as soldiers in their youth. A fictional echo of the same preoccupations is found in the elderly Prince Nikolai Bolkonsky in Tolstoy's *War and Peace*, who lives on his early-nineteenth-century country estate where his daily routines included writing his memoirs, studying mathematics, working in the garden and turning wooden snuff boxes on a lathe in his study.[24]

Woodcarving, like lapidary or lathe turning, involved hand skills and masculine tools that attracted wealthy amateurs. It was encouraged as a 'native craft' in many parts of the Highlands in the later nineteenth century to bring much needed income to local people, and it was also a popular hobby for some local elites. One of these was Sir Malcolm M'Neill of Colonsay, who, like many lairds, sold his estate to live in Edinburgh where he made a career in government administration. His *Scotsman* obituary of 1919 praised his public service, but also underscored the preoccupations of his private life. The emphasis on his emotional relationship with the Scottish landscape and with the Celtic past has a romantic resonance that is different to the science that underpinned the lapidary work of Francis Gray and his contemporaries, but both forms of amateur craft were popular amongst men pursuing desk-bound careers, who had the money to purchase the necessary equipment and the time and space to indulge their interests.

> Outside his official work Sir Malcolm M'Neill's chief interest lay in archaeology. The sand dunes of Colonsay and Oransay, with their buried pre-historic remains, were his first happy hunting ground. He loved the Celtic sculptured stones of the Highlands and Islands with a love that not only prompted him to take rubbings and fill note-books with careful outline drawings of their intricate designs, but induced him to learn the craft of wood-carving, so that he might reproduce their often quaint and oftener beautiful designs into the furnishings of his residence at Manor Place. Thus even his home breathed the atmosphere of Oransay and Iona, of Islay and many a lonely spot on the mainland where he had discovered a gem of Celtic art.[25]

Elite men and women cultivated craft practice as a personal creative pursuit and gave patronage to craft as paid employment on their estates or more widely. The two aims often went hand in hand. The Dowager Countess of Dunmore mid century not only supported Peter Gardner's highly successful Dunmore Pottery in Stirlingshire, her daughter-in-law collaborated with Gardner, providing designs for some of his celebrated exhibition pieces and taking a practical interest in ceramics.[26] Countess Ishbel Aberdeen, who sponsored Irish and Highland craft villages at exhibitions and founded craft-training schools in rural Aberdeenshire, in her later memoirs recorded that as a child in the 1850s she spent part of the year on the family estate in Inverness-shire, where she learned the 'mysteries' of spinning from an old peasant woman and 'from the wool of our own sheep, spun black and white plaids for my father, and for such special friends as Mr Gladstone and the old Duke of Westminster'.[27] Lady Anne Speirs of Houston House in Renfrewshire, patron of the domestic embroidery industry, was a fine practitioner of the craft in her own right who also sponsored and managed exhibition displays of goods made by local women, including in Chicago in 1893.[28] Understanding the meaning of these practices in connection with patronage can only be speculation, yet it appears there was a romantic form of escapism embedded in such craftworking amongst elite practitioners, for not only did the crafts fulfil the functions of creative 'hobbies', sometimes with health benefits since they required physical application, they also provided connections, however fanciful, with people, land and a sense of the past.

SHOPS, BOOKS AND MAGAZINES

Various shops catered for the needs of the amateur crafter. A type of business that had flourished in big cities since the later eighteenth century were the artists' suppliers, who were often also print sellers and had stocks of materials for painting and drawing, for stencilling, gilding and japanning and for the popular paper crafts favoured by women such as silhouette cutting, découpage and artificial flower making.[29] One such shop was owned by John Steell, carver, gilder and print seller in Edinburgh who went bankrupt in 1819. The lengthy and well-documented sequestration process reveals his retail stock in fashionable Hanover Street and before that in his shop in Aberdeen. He sold articles for ladies' fancy work, sketch books and artist materials intended mainly for the amateur.[30] There were ornamental, patterned and fancy papers, ladies' workboxes, screens for decorating, which was a popular hobby of the day, and ivory handles for the screens.[31] An Edinburgh contemporary in nearby Princes Street called his shop the 'Amateur and Artists' Repository' and newspaper advertising called attention 'to his stock of fancy goods, consisting of coloured and ornamental papers, fire screens, card pack white wood work etc he would solicit the attention of the ladies'.[32] The interiors of shops such as these were comfortably furnished to encourage leisurely browsing. A later business catering for the wealthy amateur was that owned by William Macgill, which was founded in Hanover Street in 1841 and moved to Princes Street in 1866. Macgill traded as an artists' colourman selling paints and papers, card and mounting boards, small, prepared pieces of ivory for painting on, and cases and frames for displaying miniatures. Some of his stock comprised brand-named Windsor & Newton artist materials for the amateur, including paint in tubes and prepared paint boxes, which simplified the painting process for those without the technical ability to make up their own paints from the raw materials and kept materials fresh and accessible for the weekend artist.[33]

Macgill published a catalogue for mail orders in the 1850s, which was appended to a guidebook titled *The Art of Flower Painting* and from the 1860s his Princes Street premises included a photographic studio.[34] Another Edinburgh shop, whose attractive exterior appearance and window display for browsing can be gauged from an elaborately illustrated advertising sheet, was that owned by Daniel Macintosh, which he called the 'Repository of Arts'.[35] Macintosh was the publisher in 1816 of a small volume titled *Twelve Etchings of Views in Edinburgh by an Amateur*. It is possible the 'amateur' was himself or his wife. Similar shops could also be found in fashionable parts of Glasgow and in some smaller towns. Dumfries in south-west Scotland, for instance, was the place of business for Thomas A. Currie, a bookseller, stationer and artists' colourman, who died in 1856 with his extensive stock-in-trade, including artists' materials, fancy papers, papier mâché goods, writing and work desks, sold by auction in Glasgow.[36]

Shops selling fancy textile and embroidery supplies were found in all significant towns and cities. Their stock included Berlin wool for tapestry work, which was popular amongst amateurs from the 1840s. The wool came from Merino sheep and was soft and easy to use, but its appeal was also fuelled by advances in the German aniline dying industry from the 1830s, with this type of wool available in a wide variety of bright colours. German manufacturers produced tapestry design charts as single sheets with colour guides for the novice.[37] A surviving bill of 1845 issued to the Marchioness of Breadalbane by A. Mullar & Co.'s Berlin Warehouse at 44 Princes Street for £17 4s 11d suggests a hobby that was undertaken by women of the highest ranks.[38] The illustrated billhead features the shopfront with window displays of textile panels and decorated fire screens of a sort that might have been made by the amateur. John Taylor & Sons, Edinburgh cabinetmakers, designed and retailed Berlin work footstools with embroidered tops ready-made, but they also offered a bespoke service for making up furnishing items using amateur-produced tapestry and embroidery, as it announced in 1855 as part of a larger advertisement for their 'cabinet furniture manufactured in their own works'. 'T. & S. devote great attention to the Making Up of SEWED WORK into CHAIRS, OTTOMANS, CUSHIONS, FENDER and FOOTSTOOLS and they execute Designs specially to suit the WORK.'[39]

Berlin wool retail was often combined with private classes for perfecting fancy needlework techniques, particularly in Edinburgh as advertised in the *Scotsman* in 1863: 'New Berlin Wool Repository, 7 Dublin Street, Opened by Mrs J. Matheson (late Miss Jane Mitchell), for many years with Miss McKerrecher, 50 Frederick Street. Instructions given in Knitting, Netting, Crochet, etc. Terms Moderate.'[40] The same sorts of retail outlets also advertised exhibitions and competitions for the amateur craftswoman in the later nineteenth century: 'Edinburgh and Mid-Lothian 3rd Annual Homeworkers' Competitive Industrial Exhibition in Waverley Market. £300 in prizes for work of every description . . . [details] to be had everywhere from Fancy and Berlin Wool Shops.'[41]

In another advertisement aimed at leisured women interested in 'painting on glass and velvet', Mrs John Ball, who travelled from city to city including both Edinburgh and Glasgow and described herself as 'Professor of Painting' with royal and aristocratic patronage, undertook to teach women this 'elegant accomplishment' in just four days by a 'method peculiar to herself'. She advised her clients that 'prepared velvet, colour and every requisite for painting can be purchased of Mrs John Ball at her residence'.[42]

Tools and materials aimed at the amateur craftsman were advertised by retailers, as in 1843 when Thomas Russell of Hunter Square in Edinburgh, who was listed as an ironmonger in the *City Directory*, placed a notice in the *Scotsman* for 'Artists' and Mechanics' Tools'. He invited his 'subscribers' to inspect his present stock which, 'whether it respects quality, extent, or variety, will be found worthy of the attention alike of the amateur as of the ordinary artist or mechanic'.[43] That middle-class men acquired such tools and they were also available through second-hand sales is evident from household auctions, as in April 1861 when the contents of a house at 42 Moray Place, Edinburgh, was advertised and included 'substantial and elegant furniture, magnificent mirrors, range of bookcases, amateur turning lathe and the usual requisites for dining, drawing and bedrooms, library, lobby, kitchen etc'.[44] In Glasgow a few years later a collection of 'excellent household furniture' for sale, 'of a family moving to the country', included 'two excellent tool chests, with a superior assortment of gentleman's jobbing tools of the best quality'.[45] On the same day, another sale of household furniture belonging to the late Thomas Hutchins Esq. listed a large array of comfortable effects from a west-end townhouse, along with 'an elegant small turning lathe, with polished oak frame, lapidary's lathe etc.'[46] As we have seen, cutting and polishing stones using a lapidary's lathe, which featured in the range of skills favoured by Scottish jewellers, was a popular hobby in Scotland amongst those who also collected stones and natural specimens as amateur geologists. Thomas Hutchins was a surgeon and with his scientific background may well have made an amateur study of rocks and minerals of the sort that is easily found in Scotland and when polished makes an attractive display in specimen cabinets.[47]

In addition to advertising craft materials and tools for the amateur, local newspapers gave frequent notices and reviews of books of instruction. These included, in 1851, a review of *Turning and Mechanical Manipulation, Intended as a Work of General Reference and Practical Instruction on the Lathe, and the Various Mechanical Pursuits Followed by Amateurs*, by Charles Holtzapffel, which was intended for gentlemen interested in woodworking, small-scale metalworking, polishing and grinding.[48] Serial publications moved into the hobby-craft field in the 1880s, with widely advertised journals such as *Amateur Work Illustrated*, which was 'edited by the author of *Every Man His Own Mechanic* and included designs and working drawing for wood models and small-scale engineering projects. It offered advice on tools and home-handyman repairs and answered readers' letters and queries.[49] The *Scotsman* published regular lists of books and magazines offering 'useful employments for leisure hours' such as a *Manual of Wood-Carving, Fret-Cutting and Perforated Carving* or *Paper-Rosette Work*.[50] Or there was the journal *Useful Arts and Handicrafts*, which in 1900 highlighted the use of bent iron for decoration and sought to show 'how the amateur may, with comparative ease, acquire proficiency in making many little knick-knacks for the home with strips of bent iron, copper, or brass, which can be purchased in cut sizes from dealers. The tools needed are few and inexpensive.'[51] Other editions of the same serial in the same year were focused on glass painting and leading and also 'pyrography', which claimed that 'by a small poker heated by vapour, gas, or electricity, beautiful designs can be burned on the surface of wood, as well as pictorial work, in the shape of panels and screens'.[52] Women's magazines and newspaper columns similarly advised on craft pursuits and techniques. The *Lady's Realm*, an illustrated monthly published in London from the 1890s with the 'new woman' in mind, gave advice on decorating a child's nursery using paint and textile appliqué, Christmas cracker making and sewing needlework miniatures.[53] Several magazines with a home-craft focus that survive to the present were founded in the years immediately before the First World War, including *Woman's Weekly*, established in 1911 and noted for its knitting patterns. Publications such as these set the scene for the great flourishing post-war of numerous magazines for teaching home crafts among suburban women, where the idea of the 'housewife-citizen' responsible for creating a virtuous home was promoted through sewing, embroidery and cooking for families.[54]

CLASSES AND INSTRUCTION

Craft classes for the well-off amateur were widely available throughout the nineteenth century. Classes for the poor were fewer and rarely undertaken just for leisure. The early industrial design schools founded from the 1830s had numerous 'recreational' students, particularly teenage girls from middle-class families, who attended art, design and craft classes during the day, with early morning and evening classes attended by male students in full-time employment. At the Glasgow School of Design in 1853, there were 183 female students described as having 'no occupation', 147 schoolboy students and 638 male students in employment mainly in the textile and engineering industries. The day-time amateurs paid considerably more for their teaching than the subsidised working-class men.[55] Other institutional providers of craft training for amateurs in the first half of the century included mechanics' institutes, which was where Edinburgh carver and gilder John Steell gave classes following his retirement from retail business. Known as the Edinburgh School of Arts for the Instruction of Mechanics, it was founded in 1821 and was a pioneering part of the workers' self-improvement movement that flourished in Britain and was served by publications such as the widely distributed *Mechanics' Magazine*, with its observations on popular science and engineering. Supported by a raft of Scottish intellectuals, included those linked to the *Edinburgh Review*, it operated in part around a system of member self-instruction, with, for instance, classes in geometry taught by a local joiner and a cabinetmaker. Within a few months of foundation, the School of Arts for Mechanics had attracted 450 students, all men, who paid 15s a year for mainly evening instruction and access to a library.[56] Classes were held in the Freemasons' Hall in Niddry Street in the Old Town.[57] The main aims of the mechanics' institutes was the practical application of science, but along the way craft instruction in areas like carving, modelling and drawing was also given for self-improvement and 'agreeable, harmless and rational recreation for leisure hours'.[58] In the later 1830s, John Steell's 'ornamental modelling class' was held weekly during the winter sessions on Tuesdays and Thursdays starting at 8.30 p.m.[59]

For the working population, participation in purely amateur and non-remunerative craftwork was a rare luxury because of the cost of materials and access to tools. Not surprisingly, therefore, most of those who attended mechanics' institute classes were drawn from the labouring elite with good employment and incomes. Yet there is ample evidence of interest in making and exhibiting elsewhere which meant that certain forms of craft instruction was supplied by charities. Craft classes for the

poorer working population were developed in a systematic way by the
Home Arts and Industries Association, a philanthropic and activist body
operating across Britain. Founded in 1884 as the Cottage Arts Association and connected in some of its aims and supporters with the Arts and
Crafts movement, it was described as intended for 'reviving and teaching the practice of village arts and handiwork of all kinds, and for the
encouragement of those who were glad to use their spare time in making
useful and pretty things for their own homes'.[60] The Association was set
up by Eglantyne Louisa Jebb in Shropshire following a model created
in the United States, with royal patronage, headquarters in the Royal
Albert Hall in London and instruction from trained volunteers. By 1913
it was operating c.200 classes with about 5,000 students engaged in a
range of crafts that embraced,

> simple carpentry, wood-carving, inlaying and veneering, wrought-iron work,
> hand-beaten silver and other metal work, basket-work, rush matting, hand-
> weaving and spinning, carpet and rug making, toy-making, lace-making,
> embroidery, smocking, knitting, pottery, plain and ornamental leather-work,
> bookbinding, stencilling etc.[61]

The intended students included ordinary working men and women,
mostly taking classes for recreation and the disabled and military veter-
ans hoping to develop remunerative skills. A revival of the body and its
classes following the First World War was focused on the needs of injured
ex-servicemen.[62] In parts of rural Britain the emphasis was on teaching
young people who could then move into craft employment, with clusters
of such workers established in the West Country where there was a revival
of Honiton lace making and there were groups of weavers and wool spin-
ners in rural Wiltshire and Dorset. In other areas the target group was
teenage boys and men, with the philanthropic and patronising intent of
giving them rewarding ways of spending their free time. 'The work is
meant to be to these rough lads and men what our music and picture-
galleries and our water-colour sketching and, in part, what our reading of
novels and poetry, are to us . . .'[63] The Association gave training to its volunteer teachers, who were mostly middle-class women and emphasised
design and drawing as the basis of instruction with the aim of encouraging creativity in the pupils, though according to one observer, most of the
male students were only interested in 'tool work'.[64] The classes, which
were free, provided both equipment and materials, though students were
expected to pay for the latter if they sold what they made.

A particular aim of the Home Arts and Industries Association in its first
incarnation was 'to provide pleasant and sympathetic intercourse between
the educated and the poor, and to enable the possessors of Art knowledge

and culture to impart their gifts to those who are without either'.[65] A moralising agenda was especially apparent in rural situations where peasant populations were the primary objectives. The Irish and Highland manifestations of the HAIA were developed by female aristocrats including Lady Aberdeen and the Duchess of Sutherland as patronage devices for support of 'traditional' peasant production such as lacemaking, tweed or knitwear and an emphasis on sales through city shops and international exhibitions.[66] With a different moralising intent, Lady Victoria Campbell, a pious spinster closely associated with the Scottish Celtic Christian revival, sponsored local training in woodcarving for the beautification of the churches she founded.[67] These often-criticised interventions in the lives of the rural poor were different in spirit to the work of the Home Arts and Industries Association in urban places where the working-class amateur and his or her recreation was the primary objective, as described with reference to an exhibition that was organised by the Kirkcaldy HAIA, which had 'opened up possibilities of happy hours spent in the delight of absorbing occupation and artistic production'.[68]

It was not only traditional elites who sponsored craft training as recreation for the poor but also the intellectual middle classes living in cities. The Edinburgh Social Union was established in 1884 with multiple objectives to ameliorate the lot of the urban working class, including inner-city renewal, improved housing and social reform. Patrick Geddes was one of the founders. The model for the body was Octavia Hill's Kyrle Society in London, which sought to improve surroundings and 'bring beauty home to the people'.[69] A branch of the Kryle Society was established in Glasgow, though the cultural ambition was soon sidelined as the scale of urban degeneration came to dominate its philanthropic agendas.[70] In Edinburgh, however, cultural enhancement and beautification remained a feature of the work of the Social Union, which included garden and window-box planting, the decorating of public buildings and the teaching of art and craft classes. The aim of the Edinburgh Social Union was to generate a 'more co-operative, egalitarian and cultured society' and it was heavily influenced by prevailing social philosophies such as Secular Positivism and the Arts and Crafts movement, with a socialist slant.[71] At the founding meeting, one of the three major strands of ESU activity was established in the form of craft classes to be organised across the city. In March 1885, for example, woodcarving lessons were begun by Florence Sellar from studios in Lynedoch Place and Shandwick Place in the fashionable west end, whilst Mary Louise Maclagan, a bookbinder, gave classes in bookbinding mainly to women. The second annual account of the work of the ESU, which was widely reported in the press, noted that the art and craft classes had been brought under the superintendence of Professor Baldwin Brown of the University and now included woodcarving, embossed work in brass and copper, clay modelling and metal repoussé work, with plans for embossed leather work and mosaic underway. Classes in Corstophine and Murrayfield were described as flourishing and it was also reported that the Edinburgh organisation had supplied models and patterns for an offshoot in Rothsay on the Isle of Bute. There was another branch in Dalry in Ayrshire.[72] Parallel 'Recreative Evening School' classes for children in working-class districts of Edinburgh included ESU-sponsored woodcarving for boys and needlework for girls.[73] Yet despite the overt aim to provide classes for the poor, the shifting agenda of the ESU towards a middle-class and professional client group in its provision of what were termed 'industrial art classes' was captured in a short report in the *Edinburgh Evening News* in December 1890:

> The Social Union now rents from Mr D. W. Stevenson, RSA, the lower portion of the Dean Studios, Lyndoch Place. A forge has been constructed in a convenient position, where the simpler processes of wrought iron work may be studied under a professional teacher . . . The society believes that there are many members of the artistic professions in Edinburgh, especially those studying, or in the practice of architecture, who will be glad of the opportunity of becoming practically acquainted with the use of some of the chief decorative materials.[74]

Moreover, some branches of the training were so successful that participants became commercially motivated professionals in all but name. Notable here was the bookbinding class, with work undertaken by the mainly lady participants widely displayed beyond Edinburgh, as in Liverpool in May 1899 as part of the exhibition of the Guild of Women Binders.[75]

Despite its sometimes-conflicted ambitions to teach amateur crafts with recreation in mind, examples of craftwork from the ESU were exhibited at the Edinburgh International Exhibition of 1886, including 'six decorative panels in oil monochrome prepared for Ward 30, Royal Infirmary, carvings etc, all done by ladies'.[76] The same group displayed their efforts at the Decorative Arts Exhibition in Edinburgh in November 1888, though the quality of the 'workmanship' did not impress one exhibition reviewer.[77] The Outlook Tower on Castlehill, which was established by Patrick Geddes in 1892 as a centre for education, also provided a venue for exhibitions and sales of craftwork from the classes hosted by the ESU.[78] But class ambiguities were rife. By the mid 1890s exhibitions such as the one at the Lower Dean Studio in Lyndoch Place distinguished between displays of craftworks undertaken for an 'artisan section' by the 'lads and girls of the working classes' who practised 'simple forms of handicraft' and those produced by 'young ladies' who were nominally amateurs, though their numbers included Phoebe Traquair, the celebrated artist, and Hannah Lorimer, sister of the architect, a painter, sculptor and embroiderer with a university education who taught art in her own right and also ran postal art classes.[79]

AMATEUR EXHIBITION

Amateur painters were favoured with venues for exhibition long before it became commonplace to see amateur craftworks on public display. Some of these exhibitions from the 1820s or 1830s were connected to the art schools or the private teachers who gave classes. Prominent amongst the latter were the daughters of Edinburgh landscape artist Alexander Nasmyth, whose work was regularly displayed in a semi-professional capacity in the annual Royal Institution winter exhibition alongside that of their genteel female tutees.[80]

Other than student work exhibited through the design schools, there seems to be little record of amateur craftwork on public display before the 1851 Great Exhibition, when a number of items made by individuals, both professional and amateur, were forwarded by local committees for consideration by a London selection panel. They included as exhibit number 218, a 'table-cover, consisting of 2,000 pieces of cloth, arranged into twenty-three historical and imagined characters . . . The design and execution is the sole work of the exhibitor, and has occupied his leisure hours for eighteen years' submitted by J. Johnstone of 102 Graham Street, Airdrie.[81] This section of the Great Exhibition, covering 'tapestry, carpets, floor cloths, laces and embroidery' attracted many amateur entries, such as exhibit number 139, a 'carpet of thirty squares, bordered, worked in Berlin wool by the exhibitor and her friends'. Or, 117 from M. Burton, of Liberton Bank, Edinburgh, 'a shawl, table-cover, rug etc., knitted on wires by an aged person'.[82] The personal circumstance of the craft practitioner was clearly an important part of the narrative attached to objects on display, whether they were produced during the leisure hours of a working man or by an 'aged person'. The second half of the nineteenth century saw countless opportunities for the amateur exhibitor, with a powerful set of cultural associations drawn in exhibition catalogues between the object and the circumstances or context that gave rise to such craftsmanship. The second London International Exhibition in 1862 included a notable

body of photographic work submitted by Scots who were members of the
Amateur Photographic Association as well as several amateurs listed in
the woodcarving section.[83]

National exhibitions mounted in Edinburgh sometimes included
amateur sections for mainly middle-class and elite enthusiasts. Displays
of amateur carving were prominent at the Edinburgh Decorative Arts
Exhibition in 1888.

> There are several fine panels carved by Dr and Mrs M'Laren, an antique
> chair by Mrs Dundas of Auchtertyre and a beautiful inlaid ebony and ivory
> cabinet by General Sir F. W. Hamilton, carvings of heads and vine leaves
> by Miss Lorimer, sister of the artist, and an oak cabinet by Mr T. Reekie,
> Bonnington.[84]

But it was the local exhibitions that took a decisive shift in emphasis
towards the complex agendas represented by the working-class amateur,
including the 1865 Industrial Exhibition in Glasgow that was mounted
by the Central Working Men's Club and Institute of 153 Trongate and
advertised as an 'exhibition of works of art and skill by the working
people of Glasgow and neighbouring towns'.[85] At the opening in mid
December 1865, speeches of praise were given in favour of workers'
rights and collective action though little was said about the purposes
of the exhibition itself.[86] Some of the objectives behind the exhibition,
which attracted over 400 individual entries, were laid bare in a public
presentation to a 'Working Men's Temperance Society' in Dumfries a few
months later.

> Mr David Fortune gave an interesting account of the Central Working Men's
> Club and Exhibition in Glasgow, of which he is secretary, and afterwards
> delivered a most stirring temperance address, in which he delineated the
> evils of the intoxicating cup in a very forcible manner. He also dilated upon
> the beneficial influences exercised by such institutions as he had described,
> and eloquently advocated their extension to provincial towns like Dumfries.
> He felt convinced that great comfort would thereby accrue to the working-
> classes; and that such means, operating in conjunction with other agencies,
> would tend to elevate them morally and socially.[87]

The aims, which clearly included collective moral and social improvement for the working classes, the principles of rational recreation and
a strong temperance message, were reflected in some of the Glasgow
1865 catalogue entries with their stress on evening work undertaken at
home. Following the closure of the exhibition, some exhibits were put
on permanent display, 'their object being . . . to provide a place of profitable resort for the working classes, who form a large proportion of the

population and for whom but few places of recreation of an elevating tendency are provided'.[88]

Commentators on amateur exhibitions elsewhere in Britain elaborated on the moral and improving value they represented for both the visitor and the exhibitor. For the working-class spectator, they were a source of enjoyment and of 'cheerfulness with which they will return to their labour'. The wealthy 'will see in it with what passionate interest the poor man can follow out some small work, perhaps of no importance in itself, but which has been the occupation of many a leisure hour and the thought of many a wakeful night'. And for the amateur craftworker themselves,

> It is a new and interesting feature of these exhibitions that they afford to the artisan class the opportunity of exhibiting any works which they may have produced and which are not peculiar to their trades . . . it is a great thing for a man to feel that he is not a mere machine, or part of a machine . . . there is something divine in him which gives him the power of understanding and appreciating other things besides his mechanical work, and which thus places him in conjunction and sympathy with minds higher than his own.[89]

Exhibitions organised locally by trades bodies or working men's institutes remained a feature of amateur craft practice through the second half of the nineteenth century and beyond. They included the 1887 Dundee Exhibition of Industry, sponsored by the Dundee and District United Trades Council, which was focused on 'ingenious' exhibits with patent aspirations and the 'skilful workman and amateur'.[90] The Aberdeen Industrial Exhibition was held in 1891 and in addition to many objects submitted by working men and women, also included a newly fashionable Arts and Crafts agenda driven by reforming middle classes.[91] The previous year saw the first of a series of Glasgow East-End Industrial Exhibitions, whose main purpose was to raise funds for the creation of a 'People's Palace' in the east end of the city, with profits also going to such other charitable bodies with a working-class focus as the Royal Infirmary. According to the *Scotsman*, an event such as this was designed to give the working classes 'a much needed opportunity . . . for the production of inventions, specialities, works of utility and ingenious handicraft and in this way fulfil important functions little recognised in more imposing international exhibitions'.[92] Remarkably, this series of exhibitions was under the guidance of David Fortune, the temperance reformer who had organised the 1865 exhibition for the Central Working Men's Club in Glasgow and spent part of his long career as Keeper of the University Museum in Glasgow. Fortune, who described exhibitions as 'his hobby', was the son of a master plumber, had trained as a printer-compositor and was married to a seamstress.[93] The commitment to amateur craft exhibition as a moral good continued into the early twentieth century. The Musselburgh Industrial Exhibition of 1908, which included adult and child exhibitors and was under the patronage of the local gentry, advertised its purpose in press reports of the opening speeches given by some of the gathered dignitaries:

> Lady Helen said the object of the Association, as she understood it, was two-fold – first, to develop the aesthetic taste and creative genius of its members: and, secondly, to encourage all those forms of industry which could be carried on in the home, and which were mainly directed to increasing the beauty, the attractiveness, and well-being of home life. In this respect, the Association opposed its influence to a tendency which would make people seek amusement and interest in the outside world instead of in the home and family.[94]

ARTS AND CRAFTS MOVEMENT

Amateur craft was flourishing by the later nineteenth century, informed by multiple strands of ideology, creative self-expression and philanthropy. One connection of note was that forged with the Arts and Crafts movement in Scotland and beyond. The Arts and Crafts philosophy was expressed in some of the bodies already examined including the Home Arts and Industries Associations and the Edinburgh Social Union. Indeed, founder of the latter, Patrick Geddes, was moved to break his connection with the ESU, which he intended to be a radical agent for the betterment of the poor, because he felt it had been subsumed within a more conventional Arts and Crafts dynamic, which saw middle-class and elite women artists and crafters as the main beneficiaries of the teaching and exhibitions.[95]

As a social movement designed to reverse the demoralising impact of modern industrial production, Arts and Crafts theorists were convinced of the power of handwork to change people's lives, be they rich or poor, old or young, and including amateurs alongside the artisan who worked for a living. In 1916, in the printed catalogue to accompany the annual London Arts and Crafts exhibition, the moral and citizenship value of craftwork was claimed,

> The child who realizes by experiment the delight and obligation of workmanship will alone make the complete citizen. The man who cannot use his hands in some craft is an intellectual cripple, a deficient, and all his work suffers from that lack.[96]

The movement, which was founded in London in 1887 under the title the Arts and Crafts Exhibition Society, though the ideas behind it and many key personnel were active long before that date, was strongly committed to education and practical instruction and inevitably some of those who started as 'amateurs' became sufficiently skilled and empowered by the training and philosophy to become 'professionals', with income and recognition to match. For some, however, such as Edinburgh artist, designer and jewellery maker Phoebe Traquair, the distinction was probably irrelevant since they had sufficient means from other sources to live comfortably.[97]

Superficially and according to prevailing ideology, there should have been no cause for conflict between the professional Arts and Crafts adherents who worked for a living and the amateur. But reality was different. One cause of contemporary tension was gendered around the mainly male commercial craft practitioners and the mostly female, middle-class amateurs, the former believing that the latter should stick to traditional womanly interests, decorating their homes or making things for family members rather than public display and sale for profit.[98] This tension was made worse by the low prices that amateurs often charged for their work which undercut and devalued the craftsman or craftswoman working for a living. The problem was highlighted by Francis Newberry, head of Glasgow School of Art and an important Arts and Crafts figure in Scotland, in a published review of the Edinburgh 1888 Decorative Handiwork Exhibition:

> The popular taste is never the highest taste, and in catering for the fancy of the hour, lady amateurs who dispose of their work at a low price, should bear in mind their poorer sisters in art, whom they may drive out of the market, which, like other markets is in its lower departments greatly overstocked with applicants for employment.[99]

Another tension between the professional and the amateur, with the former identified as predominantly male and the latter as leisured and female, was focused on access to training. Under the title 'Suggested Arts Club for Women in Edinburgh' the *Scotsman* reported in December 1913 on a talk given to the Arts and Crafts Club at the Lower Dean Studio in Edinburgh by F. Morley Fletcher, Director of the Edinburgh College of Art, who was also a painter and printmaker. Having sketched the history of the Arts and Crafts movement and its role in advancing the quality of craftwork in Britain, particularly through craft training schools, he went on to remark:

> The movement had spread widely and had suffered deterioration where it had degenerated into classes for the amateur . . . He spoke of the danger to arts schools of the amateur student, as compared with the student coming from a distinct trade or profession . . . In art no less than in music the superficial amateur would always be a difficulty. Mr Fletcher regretted any harm that had been done to the classes at the Dean Studio by the College of Art, and suggested the formation of an Arts Club for women, for which there seemed a real need at present in Edinburgh.[100]

The message was clearly one that tied middle-class women amateurs to declining standards in art and craft training. The reaction of the audience, of which many, if not the majority, will have been women, is not recorded.

By the end of the nineteenth century, the world of art-craft production as represented by the Arts and Crafts movement was certainly overcrowded, with women makers increasingly prominent and the amateur's encroachment on professional reputations and sales resented. That is not to say that all craftworkers who made a living from handwork were scornful of the amateur. One of the *Scotsman*'s 'artisan reporters' on the 1878 Paris exhibition, Alexander Forrester, a master cabinetmaker, gave a detailed account of the cabinetmaker displays in Paris that included furniture and woodcarving exhibits sent from Scotland. One spectacular item caught his well-trained eye:

> The only other Scotch production we have to notice is the Helicon Fountain carved in boxwood by Mr Peter Cairns of Portobello. This has been seen by many in the Industrial Exhibition previous to it being sent off to Paris, and one has a feeling of regret that the maker should not have been a wood carver, as in all likelihood he would have excelled in that or even higher art work. It is a remarkable amateur production.[101]

The object described here has survived and is now owned by the Smith Art Gallery and Museum in Stirling. It was carved by Peter Cairns while employed as a servant of the Duke of Buccleuch at Dalkeith Palace and it reputedly took him seven years to complete, working in the evening and on days off. It was exhibited in numerous places over the course of about a decade, possibly with direct personal support from Buccleuch who was a great advocate of the exhibition movement in Scotland. A late-nineteenth-century black-and-white photograph by Stirling photographers D. & J. McEwen suggests that the boxwood carved 'Helicon Fountain' may also have been displayed in their Port Street shop window in Stirling. The object, which is in multiple separately carved pieces, was purchased posthumously from Peter Cairn's family *c*.1900 and donated to the Smith Museum at about the same time.[102]

Notes

1. For background and a twentieth-century focus see Stephen Knott, *Amateur Craft. History and Theory* (London, 2015).
2. Examples of eighteenth-century elite women's activities are given in Clive Edwards, '"Home is where the art is": Women, handicrafts and home improvements 1750–1900', *Journal of Design History*, 19:1 (2006), 11–21.

On craftwork in Bluestocking circles, see Madeleine Pelling, 'Collecting the world: Female friendship and domestic craft at Bulstrode Park', *Journal for Eighteenth-Century Studies*, 41:1 (2018), 101–20.

3. On DIY as artistic expression see the comic novel, George and Weedon Grossmith, *Diary of a Nobody* (1892).

4. Talia Schaffer, 'Women's work: The history of the Victorian domestic handicraft', in Kyriaki Hadjiafxedi and Patricia Zakreski, eds, *Crafting the Woman Professional in the Long Nineteenth Century* (Farnham, 2013), 25–42, 27; Maureen Daly Goggin and Beth Fowkes Tobin, eds, *Women and the Material Culture of Needlework and Textiles, 1750–1959* (Abingdon, 2009).

5. See Talia Schaffer, *Novel Craft: Victorian Domestic Handicraft and Nineteenth-Century Fiction* (Oxford, 2011).

6. Karen Harvey, 'Craftsmen in common: Objects, skills and masculinity in the eighteenth and nineteenth centuries', in Hannah Greig, et al., eds, *Gender and Material Culture in Britain since 1600* (London, 2016); Tim Barringer, *Men at Work: Art and Labour in Victorian England* (New Haven and London, 2005).

7. Clare Rose, 'A patchwork panel "shown at the Great Exhibition"', *V&A Online Journal*, 3:1 (2011).

8. Stephanie Downes, et al., eds, *Feeling Things: Objects and Emotions Through History* (Oxford, 2018).

9. Cynthia Bornhorst-Winslow, 'The important role played by household crafts in the lives of nineteenth-century women in Britain and America', MPhil thesis, Wright State University 2012, 15; Shu-chuan Yan, 'The art of working in hair: Hair jewellery and ornamental handiwork in Victorian Britain', *Journal of Modern Craft*, 12:2 (2019), 123–39.

10. Maya Wassall Smith, '"The fancy work what sailors make": Material and emotional creative practice in masculine seafaring communities', *Nineteenth Century Gender Studies*, 14:2 (2018).

11. McManus Museum and Gallery Dundee. Collections.

12. *Scotsman*, 8 November 1843.

13. Peter C. D. Brears, 'The York spinning wheel makers', *Furniture History*, 14 (1978), 19–22.

14. Carruthers, *Arts and Crafts Movement*, 222, photograph of ladies spinning at Melsetter House, Orkney; *Scotsman*, 10 June 1912, 'Wanted, a good spinning wheel'.

15. *Aberdeen Journal*, 7 November 1860.

16. Royal Collections Trust. RCIN 2105725 Portrait photograph of Queen Victoria by Hill and Saunders, 4 April 1865.

17. *Aberdeen Journal*, 19 July 1865.

18. J. Lewis Andrew, 'Old Sussex farmhouses and their furniture', *The Antiquary*, 34 (June 1898), 172–7. 174.

19. *Scotsman*, 25 January 1935.

20. *Scotsman*, 19 November 1842.
21. Quoted in Alexander Macpherson, *Glimpses of Church and Social Life in the Highlands in Olden Times and Other Papers*, (Edinburgh, 1893), 82.
22. NRS. GD44/51/495/10 and 11. Papers of the Gordon Family, Dukes of Gordon.
23. NRS. GD22/3/348 and 354. Papers of the Cunninghame Graham Family of Ardoch.
24. Leo Tolstoy, *War and Peace* (1869). Chapter 25 gives a description.
25. *Scotsman*, 10 March 1919.
26. *Leicester Chronicle and Leicestershire Mercury*, 27 November 1879, 'The Ladies' Column'.
27. *"We Twa": Reminiscences of Lord and Lady Aberdeen*, 2 vols (London, 1925), vol. 1, 130.
28. *The Royal Commission for the Chicago Exhibition of 1893. Official Catalogue of the British Section* (1893), 452.
29. See Edwards, 'Home is where the art is', for London examples.
30. *Aberdeen Journal*, 21 May 1806.
31. NRS. CS96/415/1. Sequestration of John Steell, Edinburgh. Sederunt books 1819–25.
32. *Scotsman*, 21 December 1825.
33. Details on Windsor & Newton given in Knott, *Amateur Craft*.
34. NPG. British Artists' Suppliers, 1650–1950, William Macgill.
35. Iain Gordon Brown, 'Daniel Macintosh and the Repository of Arts', *Book of the Old Edinburgh Club*, 7 (2008), 171–5.
36. *Glasgow Herald*, 14 April 1856.
37. Pat Berman, 'Berlin work', *Needle Pointers*, February/March 1990.
38. NRS. GD112/35/37/28. Breadalbane Papers. Account due.
39. *Scotsman*, 12 September 1855.
40. *Scotsman,* 5 December 1863.
41. *Scotsman*, 12 September 1899.
42. *Scotsman*, 19 June 1819.
43. *Scotsman*, 15 November 1843.
44. *Scotsman*, 20 April 1861.
45. *Glasgow Herald*, 18 May 1849.
46. Ibid.
47. *Glasgow Directory*, 1848, 440.
48. *Scotsman*, 4 January 1851.
49. *Amateur Work Illustrated: A Practical Magazine of Constructive and Decorative Art and Manual Labour*, was published in Britain and the US throughout the 1880s and reprinted as cheaper annual volumes in the 1890s. It was widely advertised, including in the *Scotsman*.
50. *Scotsman*, 18 October 1878.
51. *Edinburgh Evening News*, 25 January 1900.
52. Ibid.

53. *Lady's Realm*, vol. 19 (1912).

54. Fiona Hackney, 'Quiet activism and the new amateur', *Design and Culture*, 5:2 (2015), 169–93.

55. *Glasgow Herald*, 25 April 1853. See also Nenadic, 'Designers in the fancy textile industry'.

56. Mabel Tylecote, *The Mechanics Institutes of Lancashire and Yorkshire Before 1851* (Manchester, 1957), 15–17.

57. *Scotsman*, 14 September 1822.

58. 'Mechanics' Institutions', *Tait's Edinburgh Magazine*, vol. 5 (1838), 521–6, 522.

59. *Scotsman*, 28 September 1836.

60. Mary Lovelace, 'Home Arts and Industries Association', *Spectator*, 1 November 1919, 12–13.

61. Ibid.

62. Ibid.

63. Bernard Bosanquet, 'The Home Arts and Industries Association: 1 – Aim and objects', *Charity Organization Review*, 4:40 (1888), 135–40.

64. Ibid, 138.

65. *Art Workers' Quarterly*, 3 (1910), 135–38.

66. Helland, *British and Irish Home Arts and Industries*.

67. Balfour, *Lady Victoria Campbell*.

68. *Scotsman*, 23 April 1908.

69. *Spectator*, 29 January 1881; Octavia Hill, 'The Kyrle Society', *Charity Organization Review*, 18:108 (December 1905), 314–19.

70. Helen Meller, *Patrick Geddes: Social Evolutionist and City Planner* (London, 1990), 53.

71. Walter Stephen, *Learning From the Lasses: Women of the Patrick Geddes Circle* (2014), chapter 6.

72. *Glasgow Herald*, 1 February 1887.

73. *Edinburgh Evening News*, 14 October 1887.

74. *Edinburgh Evening News*, 6 December 1890.

75. *Liverpool Mercury*, 29 May 1899.

76. Quoted in Smith, 'Displaying Edinburgh in 1886', 188.

77. *Edinburgh Evening News*, 7 November 1888.

78. *Scotsman*, 19 April 1932, 'The late Professor Sir P. Geddes and the Edinburgh Social Union'.

79. *Edinburgh Evening News*, 1 June 1894; Michelle Atherton, 'The lost Lorimer. Rediscovering the extraordinary life of Hannah Lorimer – Kellie Castle', National Trust for Scotland, Kellie Castle, online essay, 18 July 2019, https://www.nts.org.uk/stories/the-lost-lorimer-rediscovering-the-extraordinary-life-of-hannah-lorimer-kellie-castle (last accessed 15 February 2021).

80. J. C. B. Cooksey, 'Nasmyth family (per.1788–1884), painters and art teachers', *ODNB*, 2004; Frances Irwin, 'Lady amateurs and their masters in Scott's Edinburgh', *The Connoisseur*, 185 (December 1974), 229–37.

81. Quoted in Rose, 'A patchwork panel'.
82. *Official Catalogue of the Great Exhibition of the Works of Industry of All Nations* (1851), 98, 99.
83. *Illustrated Catalogue of the Industrial Department, The International Exhibition of 1862* (1862).
84. *Edinburgh Evening News*, 7 November 1888. General Hamilton, aged in his seventies, was a retired Crimean War veteran who lived in rural Fife.
85. *Paisley Herald and Renfrewshire Advertiser*, 18 November 1865.
86. Ibid., 16 December 1865.
87. *Dumfries and Galloway Standard and Advertiser*, 17 January 1866.
88. *Scotsman*, 11 July 1866.
89. *Scotsman*, 2 September 1865, 'Lord Houghton on Working Men's Exhibitions'.
90. *Dundee Courier and Argus*, 13 August 1887.
91. *Aberdeen Evening Express*, 19 December 1891.
92. *Scotsman*, 6 December 1890.
93. Glasgow Museums Collections Navigator. Biography of David Fortune, 1842–1917.
94. *Scotsman*, 8 April 1908.
95. Meller, *Patrick Geddes*.
96. *Arts & Crafts Exhibition Society: Eleventh Exhibition Catalogue for 1916*, 23.
97. See Hadjiafxendi and Zakreski, eds, *Crafting the Woman Professional*, especially Schaffer, 'Women's work'. There are other relevant essays in this collection on the professional–amateur split.
98. Janice Helland, 'Good work and clever design: Early exhibitions of the Home Arts and Industries Association', *Journal of Modern Craft*, 5:3 (2012), 275–94.
99. From the *Scottish Arts Review*, quoted in Carruthers, *Arts and Crafts Movement*, 46.
100. *Scotsman*, 9 December 1913.
101. *Scotsman*, 13 January 1880, 'Artisan reports on the Paris Exhibition, 1878'.
102. Smith Art Gallery and Museum, 8 September 2017. Blog Post, Collections, Stirling Stories; *Stirling Observer*, 9 June 2017. According to the Portobello listings in the *Edinburgh Post Office Directories* for the 1890s, Peter Cairn's son, with whom he lived in retirement, was a joiner.

Conclusion: Evaluating the Craft Economy

WHEN THE SCOTTISH JOURNALIST David Bremner (*c*.1838–94) published his series of *Scotsman* articles as a book in 1869, titled *The Industries of Scotland Their Rise, Progress and Present Condition*, his purpose was to 'describe the actual state of the chief branches of industry in Scotland' with a view to better informing those charged with managing the industrial economy and the public more widely, in light of increasing competition from Europe.[1] Starting with coal mining and the metal and engineering industries and with extensive discussion of factory-based textile production, Bremner's pioneering commentaries, based on numerous site visits and conversations with businessmen, were well received at the time and have been a source of information since. Though modern industry dominated, Bremner was an accurate reporter on the role of craft processes in factory production – seen, for instance, in the persistence of quality cotton printing done by hand using engraved wood blocks alongside machine printing – and several chapters focus on sectors where craftwork was the norm. They include the manufacture of plate and jewellery, sewed muslin and tweed making, glass cutting, engraving and staining. Aspects of pottery manufacture, which he reported in detail, wrought-iron making and even the fast-changing book printing industry were craft-based in the later nineteenth century. Bremner delineated numerous craft processes and offered insights into skilled workers' distinctive social characteristics and training. An example is furnished in his account of the slate works in northern Argyll: 'The workmen are all natives of Ballachulish or of the hamlet of Glencoe, which lies about a mile inland . . . One reason why there are so few strangers is, that no adult can learn to split and dress slates so expertly as those who have been trained to the work from boyhood.'[2] His observations as a well-informed journalist underscored a commonplace understanding of the day, that the modern Scottish economy was only partly mechanised and factories co-existed with smaller workplaces or skilled self-employment making use of traditional hand technologies. Bremner recognised change and his commentaries are framed by narratives explaining the history of each industry. But he also saw the degree to which craft practice and culture was embedded in individual businesses, including, in some instances, noting the craft background and skills of the businessmen whose firms he visited. The apprentice training of craftworkers was described by Bremner along with trade union activity to protect wages and know-how. He gave considerable attention to the exhibition of goods, reinforcing relationships between craftwork and hand skills and the presence in Scotland of vibrant and competitive modern industries. Whilst he did not call this phenomenon 'flexible specialisation', that is what he described.

David Bremner's industrial survey of Scotland was unique for the time, but had he looked further afield to England, Europe or North America he would have seen similar. Flexible specialisation was usual everywhere because it was defined by technologies and rational economic organisation. The application of new techniques was uneven and handwork survived and thrived alongside factory production, as classic studies of England and France have found.[3] Workshop situations defined by flexible specialisation and artisan-led industrialisation are apparent in North America as a detailed analysis of Hamilton, Ontario, has revealed, showing many parallels with Scotland, which is perhaps not surprising when so many Scots migrated to Canada and workplace cultures owe much to this diaspora.[4] Comparative studies of industrial modernisation in Britain, Europe and Asia reveal many parallels.[5] In India, where it has long been assumed the British empire project effectively destroyed local craft, recent research suggests otherwise with considerable craftworker resilience and thriving traditional industries that survive to the present, particularly in textiles.[6] The Arts and Crafts movement flourished in various but recognisable forms throughout the West and also in India, often drawing inspiration from the same British writers and reacting to the same crisis of modernism.[7] Tourists everywhere, and many were British, expected to buy souvenirs.[8] England had its Whitby jet jewellery makers, there were handmade linen weavers in the Lake District, and Ireland had its bog oak carvers and lacemakers. All represented localised clusters of adaptive craft businesses serving the tourist market of a similar sort to those found in Scotland.

Of course, there were differences also. Tensions between industrialisation and the persistence of craftworkers was politicised elsewhere in ways unseen in Scotland or England. Guild structures were tenacious in many parts of Europe, ensuring a greater presence of craftworkers and their interests in local politics, trade protection and citizenship debates.[9] The role of women craftworkers in family business contexts could vary.[10] Artisan making and craftworker authority were particularly strong in cities with long traditions of luxury goods production, particularly in Paris as was noted by the several 'artisan reporters' sent from Scotland to the Paris international exhibition of 1878. Political turmoil in nineteenth-century Europe hit craftworkers hard, with much displacement across the continent following the revolutions of 1848, which led, amongst other migrations, to the movement of many Bohemian glassworkers to Britain.[11] British artisans also emigrated to Europe, as with craft lacemakers from the Nottingham area who, driven out of work by factory-made lace in the 1820s and 1830s, settled across Europe and especially in Calais, taking their mix of small-scale machinery and hand production and adapting output to local markets. Their fortunes collapsed with the upheavals of 1848, when anti-British feelings set in.[12] The role of folk craft in Europe was also different to that in Scotland, with stronger connections with national identities at a time of fractious state formation. Folk revivals were politicised in Germany, Hungary and across Scandinavia.[13] Material culture in the form of traditional craft-made clothing or decorative techniques kept the idea of the nation alive in Poland when the country was subject to decades of foreign control.[14] With later and swifter industrialisation in many countries, home-based peasant production of folk crafts underwent a more rapid decline than Britain experienced a century before and prompted more concerted efforts to keep them alive. Sometimes, as in Scotland and Ireland, it was elite landowners and women especially who took the initiative. Russian nobles in the last few decades of the nineteenth century supported folk-art revivals on their estates on a remarkable scale.[15] The 'peasant art movement' was manifested in different ways in its different contexts even within Britain, shaped by politics and issues of identity and with differing manifestations of authenticity and cultural appropriation.[16] Those most modern of mass industrial spectacles, the international exhibitions, held popular displays of craft which were not just of Scottish Highland or Irish peasant origin, though these were seen across Europe and North America. Scottish exhibitions included European lacemakers as well as Indian artisans in traditional dress and displays of peasant dress and folk art were witnessed across Europe.[17]

The richness of Bremner's commentaries when viewed through a broader international lens underlines the degree to which it is hard to disentangle the world of craft production and its contribution to the

Scottish economy from machine production. This final chapter does, however, seek to arrive at some conclusions on the significance of artisans and craftwork for later-nineteenth- and early-twentieth-century Scotland.

EMPLOYMENT

We can start by considering the importance of different forms of craft employment by the end of the century. In some parts of the country, particularly where the home industries movement was active, craft production provided employment for women and men where none other existed. In the Highlands and Islands in 1914 the considered response from the government investigator into 'home industries' employment, economist W. R. Scott, was that there were 'good grounds for regarding the future of these industries with a considerable degree of confidence, providing their development is guided wisely'.[18] But Scott, a university professor, also observed how remuneration was low, middlemen sometimes made excessive and much-resented profits at the expense of workers and fashion-driven demand for consumer goods such as fine textiles was fickle. The numbers of different craft-based industries that then existed in the Highlands was considerable, employing large numbers of people, with the female-dominated tweed-weaving and hand-knitting sectors particularly prominent. Yet in numerous places, according to Scott, the long hours of unpaid input from philanthropic volunteers who arranged the marketing and exhibitions of goods for sale undermined the essential commercial viability of many home crafts. In the final analysis, the value was not always to be measured in economic terms, as the following quotation from Scott's report neatly suggests:

> So far the question of rural industries has been considered from the purely economic standpoint. These occupations, to my mind, are even more valuable on wider general grounds of a social nature. It is good for the population of any district to be busy. The children learn a most valuable lesson quite unconsciously from the example of their elders . . . In country districts, training in habits of industry and application must, to a very large extent, be given in the home: and it is for this reason that home industries may be said to possess an educational value.[19]

The situation in the Highlands and Islands was ambiguous, yet in other rural places the picture was more emphatically positive. In Ayrshire, a county of small towns and mixed employment, with numerous smaller gentry estates as well as the vast landholdings of the Earl of Bute, the craft economy was robust and growing throughout the nineteenth century. Although the clothing trades dominated here as elsewhere, the numbers of cabinetmakers and associated fine wood trades such as treen makers, was 215 in 1831, more than doubling to 471 in 1861 and 1,387 by 1891, an increase of well over 500 per cent over 60 years. The manufacture of earthenware, china and pottery, which was largely craft-workshop-based outside the cities, consisted of 24 workers in Ayrshire in 1831, was much the same in 1861, but had risen to 126 workers, almost certainly all associated with Cumnock motto ware manufacture, by 1891. Though the numbers are small, the rise was over 400 per cent.[20] Fife and Stirlingshire had similar profiles as did much of the Lowland north-east and though the crafts that were practised in rural Aberdeenshire were less varied than elsewhere, that county manifested an equally vibrant craft economy that existed and flourished in parallel with modern factories.

If craftwork was a flourishing phenomenon in terms of employee numbers in rural counties, in the big cities it was also identified with significant growth over the course of the nineteenth century. This is apparent through business listings given in Post Office directories for Glasgow and Edinburgh, as shown in the chapters devoted to those cities and also elsewhere, as in Dundee, where local economic conditions were more intensely industrial than in most of urban Scotland and the middle class smaller, but where the craft sector still thrived. In the years between 1820 and 1875 the Dundee population more than tripled to 110,000, rising again to 160,000 by 1900 and the numbers of craft businesses, whilst lower per head of population than in the major cities, kept pace with this growth. There were, for instance, 38 cabinetmaking and joinery firms in the city in 1818 and the number had risen to 98 by 1875, though it then started a slow decline as furniture making became mechanised and larger units emerged. Jewellers, clockmakers and watchmakers numbered 12 in 1818, 37 in 1875 and 47 by 1900. Carvers and gilders were fewer but also increased over the century as did umbrella and parasol makers.[21]

The transport infrastructure that supported Scotland's high-technology industries also facilitated the craft sector. The railway allowed some craft clusters to flourish in unexpected places, such as in the small town of Beith in North Ayrshire, which was a centre of quality furniture making from the mid 1840s to the 1980s. Some craft sectors were closely connected to tourism, especially in south-west Scotland, including Ayrshire, where the making of tourist souvenirs was a big employer through much of the nineteenth century. The tourist industry was an increasingly important feature of the Scottish economy, but here, as elsewhere, the

demand was for ever-cheaper goods and not the finely made and inevitably expensive souvenirs that supported well-paid craft jobs, and the
gap was filled not by local makers but by factory produce, often supplied
from England. Some craft entrepreneurs, like the Ritchie silver and brass
Celtic art workers on Iona, controlled this lower-quality production by
commissioning factory goods to their own designs, but that was rare.
In other instances, court cases were taken by noble patrons to protect
Scottish quality goods and maintain brand identity, as with Harris
tweed, but again that was rare. Moreover, the compromising of Scottish
high-quality craftwork as popularity increased was not always by lower-
quality or shoddy goods. In a curious twist to the Ayrshire whitework
story, demand, which flourished with the Victorian fashion for embroidered christening gowns, was partly supplied under the fraudulent
guise of genuine Ayrshire manufacture by nuns working in convents in
Germany, where costs were low but quality was high and hence impossible to differentiate from local production.[22] The Scottish craft businesses
that did best in economic terms were mostly those based in big towns
and cities, such as decorative woodworkers Scott Morton & Co. in Edinburgh or the large numbers of building craftsmen based in Aberdeen
to serve the considerable country-house building market in that part of
Scotland. It was also in the big cities that complex, highly entrepreneurial family networks engaged in connected craft employments over several
generations were found. One that is particularly well documented was the
Murphy family in Glasgow from the 1840s to 1870s, who in several generations, both male and female, and through multiple overlapping small
businesses engaged in connected aspects of the textile industry including
pattern drawing and print cutting, muslin and lace printing and embroidery organising, loom pattern design and damask pattern design.[23] One
member of the family, the ingenious James Murphy, described as a pattern designer, was also an inventor who secured a lucrative patent for
loom improvements in 1862.[24]

    The modernising economy made significant demands on craftworkers
of various kinds and in country areas especially a whole layer of skilled
men, often connected by marriage, dominated local social networks.
The case of Robert Davidson, blacksmith at Woodfoot near Hawick in
Roxburghshire in the later nineteenth century and his extended family
provides an illustration.[25] Robert's grandfather, father and elder brother
were all blacksmiths and other members of his family worked in the
joinery trade, but his employment included close relations with modern
industry. As a journeyman working for a woollen mill, he was part of a
sizeable community, largely made up of factory workers connected with

the firm of Peter Wilson & Co., a hosiery yarn factory and four other smaller works. The main manufactures of the parish were lambs' wool yarn and hosiery, blankets, plaidings, flannels and tartan shawls.[26] His work was focused on machine and vehicle maintenance for the works and he was part of a skilled trade that gave rise to an early collective body, founded in Glasgow in 1857, called the Scottish United Operative Blacksmiths' Protective and Friendly Society.[27]

Families such as the Murphys in Glasgow or the Davidsons in rural Roxburghshire, with their connected interests and evolving craft skills, underscored the vitality of the craft economy and its links with the modern world. These histories, though remarkable for being well detailed, were not unusual in nineteenth- and early-twentieth-century Scotland, though, as in the last case, the First World War seems to have acted as a disjuncture when key younger family members were killed in action. Of course, disjuncture in craft employment within families and communities was occasioned by various causes long before the First World War swept away a generation of Scottish artisans. For some and sometimes with devastating effects, it was the impact of new technologies as in the iconic early-nineteenth-century Paisley shawl hand-weaving industry, or later in the nineteenth century when the mass production of machine-turned furniture undermined some branches of the cabinetmaking trades. For others it was the overproduction of skilled workers, leading to saturated labour market and migration into other trades or, indeed, physical migration out of Scotland to England or emigration to North America or Australia. The emigration of craftworkers from Scotland was not new, with many skilled young men tempted to try their luck in the Caribbean in the eighteenth century and often doing so in male sibling groups.[28] Disappointment in job prospects and earnings at home generated growing emigration over the century, which was actively encouraged in the later nineteenth century by trade unions, with press reports frequently given on opportunities abroad, especially during economic slumps when employment at home was difficult.[29] Of course, migration outwards was matched in some sectors by the migration inwards of skilled workers from Europe, such as the glass engravers who revitalised the glass and ceramics industry in Edinburgh and Fife. Awareness of an increasingly international market for skilled labour and work and its implications for domestic craftsmen sometimes erupted into bitter disputes. This was seen in Glasgow in 1861 when a town council plan to install new painted glass windows in Glasgow Cathedral in celebration of the life and history of the city – and give the commission to the artists of the famous Royal Bavarian Stained Glass Manufactory in Munich – generated condemnation from the Glasgow Trades House over the preference for foreign workers over British. Alternatives were suggested, mostly London-based firms, but including James Ballantine of Edinburgh, who had worked on some of the stained-glass windows in the Houses of Parliament and was favoured by the Glasgow Trades. However, the original plans were carried out and as a consequence the Trades House declined to be represented on the oversight committee or in the designs, their arguments and ire fully aired in the local press.[30] By 1900, Glasgow had its own flourishing craft-based stained-glass industry and a stronger nationalist spirit kept such commissions at home.

Behind the growth of the craft economy lay some of the same dynamics as those that generated demand for machine-made goods. Expanding cohorts of middle-class consumers with bigger suburban houses – and values that favoured conspicuous cultivation of domestic comfort through the material culture of home – sought to own new and ever more elaborate 'things' made by both factories and the artisan producer. Increased disposable income promoted an appetite for craftwork, as is apparent from the popularity of craft displays in the great exhibitions and demand for holiday souvenirs. It was the mainly middle-class consumers who supported the Shetland lacemaking industry, or Orkney chair production and Harris tweed. So great was the demand for jewellery in this middle market that certain producers protected their output through the copyright registration of their designs, particularly for the quintessential 'Scotch pebble' brooches and bracelets made by firms like Rettie & Sons of Aberdeen.[31] Consumer culture built on window shopping for leisure and a desire for instant gratification through the retail purchase of luxury goods meant that there was an incentive for craft businesses to buy in handmade goods or standardised components from elsewhere, to expedite their own in-house production and keep high-demand items in stock. This gave rise to complex networks of production and stock purchase in even the most skilled of the craft sectors including jewellery, watch- and clockmaking, and cabinetmaking, with London manufacturing firms employing many skilled artisans producing mainly for the wholesale trade through catalogues or later via travelling salesmen who took orders. A case in point was the wholesale trade undertaken by silversmithing firm of Edward Barnard & Sons of Angel Street, London, which for over a century made and supplied beautifully designed and crafted stock items and components to numerous provincial firms who had their own workshops and retail premises, including several long-established businesses in Edinburgh and Glasgow.[32]

APPRENTICESHIP AND TRAINING

In the years before the First World War, craftwork thrived in many areas and apprenticeships were sought by parents seeking well-paid skilled employment for children. Publications that would today be called 'career guides' had been popular since the mid eighteenth century, giving details on the character of training, work and income for different craft groups.[33] One of these, which included insights from contemporary Scotland, was published in 1908 under the title *A Handbook of Employments Specially Prepared for the Use of Boys and Girls on Entering the Trades, Industries and Professions.* The author was Maria Ogilvie-Gordon, a Scots-born geologist and social activist, married to a medical practitioner and living in Aberdeen.[34] Her purpose was to advocate for local employment offices for young people, supported by the school boards and councils and to this end she 'instituted an inquiry among the employers in our chief cities, with regard to the positions open to young workers in their employment, the periods of training required, the rates of wages, and prospects after training'.[35] The evidence that informed the publication came from volunteer researchers including R. H. Tawney, a young assistant in the economics department at Glasgow University who would later find fame as an economic historian and social reformer. In Edinburgh, Miss Chrystal Macmillan a notable lawyer and suffrage pioneer, provided some research input. Mrs Carlaw Martin, a member of the Dundee School Board conducted a survey in Dundee and in Aberdeen the work was undertaken by Miss Elliot Ogston Clark, 'visiting all employers personally, and eliciting from many of them a free expression of their views and options regarding the best way of training the young'.[36] In the process of compiling the record, Ogilvie-Gordon provided a familiar account of machinery that robbed workers of job satisfaction and undermined apprenticeships. But she also indicated many areas of craftwork that were vibrant and well rewarded.

The 1908 *Handbook of Employments* is divided into two sections defined by skill levels, comprising occupations requiring 'short periods of training' and those with 'long periods of training'. These were arranged in tables showing the usual age of entry, which for most was between 14 and 16 years, the wages earned by beginners and the 'full average wage per week'. Occupations requiring apprenticeships or some form of longer training ranged from accountants and architects to wire-weavers and dressers and along the way embraced the usually recognised crafts such as blacksmiths, cabinetmakers, iron founders, pottery workers and tailors. The majority, in common with most areas of craft that are detailed, earned 30s–35s per week when fully trained, with the best paid, the iron founders and pottery workers, earning up to 40s per week. These incomes compare with £50–£80 per year for railway clerks or draper's assistants, both desirable occupations for the aspirant working classes, though paying similar wages to skilled manual workers. Clerks in commercial offices required a good education and could earn up to £100 per year, though many were paid less.[37]

The narratives given for individual employments are interesting for noting the degree to which entry to craftwork was trade union controlled; the ratio of apprentices to journeymen was closely regulated by some, though not all workplaces observed the regulations and indentures with premiums paid by parents seem to be rare. Trade union controls continued through the interwar years and were a source of growing concern over the power of such restrictive forces on the training and availability of artisanal labour.[38] The sector narratives for 1908, as detailed by Ogilvie-Gordon, revealed the current position of the different areas of work and the key changes taking place. There were winners and losers due to new technologies or new forms of organisation. Across the board there was evidence of decline in formal apprenticeships in favour of on-the-job training supplemented with day release or evening classes. Another feature of change was the growing importance of corporate bodies as employers of multiple craft groups, including local municipal authorities, railway companies and shipyards. The latter, for instance, employed metalworking craftsmen who specialised in riveting, plating or boiler making, but there were also carpenters, joiners and blacksmiths in shipyards along with various types of engineers, patternmakers and machine men.[39]

Some of the changes impacting on one craft could be the product of changes in another elsewhere as illustrated by tool making. This sector, making woodworking tools for use by joiners, cabinetmakers and coopers, was historically based in small workshops that were found throughout the country and the craftsmen involved 'counted their trade sure and steady'.[40] But small workshops declined as tools came to be made by machinery requiring bigger workplace units and some of the tradesmen who purchased these tools had also changed with implications for the local craft-trained tool maker.

The cabinetmakers used to make the mouldings for walls and furniture by hand, and the planes they required for this purpose were made in considerable number by the local tool maker. Now machine moulding planes are used in all the larger cabinetmaking workshops, and these can turn out more mouldings in a day than a workman could formerly have done by hand in a week. In this way, the demand for hand-made tools is being reduced every year, and as the small toolmakers die out, their workshops are seldom continued.[41]

The last observation reinforced another feature of the craft workforce that accompanied the decline in handwork – the tendency for fading crafts to be identified with older practitioners. Conversely, however, some crafts were augmented by new opportunities, the product of changing technologies or ways of working, which made them attractive to the young. An instance described by Ogilvie-Gordon was the hybrid category of craftsman called 'bell and blind hangers and locksmiths' which had expanded to embrace novel skills since the wide introduction of electric bells and lighting, with newer firms dedicated to making and fitting electric bells and telephone systems. Additionally, there was a growing subsection of the craft providing 'tube-work, wire-work and electric fittings' for ships in the main shipbuilding ports.[42] Boys apprenticed in this area were required to have 'strength and intelligence' together with a 'good knowledge of arithmetic and some skill in drawing'. According to the 1908 report, those who were trained in shops where 'machinery is not much used' got a better all-round training than elsewhere, which favoured skillsets from apprenticeships in smaller workplaces in Aberdeen or Dundee over those in Glasgow and Edinburgh. It was a flourishing sector with little unemployment where men could continue to work until old and 'employers say that a "steady man never wants a job"'.[43]

Another area of changing technologies with implications for craftsmen was connected to piped municipal water and gas supplies, which led to growing demands for plumbers and sanitary engineers, with many of the former also undertaking electrical work as 'electricity is taking the place of gas in many departments'. 'A man who can draw out plans for the sanitary arrangements of a villa or tenement is invaluable' was the opinion of employers consulted in the 1908 survey, with such men expected to have 'good eye-sight, hearing and steady nerves'. However, the traditional plumber's prized skill in manipulating metals, particularly lead, as illustrated by later-nineteenth-century exhibition displays, was now undermined by factory-made cheap standardised pipes and fittings.[44] Apprentices in this sector, which still included large numbers of small firms, usually supplemented on-the-job training with evening schools or technical college classes and had to pass City and Guilds examinations to qualify for the trade. Plumbers were subject to strict union control and increased application of safety regulations and inspection regimes.[45]

Of course, all artisanal trades were changing in some degree by the early twentieth century – but workplace and skill changes were not unique to this time. Blacksmiths were described as having a greater variety of work than any other trade, ranging from horse-shoeing which was frequently combined with cartwright work, to ironwork in the shipbuilding yard or domestic work in high-street ironmongers shops.[46] Among jewellers and silversmiths, which was always a small trade and one that was increasingly superseded by English makers with retail businesses in Scottish towns, the 'chasers', who also engraved silver, were a particularly flourishing subgroup because such silverware was 'at present very fashionable'. Hence, it was observed that £2 weekly was an average wage in Scotland as well as in London and that some firms paid as much as £4 to £5 for their most skilled 'chasers'.[47] Another group of well-paid fine metalworkers, particularly in Edinburgh with its links to medical education, were the surgical and scientific instrument makers, a category of skilled tradesman that was also connected to optical grinding for lenses and spectacles. The educational requirements for this area of employment were high, and 'it is usual for employers to apply to headmasters of the public elementary schools for suitable apprentices, as they specially desire lads who are of the best artisan class and good scholars'.[48]

Certain trades now barely existed as distinctive, commercially viable and widespread crafts. They included bookbinding, though the rise of a small but highly skilled amateur sector of lady Arts and Crafts bookbinders is noted elsewhere.[49] Boots and shoes were machine-made by the early twentieth century and frequently imported from England and America, though skilled workmen were still employed as leather cutters in Scotland and a small group of bespoke boot- and shoemakers found employment in big cities. As a contracting and ageing trade group, the craftsmen who were still involved took on few apprentices and were detached from retail. As observed in 1908, 'owing to high rents, there is generally no workshop attached to the showrooms, and practical shoemakers do their work either in their own homes or in workshops hired in common by several men'.[50] The tailoring and dressmaking sectors were similarly diverging, with a small bespoke trade still led by skilled craftsmen and craftswomen, some working from within department stores and all now making use of sewing machines, and growing factory production of clothing for the ready-made trade.[51]

Some craft areas retained their idiosyncratic characteristics, seen, for instance, in pottery works where it was observed by Ogilvie-Gordon in 1908, 'there is an inclination among journeymen potters to keep the trade in their own families as much as possible, and, in accordance with this, some employers give preference to the sons of employees when a vacancy occurs'.[52] But here, as in other crafts, boys were taken on for a trial period before being offered apprenticeships and those who lacked ability were soon turned out. The building crafts, though operating in much the same way as half a century before, found it difficult to recruit apprentices due to harsh working conditions, the need for considerable strength and, in some areas, such as stone cutting, a growing appreciation of the health implications of long-term exposure to toxic stone dust.[53] Printers and compositors for the book trade were important areas of skilled employment especially in Edinburgh, where the expansion of employment in the sector was matched by others in decline, such as fine glassmaking.[54] Indeed, in 1908, the printing industry employed the second largest number of craftsmen in Edinburgh, exceeded only by the joinery trade which flourished alongside high rates of new house building. Cabinetmakers still existed in small firms the length of the country doing fine bespoke work of the sort typified by Danny Thompson's workshop in Tain.[55] But increasingly, craftsmen were based in factories where the work was highly specialised and segmented – a feature of iron and brass founding also – with apprentices usually fixed in one department only, which might be the machine shop, or chair making, French polishing, upholstery or woodcarving, with no opportunity for gaining a range of complementary skills as typically seen in more traditionally organised smaller workshops. As in the past, woodcarving, which remained fashionable in furniture, required apprentices with 'artistic qualities' and talented workmen could progress to modelling and even furniture design, the latter in demand, though requiring small numbers, in large machine-based furniture-making firms with their own product lines.[56]

As noted above, the 1908 *Handbook* report was prompted by concern in Scotland with employment for the young and it featured considerable discussion of the character of training and details of apprentice experience. A similar concern was mirrored elsewhere including within the municipal authorities that ran the state schooling system and this gave rise to new schemes for bringing the skills training of youths under more systematic control. In Edinburgh in 1912, a joint committee representing the Merchants Company, George Heriot's Trust, the Edinburgh School Board and the Edinburgh College of Art embarked on its own investigations, focused on four illustrative trades – printing, house painting, joinery and brass moulding and finishing – and concluded that though there was much variation between trades, as, indeed, the 1908 report had revealed, there were certain commonalities that could be improved through better organisation. They recommended that each trade should form an 'apprentice training committee' to keep a list of the apprentices in their area in the city and to frame a more systematic and effective scheme of education for the boys involved.[57] The challenge, of course, was to engage the interests of employers and a unionised workforce. Amongst the latter, such intervention from municipal interests was seen by many as an attempt to revive controls over training that had long vanished and were 'a relic of the old guilds and trade monopolies and against all the tenets of Trade Unionism'.[58] Introduced on the eve of war and resisted by unions, the scheme had limited success in Edinburgh or elsewhere.

FIRST WORLD WAR AND BEYOND

Preoccupations with apprentices continued during and after the First World War. The interruption to training that came as young men went into military service was much debated and post-war there was new concern that the skilled work available in some sectors, such as the building trades, was not sufficient to support good apprenticeships.[59] The problem was neatly captured in a speech made in 1931 by Gilbert Archer, Master of the Edinburgh Merchant Company, at an event designed for prize and certificate presentation for apprentices in the wood-working and house-painting trades, which was under the sponsorship of the Merchant Company Apprentice Training Committees.

> Mr Forrest said that he could not help feeling that at the present time apprentices were not getting the best chance – certainly not the chance they had before the war. To-day there were so many substitutes, and so much was done by machinery, that there seemed little chance for craftmanship. Nevertheless, he was a great believer in craftsmanship, and he felt sure that it would come into its own again . . . At the present moment craftsmanship had little chance in, say Corporation houses, but they should not forget that these houses were a blessing to the people . . . they must not forget that in these difficult days the efficient man had far more chance to get any job that was going than had the inefficient man.[60]

The impact of the First World War on craftworkers is hard to quantify, though it was clearly disruptive of artisan employment with many women taking male jobs and new technologies undermining hand skills. For instance, advances in demand for motorised vehicles accelerated the fall in use of horses for transport, with implications for a range of skilled craftsmen from blacksmiths to carriage makers. Prior to the war, motor-vehicle makers employed a highly trained workforce, but expanding output corresponded with de-skilling across the sector which increased with the introduction of American production line techniques in the 1920s. The loss of a generation of young men through death in service was also important for what subsequently happened during the interwar years. A high toll on craftsmen who became soldiers was reinforced by the early recruitment success of the 'pals' regiments, where men from a single location and employer or trade joined together to form a distinct fighting unit. An account of recruitment activity in Dundee stressed the popularity of these regiments 'among young men who have worked together or been associated socially' and also detailed how 'men in the professions and skilled trades besides responding to the call of their country, can fill the role of recruiting officers in offices and workshops'.[61] In Glasgow, one of the four companies of the newly formed 17th Highland Light Infantry was entirely made up of students from the Royal Glasgow Technical College, which had grown out of the mechanics' institute and trained many young engineers.[62] As in this case, the indiscriminate early recruitment of skilled men into the army, when they were needed for war work at home in areas like shipbuilding, was soon apparent and avoided in 1939.[63]

In many craft businesses the deployment and subsequent death of skilled employees was devastating, as seen at the Dovecot Tapestry Studio in Edinburgh. The Dovecot was created in 1912 by the Marquis of Bute, with two founder master weavers, John Glassbrook and Gordon Berry, both in their early twenties, recruited from the workshops of William Morris at Merton Abbey near London. Their work was mostly based on traditional and Arts and Crafts designs, with many of the tapestries intended to decorate Bute's houses in Scotland. Several local apprentices were also recruited in 1912, but the work of the studio was suspended when the men and boys all joined the forces. Glassbrook and Berry both died in France in 1917 and it proved hard to find replacement master weavers when such men were mostly older, based in the south of England and unwilling to move to Edinburgh. It was several years before the Dovecot tapestry workshop resumed production, but the absence was not forgotten.[64] Indeed, the erection of countless war memorials and rolls of honour in places of work is testament to the passing of a generation and profound sense of loss.

Most areas of craft production, though intrinsically evolving from the later nineteenth century, continued with only short-term disruption in the interwar years and certain prestige projects were testament to the sustained existence of remarkable hand skills. Perhaps the most notable in Scotland was the creation from 1924 of a National War Memorial at Edinburgh Castle, designed by Sir Robert Lorimer. The memorial employed c.200 artists, craftsmen and craftswomen, including stained-glass makers, stone- and woodcarvers, brass founders and fine paper makers. Firms that had worked with Lorimer for decades and had advertised in the 1913 *Country Life* special feature on the architect and his projects, were involved in the great memorial. They included Thomas Hadden, the Edinburgh decorative ironworker, and the wood-carving firm of W. and A. Clow.[65] Lorimer, whose pre-war practice was mainly in country houses, designed several memorials in the 1920s and this type of building work called on the skills of craftworkers. But the building sector was changed, with few country houses or prestigious offices built in the interwar years and the biggest investment in money and labour now going into council-house building, which used stan-dardised elements made off-site and construction by mostly semi-skilled labour, as the previous quote from Gilbert Archer on the fall in demand for 'craftsmanship' reveals.

Despite the continued popular appeal of Arts and Crafts design, a shift in elite taste and values that saw a rejection of the material his-toricism that dominated the nineteenth century and a renewed focus on science and the modern also undermined craftmanship in favour of the machine-made. Modernist aesthetics could still incorporate the work of craftsmen, but when combined with fashionable man-made materials and mass factory production the impact was significant.[66] Conversely, however, craft making was encouraged in other ways through links to socialism and rural lifestyles. Indeed, the interwar years saw significant government investment in the rural craft sector as part of a broader eco-nomic agenda, which was matched by cultural and political movements connected with return-to-the-land nostalgia.[67] The interventions and interests of paternalistic Scottish aristocrats kept many pockets of craft alive in the countryside. Also, amateur craft connected with working-class home-making was given a new boost by the post-war housing boom. The decisive collapse in a craft economy based on apprentice-trained men and skilled artisans was in the 1950s and not the interwar years, but it did not vanish completely and there were subsequent reviv-als. Post Second World War, other than in some areas of textiles such as handmade knitwear or tweed or in a narrowing spectrum of build-ing crafts, often linked to heritage conservation, a very different type of product made by studio-based craft artists came to dominate the craft economy. These practitioners, who had their antecedents in the early twentieth century, were sometimes rural and were occasionally supported on great estates where craft workshops can still be found today.[68] But they were mostly urban, middle class and art-college trained, funded by the state to a great extent through its cultural agencies, often supplying state patrons such as museum or gallery collections or responding to demand for unique items of decorative ware.

In the 1970s there was a distinctive craft revival generated by anxiety with the modern world and supported by government initiatives to incubate new forms of work in the face of changing employment.[69] Today we are living with another cycle of craft revival linked to shifts in workplace practices, more democratic and popular in character than before, which, despite a tightening of state support for the arts is sustained by mainstream corporate interests and a recognition of craft's role in a cultural economy. This is not a uniquely British phenomenon, with similar initiatives elsewhere in Europe and North America. According to the most recent government report, the craft sector was the fastest-growing component of Britain's 'creative industries', increasing by almost 50 per cent in the previous five years and contributing £420 million of gross value to the economy.[70] The market for craftwork today is dominated by middle-aged, middle-class women whose motives are driven by gift-buying coupled with admiration for the skills involved, which they often practise themselves as amateurs, along with desires to possess things that are 'beautiful'.[71] But this 'cosy' and backward-referencing appreciation of craft, which is modern but also echoes Arts and Crafts sensibilities of over a century ago, does not tell the whole story. Crafts Council studies have also shown that craft skills, techniques and materials are not just about making lovely decorative objects and things, they are embedded in the science and technology sectors with a significant migration of expertise into future-facing businesses.[72] The craft economy and the craftworkers who sustain it have relevance today as they had in the past and are constantly evolving.

Notes

1. When he wrote his articles on industry, Bremner was employed as a sub-editor on the *Scotsman*. He departed Edinburgh for Manchester in 1870 to take up an editorial role with the *Manchester Examiner and Times*. He wrote an extended account of 'the early history of the manufacture of cotton' for a collection of essays titled *The Great Industries of Great Britain, pt 1*, published in 1878. He also wrote for children's magazines, was an active member of the National Association of Journalists and ended his career in London as *Times* chief sub-editor. *John O'Groat Journal*, 3 March 1870, 'Farewell dinner to Mr David Bremner of the "Scotsman"'; *Capital and Labour*, 30 January 1878, book reviews; David Bremner, 'My Lady's Workbox, and Some of its Wonders. II – Buttons', *Little Folks*, 1 February 1884. His death and posthumous article on 'petroleum' in the magazine *Science for All*, was reported in the *Hampshire Advertiser*, 19 May 1894.

2. Bremner, *Industries of Scotland*, 431.
3. Raphael Samuel, 'Workshop of the world: Steam power and hand technology in mid-Victorian Britain', *History Workshop Journal* (Spring 1977), 6–72; Patrick O'Brien and Caglar Keydar, *Economic Growth in Britain and France, 1780–1914: Two Paths to the Twentieth Century* (London, 1978).
4. Robert B. Kristofferson, *Craft Capitalism: Craftworkers and Early Industrialization in Hamilton, Ontario, 1840–1872* (Toronto, 2007).
5. Maxine Berg, 'Skill, craft and histories of industrialisation in Europe and Asia', *Transactions of the Royal Historical Society*, 24 (2014), 127–48.
6. Tirthankar Roy, *Traditional Industry in the Economy of Colonial India* (Cambridge, 1999). Tirthankar Roy, *The Crafts and Capitalism: Handloom Weaving Industry in Colonial India* (Abingdon, 2020).
7. Wendy Kaplan, ed. *The Arts and Crafts Movement in Europe and America, 1880–1920* (New York, 2004).
8. See, for example, Ruth B. Phillips, *Trading Identities: The Souvenir in Native North American Art from the Northeast, 1700–1900* (Seattle, 1998).
9. Marcel Hoogenboom, et al., 'Guilds in the transition to modernity: The case of Germany, United Kingdom and the Netherlands', *Theory and Society*, 47 (2018), 255–91.
10. Juanjo Romero-Martin, 'Craftswomen in times of change: Artisan family strategies in nineteenth-century Barcelona', *Mélanges de l'École française de Rome*, 128:1 (2016).
11. Rudiger Hatchmann, 'Artisans and artisan movements (Germany)', in James G. Chastain, *Encyclopaedia of 1848 Revolutions* (2005).
12. Fabrice Bensimon, 'The emigration of British lacemakers to continental Europe (1816–1860s)', *Continuity and Change*, 34:1 (2019), 15–41.
13. Juliet Kinchin, 'Hungary. Shaping a national conscious', in Kaplan, *Arts and Crafts Movement*.
14. Edyta Barucka, 'Redefining Polishness: The revival of crafts in Galicia around 1900', *Acta Slavica Iaponica*, 28 (2010), 71–99.
15. Wendy R. Salmond, *Arts and Crafts in Late Imperial Russia: Reviving the Kunstar Art Industries, 1870–1917* (Cambridge, 1996). See also Hanna Chuchvaha, 'Quiet feminists: Women collectors, exhibitors and patrons of embroidery, lace and needlework in late imperial Russia (1860–1917)', *West 86th*, 27:1 (2020), 45–72.
16. Amy Palmer, 'Radical conservatism and international nationalism: The peasant arts movement and its search for the country heart of England', *Cultural and Social History*, 15:5 (2018), 663–80.
17. Lou Taylor, 'Displays of European peasant dress and textiles in the Paris international exhibitions, 1862–1900', in David Crowley and Lou Taylor, eds, *The Lost Arts of Europe* (Haslemere, 2000).
18. *Report on Home Industries*, 136–7.
19. Ibid., 145.
20. Comparative statistics collated from published census abstracts.

21. *Dundee Directory for 1818* (Dundee, 1818); *Dundee Directory for 1874–5* (Dundee, 1875); *Dundee Directory, 1900–1901* (Dundee, 1900).
22. Joslyn M. Baker, 'The Moravians. An Alternative Perspective on White-work Embroidery, 1780–1950', MA dissertation, Winchester School of Art, 1995.
23. Nenadic, 'Designers in the nineteenth century', 117.
24. *Glasgow Herald*, 17 October 1862.
25. Detailed in Chapter 3.
26. Samuel Lewis, *A Topographical Dictionary of Scotland with Historical and Statistical Descriptions Vol. 1* (London, 1851), 609.
27. University of Warwick Library. Modern Records Centre. MSS. 192/AB/23–80. Records of the Associated Blacksmiths' Forge and Smithy Workers' Society. The records include a 'Roll of Honour' of members who died on active service in every year from 1916 to 1919.
28. Chapter 5. See also Stephen Mullen, 'Scots in the West Indies in the Colonial period: A view from the archives', *Scottish Archives*, 22 (2016), 7–16.
29. As penned by patternmaker Andrew McIlwraith, whose life is detailed in Chapter 3.
30. *Glasgow Herald*, 19 February 1861.
31. See Chapter 4.
32. V&A Archive of Art and Design. AAD/1979/7. Edward Barnard and Sons, Manufacturing Silversmiths, London. Business Records 1805–2006.
33. One of the earliest was Robert Campbell's *Complete Tradesman*, published in London in 1749. For the nineteenth century, see J. C. Hudson, *The Parent's Handbook* (London, 1842); F. Davenant, *What Shall My Son Be? Hints to Parents on the Choice of a Profession or Trade* (London, 1870).
34. Mary R. S. Creese, 'Dame Maria Gordon, [née Ogilvie] (1864–1939)', *ODNB*, 2004.
35. Ogilvie-Gordon, *Handbook of Employments*.
36. Ibid., 20.
37. Ibid., 29–33.
38. *Scotsman*, 29 March 1924, 'Remove the restrictions'.
39. Ogilvie-Gordon, *Handbook of Employments*, 338–42.
40. Ibid., 376.
41. Ibid.,
42. Ibid., 145.
43. Ibid.,
44. See the case of Haddington plumber and enthusiastic exhibitor, Tommy Ross, detailed in Chapter 6.
45. Ogilvie-Gordon, *Handbook of Employments*, 298.
46. Ibid., 147.
47. Ibid., 251.
48. Ibid., 354–5.
49. Ibid., 149.

50. Ibid., 155–6.
51. Nenadic, 'Social shaping of business behaviour'; Katrina Honeyman, *Well Suited. A History of the Leeds Clothing Industry, 1850–1990* (Oxford, 2000).
52. Ogilvie-Gordon, *Handbook of Employments*, 309.
53. Donaldson, 'Death in the New Town'.
54. Ogilvie-Gordon, *Handbook of Employments*, 312–13.
55. See Chapter 3.
56. Ogilvie-Gordon, *Handbook of Employments*, 169–74.
57. *Scotsman*, 26 January 1912.
58. *Scotsman*, 10 January 1913.
59. *Scotsman*, 13 November 1914, 'The apprentice problem: Opinions of the Edinburgh Apprentice Training Committees'; *Scotsman*, 10 July 1919, 'Apprentice training: Edinburgh inter-shop competitions'.
60. *Scotsman*, 30 July 1931, 'Training of apprentices: The decline of craftsmanship'.
61. *Courier and Argus*, 7 September 1914.
62. Peter Simkins, *Kitchener's Army: The Raising of the New Armies, 1914–16* (Manchester, 1988), 89.
63. Juliette Pattinson, '"Shirkers", "Scrimjacks" and "Scrimshanks"? British civilian masculinity and reserved occupations, 1914–45', *Gender and History*, 28:3 (2016), 209–27.
64. David Saxby, 'From Merton Abbey to Scotland. Weaving Scotland's first tapestry', *William Morris Society Magazine* (Spring 2017), 2–6. The Dovecot Studio mounted an exhibition in 2017 – titled 'The Weaver's Apprentice' – to commemorate the lives of John Glassbrook and Gordon Berry.
65. *Edinburgh Castle: Scottish National War Memorial*, Historic Scotland Statement of Significance.
66. George H. Marcus, 'Disavowing craft at the Bauhaus: Hiding the hand to suggest machine manufacture', *Journal of Modern Craft*, 1:3 (2008), 345–56.
67. Christopher Bailey, 'Progress and preservation: The role of rural industries in the making of the modern image of the countryside', *Journal of Design History*, 9 (1996), 35–53.
68. See Harrod, *Crafts in Britain*; Harrod, *The Last Sane Man*.
69. Andrea Peach, 'What goes around comes around? Craft revival, the 1970s and today', *Craft Research*, 4:2 (2013), 161–79.
70. *Telegraph*, 14 January 2018.
71. McIntyre, *Consuming Craft*, Crafts Council Report, 2010, 16.
72. *Measuring the Craft Economy*, Crafts Council Report, 2014.

Bibliography

UNPUBLISHED PRIMARY SOURCES

Abbotsford, Galashiels
Abbotsford House Building Work Ledger and Letter Book, *c*.1816–32.

Borders Regional Archive, Hawick
SBA/183/1. James Mein, Cabinetmaker, Kelso. Business Papers, *c*.1800–1830.

British Library
Additional Manuscript 42556, fol. 2. Diary of Samuel Kevan, Journeyman of
    Southwark.
1807 a.4 74/1. *Catalogue: Section 1 Stoves, Hearths, etc. Manufactured by
    Carron Company*, 1883.

Edinburgh University Library Special Collections
GB237-Coll329. Papers of David Ramsay Hay (1798–1866), Decorative Artist
    and Author.
Gen 1070 (204). Letters from John Broomfield to Robert Waugh of Melrose,
    1810.

London Metropolitan Archives
MS 11936–7. Sun Insurance Company Registers, 1710–1863.

Mount Stuart Archive, Bute
BU/88. William Frame (1848–1906), Architect. Letter Books.

National Archives, Kew
BT42–51. Board of Trade Registers of Patents, Designs and Trade Marks,
    1842–1908.
PROB 11/1886. Will of Robert Waugh of Melrose, 1837.

National Library of Scotland
MS, Acc 4006. Sanderson and Paterson, Builders and Timber Merchants, Galashiels. Ledger 1806–35.
MS, Acc 7603. Records of Dowells Ltd, Auctioneers, Edinburgh.

National Museums Scotland
Scottish Life Archive. W.MS. 1997. James Simpson, Joiner, Fala Dam, Business Papers, 1912–22.
Society of Antiquaries of Scotland Archive. UC17. Papers Relating to Donations to and Purchases for the Museum.

National Records of Scotland
CS96/204. Sequestration of James Watson, Cabinet Maker, Edinburgh. Wages Book 1844–52.
CS96/415/1. Sequestration of John Steele, Gilder and Print Dealer, Edinburgh. Sederunt books 1819–25.
CS96/452. Sequestration of James Dowell, Cabinetmaker, Edinburgh 1829–31.
CS96/1246. Sequestration of David Gullan, Cabinetmaker, Musselburgh. Sederunt Book, 1813–15.
CS280/42. Sequestration of John Black, Builder, Kirkcaldy, 1843–56.
GD1/1164. Miscellaneous Papers. Contract between John Stainton Manager of Carron Company and George Smith, 1817.
GD1/1208. Invercreran Photograph Album, 'Our Glen', 1866.
GD22/1. Papers of the Cunninghame Graham Family of Ardoch.
GD27/7/323. Papers relative to building Dalquharran House to designs by Robert Adam, 1787–90.
GD44. Papers of the Gordon Family, Dukes of Gordon.
GD45. Papers of the Maule family, Earls of Dalhousie.
GD58. Carron Iron Company. Business Papers.
GD112. Papers of the Campbell Family, Earls of Breadalbane.
GD113. Papers of the Innes Family of Stow.
GD152. Papers of the Hamilton Bruce Family of Grange Hill and Falkland.
GD224. Papers of the Montague-Douglas-Scott Family, Dukes of Buccleuch, with permission from the Duke of Buccleuch and Queensberry KT.
NG1. Board of Manufactures, General and Manufacturing Records, 1727–1930.
RH15/69. Duncan Campbell, Indigo Merchant, London and Edinburgh. Business Papers and Correspondence, 1726–51.
SC20/50/96. Cupar Sheriff Court, Record of Inventories. William Wheeler, Furniture Maker. Arncroach, 1914.

Orkney Library and Archives, Kirkwall
D1/33. Papers Relating to D. M. Kirkness, Chair Maker, Kirkwall. 1888–1914.
D9. Records of Frances Taylor, Straw Plait Manufacturer and Merchant in Orkney and Sandwick, *c.*1780–1850.

D20/4/19/5. Letters from Sheriff Thoms to D. M. Kirkness, 1890.
Photographic Collection. Tom Kent, 1863–1936.

Signet Library, Edinburgh
State of the Mutual Process. John Bird late of London Potter and Robert
  Dinwiddie, Merchant in London, Laurence Dinwiddie and Patrick Nisbet,
  Merchants in Glasgow and Robert Finlay Tanner There, 1 November 1750.
Petition of Laurence Dinwiddie, Merchant and Late Provost of Glasgow, Patrick
  Nisbet Merchant and Robert Finlay Tanner There, and Robert Dinwiddie
  Merchant in London. Proprietors of a Delftware Factory Lately Set Up In
  Glasgow. 8 January 1751.

University of Warwick Library
MSS. 192/AB/23–80. Records of the Associated Blacksmiths' Forge and Smithy
  Workers' Society.

V&A Archive of Art and Design
AAD/1979/7. Edward Barnard and Sons, Manufacturing Silversmiths, London.
  Business Records, 1805–2006.

NEWSPAPERS AND MAGAZINES

Aberdeen Evening Express
Aberdeen Press and Journal
Aberdeen Journal
Aberdeen Weekly Journal
Ayrshire Post
Birmingham Daily Post
Caledonian Mercury
Country Life
Daily Mail
Dumfries and Galloway Standard and Advertiser
Dundee Courier and Argus
Edinburgh Advertiser
Edinburgh Evening Courant
Edinburgh Evening News
Edinburgh Annual Register
Evening Telegraph
Gazette
Glasgow Herald
Journal of the Society of Arts
Leicester Chronicle and Leicestershire Mercury
Lincoln, Rutland and Stamford Mercury
Liverpool Mercury

Newcastle Daily Journal
North British Daily Mail
Paisley Herald and Renfrewshire Advertiser
Poor Man's Guardian
Scots Magazine
Scotsman
Sheffield and Rotherham Independent
Southern Reporter
Spectator
Tait's Edinburgh Magazine
Times

PRINTED PRIMARY SOURCES

Abram, Edmund W., 'The last Lancashire handloom-weavers', *The Leisure Hour* (September 1893), 737–41.

Andrew, J. Lewis, 'Old Sussex farmhouses and their furniture', *The Antiquary*, 34 (June 1898), 172–7.

Arts & Crafts Exhibition Society: Catalogue of the Fifth Exhibition. The New Gallery, 121 Regent St, 1896.

Balfour, Frances, *Lady Victoria Campbell. A Memoir* (London, *c*.1910).

Black's Picturesque Tourist of Scotland (Edinburgh, 1874).

Blair, Matthew, *The Paisley Shawl and the Men who Produced It* (Paisley, 1904).

Bosanquet, Bernard, 'The Home Arts and Industries Association: 1 – Aim and objects', *Charity Organization Review*, 4:40 (1888), 135–40.

Bourne, George, *Change in the Village* (New York, 1912).

Bremner, David, *The Industries of Scotland. Their Rise, Progress and Present Condition* (Edinburgh, 1869).

Brown, James, *History of Sanquhar* (Dumfries, 1891).

Campbell, Robert, *The London Tradesman: Being a Compendious View of All the Trades, Professions, Arts, both Liberal and Mechanic now Practiced in the Cities of London and Westminster* (London, 1747).

Carment's 1889 Directory for Dalkeith and District (Dalkeith, 1889).

Catalogue of the First Exhibition of the Art-Manufacture Association in the National Galleries, Edinburgh 1856 (Edinburgh, 1856).

Clelland, James, *The Rise and Progress of the City of Glasgow*, 2 vols (Glasgow, 1820).

Dalkeith District Directory and Household Almanac for 1890 (Dalkeith, 1890).

Davenant, Francis, *What Shall My Son Be? Hints to Parents on the Choice of a Profession or Trade* (London, 1870).

Day, Lewis F., 'Decorative and industrial art at the Glasgow exhibition', *Art Journal* (September 1901), 273–7.

Designs of Furniture Illustrative of Cabinet Furniture and Interior Decoration Specially Designed for James Shoolbred & Company, Tottenham House, Tottenham Court Road (1874).

Dundee Post Office Annual Directories, 1818–1900.

Dundee Exhibition of Industry (Dundee, 1887).

'The Dundee works of Messrs. Valentine and Sons, Dundee', *British Journal of Photography*, 51 (September 1904), 808–9.

Edinburgh Post Office Annual Directories, 1805–1914.

Exhibition of Decorative Handiwork, Edinburgh (Edinburgh, 1888).

Glasgow and Its Environs: A Literary, Commercial, and Social Review Past & Present with a Description of its Leading Mercantile Houses and Commercial Enterprises (1891).

Glasgow Building Trades Exchange, 1898.

Glasgow Post Office Annual Directories, 1828–1912.

Grierson, Herbert, ed., *The Letters of Sir Walter Scott*, 12 vols (1932–7).

Groome, Francis H., *Ordnance Gazetteer of Scotland: A Survey of Scottish Topography, Statistical, Biographical and Historical*, 6 vols (Edinburgh, 1884–5).

Hammond, William, *Recollections of William Hammond: A Glasgow Handloom Weaver* (Glasgow, 1905).

Hill, Octavia, 'The Kyrle Society.' *Charity Organization Review*, 18:108 (December 1905), 314–19.

Hudson, J. C., *The Parent's Handbook* (London, 1842).

Hunter, James, *Fala and Soutra* (Edinburgh, 1892).

Illustrated Catalogue of the Industrial Department, The International Exhibition of 1862 (1862).

Industrial Exhibition Catalogue (Glasgow, 1865).

Information for the Hair Dressers in Edinburgh: Against the Incorporation of Barbers, 7 March 1758. Reproduced in *Econ Journal Watch*, 15:3 (2018), 382–96.

International Exhibition of Industry, Science & Art, Edinburgh 1886. The Official Catalogue (Edinburgh, 1886).

International Exhibition, 1862. Official Catalogue of the Industrial Department (London, 1862).

International Health Exhibition, 1884. Official Catalogue (1884).

Lewis, Samuel, *A Topographical Dictionary of Scotland with Historical and Statistical Descriptions, Vol. 1.* (London, 1851).

Lockhart, John Gibson, *Memoirs of the Life of Sir Walter Scott, Bart.* 7 vols (Edinburgh, 1838).

Lovelace, Mary, 'Home Arts and Industries Association.' *Spectator*, 1 November 1919.

McEwan, Robert D., *Old Glasgow Weavers: Being Records of the Incorporation of Weavers* (Glasgow, 1908).

Macpherson, Alexander, *Glimpses of Church and Social Life in the Highlands in Olden Times and Other Papers* (Edinburgh, 1893).

Millar, A. H. *Historical and Descriptive Accounts of the Castles and Mansions of Ayrshire* (Edinburgh, 1885).

Miller, Hugh, *My Schools and School Masters, Or the Story of My Education* (London, 1845).

'New Patents Lately Enrolled. Mr William Hance's (Tooley Street) for a Method of rendering Beaver and other Hats Water-proof', *Monthly Magazine or British Register*, 23:157 (June 1807), 466.

The New Statistical Account of Scotland, 15 vols (Edinburgh, 1845).

Ogilvie-Gordon, Maria, *A Handbook of Employments Specially Prepared for the Use of Boys and Girls on Entering the Trades, Industries and Professions* (Aberdeen, 1908).

Official Catalogue of the Exhibition of Industrial and Decorative Art, 1861 (Edinburgh, 1861).

Official Catalogue of the Great Exhibition of the Works of Industry of All Nations (1851).

Official Catalogue of the International Forestry Exhibition (Edinburgh, 1884).

Pennant, Thomas, *A Tour in Scotland* (London, 1769).

Pigot and Co's National Commercial Directory of the Whole of Scotland (1825, 1837).

Report of the Committee of Management of the Art Manufacture Association for Encouraging the Application of High Art to Works of Utility and Ornament for the Year 1857–8. (Edinburgh, 1858).

The Royal Commission for the Chicago Exhibition of 1893. Official Catalogue of the British Section (1893).

Sinclair, John, ed., *The Statistical Account of Scotland*, 21 vols (Edinburgh, 1791–9).

Sketch of the Life of Peter Burnet. A Negro (Paisley, 1842).

Slater's Commercial Directory and Topography of Scotland (Manchester, 1861).

Smith, John and John Mitchell, *The Old Country Houses of the Old Glasgow Gentry* (Glasgow, 1870).

Stowe, Harriet Beecher, *Sunny Memories of Foreign Lands,* vol. 1 (Boston, 1854).

Thom, William, *Rhymes and Recollections of a Handloom Weaver* (London, 1845).

Wallis, George, *Schools of Art. Their Constitution, Management etc.* (London, 1857).

"We Twa": Reminiscences of Lord and Lady Aberdeen, 2 vols (London, 1925).

The Weavers Magazine and Literary Companion (Glasgow, 1819–20).

Wilson, Charles Heath, *Remarks on Ornamental Art and Suggestions for its Improvement. A Lecture Delivered in the National Galleries at the Request of the Committee of Management of the Art Manufacture Association on the Evening of 20 January 1857* (Edinburgh, 1857).

Yapp, G. W., *Art Industry. Metal Work Illustrating the Chief Processes of Art-Work Applied by the Goldsmith, Silversmith etc* (1878).

PARLIAMENTARY AND GOVERNMENT PAPERS

Census of Scotland, 1841. Abstract of Answers and Returns published in *Accounts and Papers*, vol. 26, 1844.

Census of Scotland, 1881. *Report*, vol. 2. 1883.
Census of Scotland, 1911. *Abstracts* vols 1 and 2. Occupations of Males and Females Aged 10 Years and upwards. 1912.
Report of a Committee of the Trustees for the Encouragement of Manufactures in Scotland, to the said Trustees, within the last Six Months. Containing A Statement of the Establishment, Funds, and Expenditure of the Board. Ordered by the House of Commons, 27 April 1830.
Report to the Board of Agriculture for Scotland on Home Industries in the Highlands and Islands. 1914 (Cd 7564),
Report from the Select Committee on Handloom Weavers' Petitions, July 1835.
Report from the Select Committee on the Arts and the Connections with Manufactures. House of Commons Papers, 1X.1, 1836.
Sessional Papers of the House of Lords in the Session 1840, vol. 32, 'Handloom Weavers'.

PUBLISHED SECONDARY SOURCES

Abrams, Lynn, 'Knitting, autonomy and identity: The role of hand-knitting in the construction of women's sense of self in an island community, Shetland, *c*.1850–2000', *Textile History*, 37:2 (2006), 149–65.
Adamson, Glenn, ed., *The Craft Reader* (Oxford, 2010).
Adamson, Glenn, *Fewer, Better Things: The Hidden Wisdom of Objects* (London, 2018).
Adamson, Glenn, *The Invention of Craft* (London, 2013).
Allen, Aaron, *Building Early Modern Edinburgh. A Social History of Craftwork and Incorporation* (Edinburgh, 2018).
Allen, Aaron, *The Locksmiths Craft in Early Modern Edinburgh* (Edinburgh, 2007).
Anderson, Christine M., 'Robert Lorimer and Scott Morton & Company', *Regional Furniture*, 19 (2005), 43–68.
Auerbach, Jeffrey A., *The Great Exhibition of 1851: A Nation on Display* (1999).
Auerbach, Jeffrey and Peter Hoffenberg, eds, *Britain, the Empire and the World at the Great Exhibition of 1851* (Aldershot, 2008).
Bailey, Christopher, 'Progress and preservation: The role of rural industries in the making of the modern image of the countryside', *Journal of Design History*, 9 (1996), 35–53.
Baker, John, *Mauchline Ware and Associated Scottish Souvenir Ware* (Princes Risborough, 1985).
Baker, Sonia, *The Country Houses, Castles and Mansions of East Lothian* (Catrine, 2009).
Bamford, Francis, 'A dictionary of Edinburgh wrights and furniture makers, 1660–1840', *Furniture History*, 19 (1983), 1–137.
Barr, Gordon, 'Maryhill Burgh Halls', *Architectural Heritage*, 28:3 (2010), 19–21.

Barringer, Tim, *Men at Work: Art and Labour in Victorian England* (New Haven and London, 2005).

Barton, Susan and Allan Brodie, eds, *Travel and Tourism in Britain, c.1780–1914* (London, 2014).

Barucka, Edyta, 'Redefining Polishness: The revival of crafts in Galicia around 1900', *Acta Slavica Iaponica*, 28 (2010), 71–99.

Bell, Bill, ed., *The Edinburgh History of the Book in Scotland vol. 2: Ambition and Industry, 1800–1880* (Edinburgh, 2007).

Bell, Quentin, *The Design School* (London, 1963).

Bensimon, Fabrice, 'The emigration of British lacemakers to continental Europe (1816–1860s)', *Continuity and Change*, 34:1 (2019), 15–41.

Berg, Maxine, 'Skill, craft and histories of industrialisation in Europe and Asia', *Transactions of the Royal Historical Society*, 24 (2014), 127–48.

Berman, Pat, 'Berlin work.' *Needle Pointers*, February/March 1990.

Black, Anthea and Nicole Burisch, eds, *The New Politics of the Handmade: Craft, Art and Design* (London, 2020).

Bort, Eberhard, 'Review: Scottish Arts and Crafts', *Scottish Affairs*, 63 (2008), 163–169.

Bowen, Jane, 'The Edinburgh International Forestry Exhibition of 1884', *Journal of the Mauchline Ware Collectors Club* (1998).

Brears, Peter C. D., 'The York spinning wheel makers', *Furniture History*, 14 (1978), 19–22.

Brown, Iain Gordon, ed., *Abbotsford and Sir Walter Scott: The Image and the Influence* (Edinburgh, 2003).

Brown, Iain Gordon, 'Daniel Macintosh and the Repository of Arts', *Book of the Old Edinburgh Club*, New Series, 7 (2008), 171–5.

Bryden, D. J., *Scottish Scientific Instrument Makers, 1600–1900* (Edinburgh, 1972).

Bunn, Stephanie J., 'Who designs Scottish vernacular baskets?' *Journal of Design History*, 29:1 (2016), 24–42.

Bunn, Stephanie and Victoria Mitchell, eds, *The Material Culture of Basketry: Practice, Skill and Embodied Knowledge* (London, 2020).

Burton, Anthony, *Vision and Accident. The Story of the Victoria and Albert Museum* (London, 1999).

Caldwell, David H. and Valerie E. Dean, 'The pottery industry at Throsk, Stirlingshire, in the 17th and early 18th century', *Post-Medieval Archaeology*, 26 (1992), 1–46.

Carnevali, Francesca, 'Fashioning luxury for factory girls. American jewelry, 1860–1914', *Business History Review* 85:2 (2011), 295–317.

Carnevali, Francesca, 'Golden opportunities: Jewellery making in Birmingham between mass production and speciality', *Enterprise and Society*, 4:2 (2003), 248–78.

Carruthers, Annette, *Arts and Crafts Movement in Scotland* (New Haven, 2013).

Carruthers, Annette, 'The social rise of the Orkney chair', *Journal of Design History*, 22:1 (2009), 27–45.

Carruthers, Annette, 'William Craigie of Kirkwall and the furnishing of Melsetter House, Hoy', *Regional Furniture*, 16:1 (2002), 108–20.

Choi, Tina Young, 'Producing the past: The native arts, mass tourism and souvenirs in Victorian India', *Lit: Literature Interpretation Theory*, 1 (2016), 50–70.

Clarke, T. N., A. D. Morrison-Low and A. D. C. Simpson, *Brass & Glass. Scientific Instrument Making Workshops in Scotland as Illustrated by Instruments from the Arthur Frank Collection at the Royal Museum of Scotland* (Edinburgh, 1989).

'The Creative Industries in History', *Business History Review*, 85:2 (2011). Special edition, edited by Walter A. Friedman and Geoffrey Jones.

Crawford, Nick, *Scottish Pebble Jewellery: Its History and the Materials from Which It Was Made* (Kingsdown, 2007).

Crossick, Geoffrey, ed., *The Artisan and the European Town, 1500–1900* (London, 1997).

Cumming, Elizabeth, *Hand, Heart and Soul: The Arts and Crafts Movement in Scotland* (Edinburgh, 2006).

Curtis, Neil G. W., 'The place of history, literature and politics in the 1911 Scottish Exhibition', *Scottish Literary Review*, 7:1 (2015), 43–74.

Dobraszczyk, Paul, *Iron, Ornament and Architecture in Victorian Britain: Myth, Modernity, Excess and Enchantment* (Farnham, 2014).

Donaldson, Ken, et al., 'Death in the New Town: Edinburgh's hidden story of stonemasons' silicosis', *Journal of the Royal College of Physicians of Edinburgh*, 47 (2017), 375–83.

Donnelly, Michael, *Scotland's Stained Glass. Making the Colours Sing* (1997).

Dormer, Peter, ed., *The Culture of Craft: Status and Future* (Manchester, 1997).

Downes, Stephanie, et al., eds, *Feeling Things: Objects and Emotions Through History* (Oxford, 2018).

Drinkall, Sophie, 'The Jamaican plantation house: Scottish influence', *Architectural Heritage*, 2:1 (1991), 56–68.

Durie, Alastair J., *Scotland for the Holidays, c.1780–1939* (East Linton, 2013).

Durie, Alastair J., *The Scottish Linen Industry in the Eighteenth Century* (Edinburgh, 1979).

Durie, Alastair J., 'Sporting tourism flowers – the development from *c*.1780 of grouse and golf as visitor attractions in Scotland and Ireland', *Journal of Tourism History* (2013), 1–15.

Durie, Alastair, *Tourism and Scotland. The Long View, 1700–2015* (London, 2017).

Edwards, Clive, *Victorian Furniture: Technology and Design* (Manchester, 1993).

Edwards, Clive, '"Home is where the art is": Women, handicrafts and home improvements 1750–1900', *Journal of Design History*, 19:1 (2006), 11–21.

Edwards, Clive, 'Vernacular craft to machine assisted industry: The division of labour and the development in machine use in vernacular chair making in High Wycombe, 1870–1920', *Proceedings of the 9th International Symposium on Wood and Furniture Conservation*, Amsterdam, 2008.

Edwards, Clive, '"Art furniture in the Old English style". The firm of Colinson and Lock, London, 1870–1900', *West 86th*, 19:1 (2012), 255–81.

Epstein, S. R., 'Craft guilds in the early modern economy: A discussion', *Economic History Review*, 61:1 (2008), 155–74.

Esterly, David, *The Lost Carving: A Journey to the Heart of Making* (London, 2012).

Fairley, J. A., *Lauriston Castle. The Estate and its Owners* (Edinburgh, 1925).

Fortescue, William Irvine, 'James Ker, Member of Parliament for Edinburgh, 1747–1754', *Book of the Old Edinburgh Club*, New Series, 10 (2014), 17–44.

Frayling, Christopher, *Craftsmanship: Towards a New Bauhaus* (London, 2011).

Gloag, John and Derek Bridgewater, *A History of Cast Iron in Architecture* (London, 1948).

Goggin, Maureen Daly and Beth Fowkes Tobin, eds, *Women and the Material Culture of Needlework and Textiles, 1750–1959* (Abingdon, 2009).

Gordon, Beverly, 'The souvenir: Messenger of the extraordinary', *Journal of Popular Culture*, 20:3 (1986), 135–46.

Guthrie, Neil, *The Material Culture of the Jacobites* (Cambridge, 2013).

Habib, Vanessa and Helen Clark, 'The linen weavers of Drumsheugh and the linen damask tablecloth woven to commemorate the visit of George IV to Scotland in 1822', *Proceedings of the Society of Antiquaries of Scotland*, 132 (2002), 529–53.

Hackney, Fiona, 'Quiet activism and the new amateur', *Design and Culture*, 5:2 (2015), 169–93.

Hadjiafxendi, Kyriaki and Patricia Zakreski, eds, *Crafting the Woman Professional in the Long Nineteenth Century* (Farnham, 2013).

Hannah, Rosemary, *The Grand Designer: Third Marquess of Bute* (Edinburgh, 2013).

Harvey, Karen, 'Craftsmen in common: Objects, skills and masculinity in the eighteenth and nineteenth centuries', in Hannah Greig et al., eds, *Gender and Material Culture in Britain since 1600* (London, 2016).

Harris, Bob and Charles McKean, *The Scottish Town in the Age of Enlightenment 1740–1820* (Edinburgh, 2014).

Harrod, Tanya, *The Crafts in Britain in the Twentieth Century* (New Haven and London, 1999).

Harrod, Tanya, *The Last Sane Man: Michael Cardew: Modern Pots, Colonialism and Counter Culture* (New Haven, 2012).

Harrod, Tanya and Miriam Rosser-Owen, 'Introduction: Middle Eastern Crafts', *Journal of Modern Craft*, 13:1 (2020), 1–5.

Hart, Imogen, *Arts and Crafts Objects* (Manchester, 2010).

Hay, Geoffrey D. and Geoffrey P. Stell, *Monuments of Industry: An Illustrated Historical Record* (Glasgow, 1986).

Helland, Janice, *British and Irish Home Arts and Industries, 1880–1914: Marketing Craft, Making Fashion* (Dublin, 2011).

Helland, Janice, 'Good work and clever design: Early exhibitions of the Home Arts and Industries Association', *Journal of Modern Craft*, 5:3 (2012), 275–94.

Hills, Richard, 'James Watt and the Delftfield Pottery, Glasgow', *Proceedings of the Society of Antiquaries of Scotland*, 131 (2001), 375–420.

Hitchcock, Michael and Ken Teague, eds, *Souvenirs: The Material Culture of Tourism* (Aldershot, 2000).

Hodges, William and Ruth Hodges, 'Fern Ware tables', *Journal of the Mauchline Ware Collector's Club*, 55 (April 2004), 7.

Hoffenberg, Peter H., 'Promoting traditional Indian art at home and abroad: The Journal of Indian Art and Industry, 1884–1917', *Victorian Periodicals Review*, 37:2 (2004), 192–213.

Holman, Andrew C. and Robert B. Kristofferson, eds, *More of a Man: Diaries of a Scottish Craftsman in Mid-Nineteenth-Century North America* (Toronto, 2013).

Hoogenboom, Marcel, et al., 'Guilds in the transition to modernity: The case of Germany, United Kingdom and the Netherlands', *Theory and Society*, 47 (2018), 255–91.

Hooper, Glen, 'Furnishing Scotland and the world. Morris & Co., Glasgow 1945–65', *Journal of Scottish Historical Studies*, 37:1 (2017), 52–72.

Ide, Jennifer M., 'John Taylor & Son, Manufacturers Edinburgh', *Mauchline Ware Newsletter*, 2011.

Irwin, Frances, 'Lady amateurs and their masters in Scott's Edinburgh', *The Connoisseur*, 185 (December 1974), 229–37.

Irwin, Frances, 'Scottish eighteenth-century chintz and its design', *The Burlington Magazine*, 107:750 (September 1965), 452–8.

Irons, Neville, 'Irish bog oak carving', *Irish Arts Review*, 4:2 (1987), 54–63.

Jackson, Stephen, 'William Trotter, cabinetmaker, entrepreneur and Lord Provost, 1772–1833', *Book of the Old Edinburgh Club*, New Series, 6 (2005), 73–90.

Jones, David, 'Coal furniture in Scotland', *Furniture History*, 23 (1987), 35–8.

Kaplan, Wendy, ed., *The Arts and Crafts Movement in Europe and America, 1880–1920* (New York, 2004).

Kinchin, Juliet, 'Hungary. Shaping a national conscious', in Wendy Kaplan, ed., *The Arts and Crafts Movement in Europe and America, 1880–1920* (New York, 2004).

Kinchin, Perilla and Juliet Kinchin, with a contribution by Neil Baxter, *Glasgow's Great Exhibitions* (Wendlebury, Bicester, 1988).

Kirkham, Pat, *The London Furniture Trade, 1700–1870* (London, 1989).

Kneebone, Roger, *Expert: Understanding the Path to Mastery* (London, 2020).

Knell, Simon J., and Michael A. Taylor, 'Hugh Miller: Fossils, landscape and literary geology', *Proceedings of the Geologists' Association*, 117 (2006), 85–98.

Knott, Stephen, *Amateur Craft. History and Theory* (London, 2015).

Knox, W. W., *Industrial Nation: Work, Culture and Society in Scotland, 1800–Present* (Edinburgh, 1999).

Korn, Peter, *Why We Make Things and Why It Matters: The Education of a Craftsman* (Boston, 2013).

Kristofferson, Robert B., *Craft Capitalism: Craftworkers and Early Industrialization in Hamilton, Ontario, 1840–1872* (Toronto, 2007).

Lears, Jackson, 'Art for life's sake. Craft and the quest for wholeness in American culture', *Journal of Modern Craft*, 12:3 (2019), 161–72.

Levene, Alysa, 'Honesty, sobriety and diligence: Master-apprentice relations in eighteenth- and nineteenth-century England', *Social History*, 33 (2008), 183–200.

Lindeman, Christina K., 'Gendered souvenirs: Anna Amalia's Grand Tourist *vedute* fans', in Jennifer G. Germann and Heidi A. Strobel, eds, *Materializing Gender in Eighteenth-Century Europe* (London, 2016), 51–66.

Logan, John C., 'The Dumbarton Glassworks Company: A study in entrepreneurship', *Business History*, 14:1 (1992), 61–81.

Luckman, Susan and Nicola Thomas, *Craft Economies* (London, 2017).

MacArthur, E. Mairi, *Iona Celtic Art: The Work of Alexander and Euphemia Ritchie* (Iona, 2003).

MacBeth, Lindsay, 'The Wheelers of Arncroach: A family of furniture makers in Fife', *Regional Furniture*, 5 (1991), 69–78.

McGovern, Alyce, *Craftivism and Yarn Bombing: A Criminological Exploration* (London, 2019).

Marcus, George H., 'Disavowing craft at the Bauhaus: Hiding the hand to suggest machine manufacture', *Journal of Modern Craft*, 1:3 (2008), 345–56.

Mason, J., 'The Edinburgh School of Design', *Book of the Old Edinburgh Club*, 27 (1949), 67–97.

Meller, Helen, *Patrick Geddes: Social Evolutionist and City Planner* (London, 1990).

Minns, Chris and Patrick Wallis, 'Rules and reality: Quantifying the practice of apprenticeship in early modern England', *Economic History Review*, 65:2 (2012), 556–79.

Munck, Bert de, 'Artisans, products and gifts: Rethinking the history of material culture in early-modern Europe', *Past and Present*, 224:1 (2014), 39–74.

Nenadic, Stana, 'Architect-builders in London and Edinburgh c.1750–1800 and the market for expertise', *Historical Journal*, 55:3 (2012), 1–21.

Nenadic, Stana, 'Designers in the nineteenth-century Scottish fancy textile industry: Education, employment and exhibition', *Journal of Design History*, 27:2 (2014), 115–31.

Nenadic, Stana, 'Exhibiting India in nineteenth-century Scotland and the impact on commerce, industry and popular culture', *Journal of Scottish Historical Studies*, 34:1 (2014), 67–89.

Nenadic, Stana, 'Gender, craftwork and the exotic in international exhibitions *c.*1880–1910', in Deborah Simonton, et al., eds, *Luxury and Gender in European Towns, 1700–1914* (Abingdon, 2015), 150–67.

Nenadic, Stana, 'Industrialisation and the Scottish people', in T. M. Devine and J. Wormald, eds, *Oxford Handbook of Modern Scottish History* (Oxford, 2012), 405–22.

Nenadic, Stana, ed., *Scots in London in the Eighteenth Century* (Lewisburg, 2010).

Nenadic, Stana, 'Selling printed cottons in mid-nineteenth-century India. John Matheson of Glasgow and Scottish Turkey red', *Enterprise and Society*, 20:2 (2019), 328–65.

Nenadic, Stana, 'The small family firm in Victorian Britain', *Business History*, 35 (1993), 86–114.

Nenadic, Stana and Sally Tuckett, 'Artisans and aristocrats in nineteenth-century Scotland', *Scottish Historical Review*, 95:2 (2016), 203–29.

Nenadic, Stana and Sally Tuckett, *Colouring the Nation. The Turkey Red Printed Cotton Industry in Nineteenth Century Scotland* (Edinburgh, 2013).

Ogilvie, Shelagh, *The European Guilds: An Economic Analysis* (Princeton, 2019).

Ottewill, David, 'Robert Weir Schultz (1860–1951). An Arts and Crafts Architect', *Architectural History*, 22 (1979), 87–115.

Palmer, Amy, 'Radical conservatism and international nationalism: The peasant arts movement and its search for the country heart of England', *Cultural and Social History*, 15:5 (2018), 663–80.

Parker, Rozsika, *The Subversive Stitch: Embroidery and the Making of the Feminine* (London, 1984).

Peach, Andrea, 'What goes around comes around? Craft revival, the 1970s and today', *Craft Research*, 4:2 (2013), 161–79.

Pelling, Madeleine, 'Collecting the world: Female friendship and domestic craft at Bulstrode Park', *Journal for Eighteenth-Century Studies*, 41:1 (2018), 101–20.

Perry, Grayson, *The Tomb of the Unknown Craftsman* (London, 2011).

Petrie, Kevin and Andrew Livingstone, eds, *The Ceramics Reader* (London, 2020).

Phillips, Ruth B., *Trading Identities: The Souvenir in Native North American Art from the Northeast, 1700–1900* (Seattle, 1998).

Phillips, R., 'The collecting and display of souvenir arts: Authenticity and the strictly commercial', in H. Morphy and M. Perkins, eds, *The Anthropology of Art: A Reader* (Oxford, 2006), 431–53.

Pittock, Murray and Christopher Whatley, 'Poems and festivals, art and artefact and the commemoration of Robert Burns, c. 1844–1896', *Scottish Historical Review*, 93:1 (2014), 56–79.

Pollanen, Sinikka, 'The meaning of craft: Craft makers' descriptions of craft as an occupation', *Scandinavian Journal of Occupational Therapy*, 20:3 (2013), 217–27.

Prothero, Iorwerth, *Radical Artisans in England and France, 1830–1870* (Cambridge, 1997).

Rickly-Boyd, J., 'Authenticity and aura. A Benjaminian approach to tourism', *Annals of Tourism Research*, 39:1 (2012), 269–89.

Riello, Giorgio, 'Nature, production and regulation in eighteenth-century Britain and France: the case of the leather industry', *Historical Research*, 81 (2008), 75–99.

Reynolds, Sian, *Britannica's Typesetters. Women Compositors in Edwardian Edinburgh* (Edinburgh, 1989).

Roads, Elizabeth, ed., *The Thistle Chapel within St Giles' Cathedral* (Edinburgh, 2009).

Romero-Martin, Juanjo, 'Craftswomen in times of change: Artisan family strategies in nineteenth-century Barcelona', *Mélanges de l'École française de Rome*, 128:1 (2016).

Roscoe, Ingrid, Emma Hardy and Greg Sullivan, *A Biographical Dictionary of Sculptors in Britain, 1660–1851* (New Haven and London, 2009).

Roy, Tirthankar, *The Crafts and Capitalism: Handloom Weaving Industry in Colonial India* (Abingdon, 2020).

Sabel, Charles and Jonathan Zeitlin, 'Historical alternatives to mass production: Politics, markets and technology in nineteenth-century industrialization', *Past and Present*, 108 (1985), 133–76.

Salmond, Wendy R., *Arts and Crafts in Late Imperial Russia: Reviving the Kunstar Art Industries, 1870–1917* (Cambridge, 1996).

Samuel, Raphael, 'Workshop of the World: Steam power and hand technology in Victorian Britain', *History Workshop Journal*, Spring 1977, 6–72.

Saxby, David, 'From Merton Abbey to Scotland. Weaving Scotland's first tapestry', *William Morris Society Magazine*, Spring 2017, 2–6.

Scarisbrick, Diana, *Scottish Jewellery: A Victorian Passion* (Milan, 2009).

Schaffer, Talia, *Novel Craft: Victorian Domestic Handicraft and Nineteenth-Century Fiction* (Oxford, 2011).

Schaffer, Talia, 'Women's work: The history of the Victorian domestic handicraft', in Kyriaki Hadjiafxedi and Patricia Zakreski, eds, *Crafting the Woman Professional in the Long Nineteenth Century* (Farnham, 2013), 25–42.

Secord, Anne, 'Science in the pub: Artisan botanists in early nineteenth century Lancashire', *History of Science*, 32 (1994), 269–315.

Sennet, Richard, *The Craftsman* (New Haven and London, 2008).

Smith, Harry, Robert J. Bennett, Carry van Lieshout and Piero Montebruno, 'Entrepreneurship in Scotland, 1851–1911', *Journal of Scottish Historical Studies*, 41:1 (2021), 38–64.

Smith, John, *Old Scottish Clockmakers from 1453 to 1850* (Edinburgh, 1921).

Smith, Kate, *Material Goods, Moving Hands: Perceiving Production in England, 1700–1830* (Manchester, 2014).

Smith, Maya Wassall, '"The fancy work what sailors make": Material and emotional creative practice in masculine seafaring communities', *Nineteenth Century Gender Studies*, 14:2 (2018). Online journal at www.ncgsjournal. com

Smout, T. C., *A Century of the Scottish People, 1830–1950* (London, 1986).

Smout, Christopher, 'Tours in the Scottish Highlands from the eighteenth to the twentieth centuries', *Northern Scotland*, 1:1 (1982), 99–121.

Speed, Jessica, 'English pictorial enamels. Battersea and Bilston enamels and their successors', *Magazine Antiques*, 6 (2007), 88–95.

Stephen, Walter, *Learning From the Lasses: Women of the Patrick Geddes Circle* (2014).

Sturt, George, *The Wheelwright's Shop* (Cambridge, 1993).

Sutherland, Paul, *Mirth, Madness and St Magnus and the Eccentric Sheriff Thoms* (Kirkwall, 2013).

Taylor, Lou, 'Displays of European peasant dress and textiles in the Paris international exhibitions, 1862–1900', in David Crowley and Lou Taylor, eds, *The Lost Arts of Europe* (Haslemere, 2000).

Trachtenberg, David and Thomas Keith, *Mauchline Ware. A Collector's Guide* (Woodbridge, 2002).

Tuckett, Sally, '"Needle crusaders". The nineteenth-century Ayrshire whitework industry', *Journal of Scottish Historical Studies*, 36:1 (2016), 60–80.

Tuckett, Sally, 'Reassessing the romance: Tartan as a popular commodity, c.1770–1830', *Scottish Historical Review*, 95:2 (2016), 182–202.

Turnbull, Jill, *From Goblets to Gaslights: The Scottish Glass Industry, 1750–2006* (Edinburgh, 2017).

Tylecote, Mabel, *The Mechanics Institutes of Lancashire and Yorkshire Before 1851* (Manchester, 1957).

Waal, Edmund de, *The White Road: A Journey into an Obsession* (2015).

Walker, Frank Arneil, *The Buildings of Scotland: Argyll and Bute* (London, 2000).

Weatherill, Lorna, *The Pottery Trade and North Staffordshire, 1660–1760* (Manchester, 1971).

White, Jerry, *A Great and Monstrous Thing: London in the Eighteenth Century* (Cambridge, MA, 2013).

Whyte, D. A., and M. H. Swain, 'Edinburgh Shawls', *The Book of the Old Edinburgh Club*, 31 (1962), 52–64.

Wilson, Richard and Alex Mackley, *Creating Paradise. The Building of the English Country House, 1660–1880* (London, 2000).

Wright, Elizabeth, 'Thomas Hadden, architectural metalworker', *Proceedings of the Society of Antiquaries of Scotland*, 121 (1992), 427–35.

Yan, Shu-chuan, 'The art of working in hair: Hair jewellery and ornamental handiwork in Victorian Britain', *Journal of Modern Craft*, 12:2 (2019), 123–39.

Youngson, A. J., *The Making of Classical Edinburgh 1750–1840* (Edinburgh, 1966).

UNPUBLISHED SECONDARY SOURCES

Baker, Joslyn M., 'The Moravians. An Alternative Perspective on Whitework Embroidery, 1780–1950', MA dissertation, Winchester School of Art, 1995.

Bornhorst-Winslow, Cynthia, 'The important role played by household crafts in the lives of nineteenth-century women in Britain and America', MPhil thesis, Wright State University, 2012.

CANMORE. National Record of the Historic Environment. www.canmore.org.uk

Cooke, Edward S., 'Rural industry, village craft: The politics of modern globalized craft', Peter Dormer Lecture at the Royal College of Arts, London, 2009.

Dictionary of Scottish Architects. www.scottisharchitects.org.uk

Dietert, Rodney R., and Janice Dietert, 'The Edinburgh Goldsmiths: Biographical Information for Freemen, Apprentices and Journeymen.' Cornell University *c.*2010.

Farrell, William, and Tim Reinke-Williams, 'Apprentice migration to early modern London: A four nations approach', Paper to the Economic History Society Annual Conference, Cambridge, April 2016.

Future Museum.co.uk: South-West Scotland, www.futuremuseum.co.uk

Haggarty, George, *Glasgow Delftfield Ceramic Resource Disk 18th Century Earthenware and Creamware*, National Museum Scotland, 2014.

Jurgens, Kristin, 'Dunmore Pottery: The Art of the Art Pottery Business', PhD thesis, University of Glasgow, 2007.

Laurenson, Sarah, 'Materials, Making and Meaning: The Jewellery Craft in Scotland, *c.*1780–1914', PhD thesis, University of Edinburgh, 2017.

Leyland, Megan, 'Patronage and the Architecture Profession. The Country House in Nineteenth-Century Northamptonshire', PhD thesis, University of Leicester, 2016.

McIntyre, Morris Hargreaves, *Consuming Craft: The Contemporary Craft Market in a Changing Economy*, Crafts Council Report, 2010.

Mapping the Practice and Profession of Sculpture in Britain and Ireland, 1851–1951, University of Glasgow and HATII Database, 2011, www.sculpture.gla.ac.uk

Maryhill Burgh Halls: Historic Stained-Glass Windows, Maryhill Burgh Halls Trust.

Measuring the Craft Economy, Crafts Council Report, 2014.

Mitchell, David Scott, 'The Development of the Architectural Iron Founding Industry in Scotland', PhD thesis, University of Edinburgh, 2013.

National Library of Scotland, Scottish Book Trade Index, www.nls.uk

National Portrait Gallery, British Artists' Suppliers, 1650–1950, www.npg.org.uk

Rock, Joe, Annotated Catalogue of the Edinburgh Dean of Guild Court, Architectural Plans, 1700–1824. www.google.com/site/edinburghdeanofguild

Smith, George Wilson, 'Displaying Edinburgh in 1886: The International Exhibition of Industry, Science and Art', PhD thesis, University of Edinburgh, 2015.

University of Glasgow, Mackintosh Architecture, Context, Making and Meaning, www.mackintosh-architecture.gla.ac.uk

University College London, Legacies of British Slave Ownership, www.ucl.ac.uk

Index

Abbotsford, 110, 114, 134, 136–40
Aberdeen, 18, 19, 33, 88, 89, 116–17
    Industrial Exhibition 1891, 204
Aberdeen, Countess Ishbel, exhibition
    sponsor, 175, 193, 200
Aberdeenshire, 151–2, 193
Aberfeldy, 85
Adamson, Glen, 2–3
amateur craftsmen, 187, 188, 191–3, 196,
    202, 203, 207
amateur craftswomen, 187–8, 189,
    190, 191, 193, 195, 202,
    203, 206
'An Clachan' Highland village, 175–6
apprenticeship guides, 18, 220–4
architects, 18, 44, 62, 133–55
    Adam, Robert, 62, 93, 136
    Atkinson, William, 134, 137, 143
    Burn, William, 134, 144–8
    Lorimer, Robert, 44, 63, 124, 150–1,
        226–7
    McKenzie, A. Marshal, 151–2
    Mackintosh, Charles Rennie, 67, 72,
        149–50
    Mylne, Robert, 18
    Schultz, Robert Weir, 134
Argyll, 84, 85, 86–8, 90, 98, 118–19,
    143, 212
Argyll, duke of, estate owner, 181
aristocracy of labour, 74
Art Manufacture Association, 165–6;
    see also Scottish Art Manufacturers
    Association
artisan courts, 7, 161, 163
artisan housing, 31, 34
artisan reporters, 178, 207

Arts and Crafts movement, 48, 63, 68,
    73, 124, 149, 162, 190, 200, 205–6,
    213, 227
    history, 4
    theory, 2, 6
Auchendrane House, 136
Ayrshire, 58, 95–6, 97, 100–2, 110, 135–6,
    215–16

Balmoral, 108, 116, 135
bankruptcy, 34, 37–40, 40–1, 42–3, 147–8
barbers, 9, 93
Barrie, J. M., novelist, 79
basket makers, 3, 125–6
Battersea wares, 109
Beil House, 134
Beith, 100–2
Berlin wool, 189, 195–6
Birmingham, 111, 118
blacksmiths, 73, 82, 85, 86, 93–5, 223
    Broomfield, Robert, Fala Dam, 82
    Davidson, Robert, Hawick, 93–5, 217
Blair, Matthew, weaver and historian,
    Paisley, 177
Board of Manufactures (Board of Trustees
    for Fisheries, Manufactures and
    Improvements), 13–17, 19, 59–60, 68,
    111, 160–1, 164, 166
bog oak carving, 114
boot and shoemakers, 223
    John Lees & Co., Maybole, 102
Breadalbane, earl and countess of, craft
    sponsors, 111, 143, 189, 195
Breadalbane estate, 84–5, 87
Bremner, David, journalist, 60, 62, 64, 67,
    212–13

Bridgeton Rambling Club, 57
Bruce, John, country house owner, 144
Bruce, Margaret Stuart Hamilton, country
    house owner, 144
Bruce, Onesiphorus Tyndall, country house
    owner, 144–5, 148
Buccleuch, duke of, craft sponsor, 122, 167,
    168, 207
Buccleuch estate, 122
building trades, 19, 133–55, 224
    Black, John, Kirkcaldy, 146, 147–8
    Kevan, Samuel, London, 19
    McGibbon, Charles and John,
        Edinburgh, 148
    Miller, Hugh, Cromarty, 4, 90–3, 115
    Miller, James, Fife, 146, 148
    Sanderson & Patterson, Galashiels, 138
    Smith Brothers, Darnick, 137–8,
        139, 141
    see also joiners, masons, painters and
        decorators, plasterers, plumbers
building project management, 133, 145–8
Bulloch, Sir George, country house
    owner, 149
Burns, Robert, poet, 113, 177
Bute, marquis of, craft sponsor, 134, 144,
    153, 215, 226

cabinetmakers, 9, 15, 29, 31, 37–48, 53–4,
    99–100, 101, 142, 164, 181, 221–2
    Aitken, William, Edinburgh, 178
    Dowell, James, Edinburgh, 40–1
    Forrester, Alexander, Edinburgh, 207
    Gullan, David, Musselburgh, 37–40
    John Taylor & Co., Edinburgh, 36, 45–6,
        168, 195
    Mein, James, Kelso, 142
    Morison & Co., Edinburgh, 43–4,
        153–4
    Shillinglaw, Joseph, Darnick, 138, 139
    Smith, Francis, Glasgow, 150
    Thomson, Danny, Tain, 99–100
    Watson, James, Edinburgh, 41–3
    Young, Trotter & Hamilton, Edinburgh,
        36, 145, 147, 153
    see also chair makers, furniture makers
        and retailers, upholsterers
Caledonian Fancy Wood Works, 112
Campbell, Lady Victoria, craft sponsor,
    117, 200
Canada, 96–7, 213
carpenters, 84, 87; see also joiners, wrights
Carron Iron Co., 31, 61–2

carvers and gilders, 29, 33–4, 47, 53–4, 198
    C. L. Dobbie & Son, Glasgow, 54
    Steell, John, Edinburgh, 33–4, 194, 198
    see also woodcarvers
cedar wood, 142–3
Celtic revival, 114, 118–19, 167, 169, 193
census, 46–7, 52–3, 73, 81, 97–8, 100, 216
chair makers, 101–2
    Caledonian Cabinet and Chair Works,
        Beith, 101
    Foubister, Robert and Lizzie, straw-
        backers, Orkney, 124–5
    Kirkness, David, Kirkwall, 123–5
    Wheeler, William, Fife, 150
    see also cabinetmakers, furniture makers
        and retailers, upholsterers
coal carving, 114
Coats, Sir Peter, country house owner and
    exhibition sponsor, 136, 177
Colonsay, 193
commemorative wares, 102, 109–10, 122,
    127, 188
consumer culture, 10, 18, 108, 219
copyright, 62; see also patents
Country Life, 125, 150–1, 153, 227
craft
    appeal, 186–7
    authenticity, 7, 120
    books and magazines, 197
    competitions, 15–16, 69, 160, 165,
        168–9, 196
    contemporary, 1–5
    demonstrations, 68, 163, 171, 174–5,
        175–6
    educators, 195–6, 198–202
    exhibitions, 15–16, 82, 95, 120–1,
        159–82
    leisure, 187, 197, 200, 201
    revivals, 228
    shops, 19–20, 33–4, 194–5
    theory, 1–4
    tools, 101, 196, 221
craftivism, 4
Crafts Council, 3, 228
CraftsScotland, 3
craftworkers
    amateurs, 186–207
    apprentices, 9, 10, 11–12, 13, 18, 19, 32,
        45, 67, 68, 94, 117, 164, 165, 168,
        220–1, 225
    community, 57–8, 88, 90, 94–5, 96–7,
        113, 152
    conflict with amateurs, 206–7

craftworkers (*cont.*)
   definitions, 5–6, 46–7
   education, 14, 67–72, 80, 164–7, 193,
      224–5
   education for amateurs, 198–202
   family, 32–3, 63, 79, 82, 90, 91,
      94–5, 96
   'golden age', 2, 6, 57, 88–9
   housing, 31, 34, 37, 40, 42, 59, 84, 88
   identity, 9, 46–8, 57–8, 74, 80, 92–3, 187–8
   journeymen, 46, 96
   masculinity, 8, 74, 92
   masters, 8, 46
   migration, 18, 56, 80, 85, 95, 96–7,
      214, 218
   numbers, 27–8, 46–8, 53–4, 73, 97–8
   social life, 96–7
   subcontractors, 42–3, 55, 61
   wages and payments, 11, 42–3, 67, 85,
      88, 91, 97, 139, 178, 221
   women, 42, 47, 64, 70, 74, 85, 97, 102–3,
      126, 174–5, 181–2, 214
   working day, 58, 89, 96, 178
creative industries, 5, 228
Cromarty, 90–1
Cumnock, 102, 110

Dalquharran Castle, 135–6
design schools, 14, 16, 33, 67–72, 164–5,
   171, 198
deskilling, 5–6, 47–8, 218, 221–2
Dinwiddie, Robert, entrepreneur, Glasgow
   and London, 11–12
DIY, 187
Dormer, Peter, 1–2
Dovecot Tapestry Studio, 226
dressmakers and milliners, 28, 52–3, 223
Dryburgh Abbey, 115
Dublin, 12, 32, 114
Dumbarton, 64–5
Dumfries, 100, 195, 203
Dundee, 216
   Exhibition of Industry 1887, 163–4, 204
Dunfermline, 68
Dunmore, countess of, craft sponsor, 122–3,
   170, 193
Dyce, William, craft educator, 164–5

economic impact, 3, 5–6, 10, 13–14, 30–1,
   52–3, 82, 121–2, 127, 215–17, 228
Edinburgh, 8, 20, 27–48, 52–4, 63, 65–6,
   91, 114, 116, 126–7, 139–40, 160–2,
   165, 178, 224–5, 226

Dean of Guild Court, 31–2
Decorative Arts Exhibition 1888, 203, 206
Industrial Museum, 172, 178
International Exhibition 1886, 117,
   161–2, 174, 176, 180, 201
International Exhibition of Science, Art
   and Industry 1890, 124
International Fisheries Exhibition 1882,
   175
International Forestry Exhibition 1884,
   172–3
National War Memorial, 226–7
New Town, 30–37
Old Assembly Close fire, 32–3
'Old Edinburgh' Court, 176
Social Union, 200–1, 205–6
Thistle Chapel, 63
employers, 41–3, 46–8, 53–4, 67, 70–1,
   85, 163
engravers, 17, 27, 32–3, 63–4
Esterly, David, 2
exhibition objectives, 161–2, 164, 177
exhibition organisers, 175
   Aberdeen, Countess Ishbel, 175
   Art Manufacture Association, 165–6
   Blair, Matthew, Paisley, 177
   Central Working Men's Club and
      Institute, 180–1, 203
   Dundee and District United Trades
      Council, 163
   Fortune, David, Glasgow, 203, 204
   Select Society, Edinburgh, 160
   Thomas, Mrs Frances, Harris and
      Edinburgh, 162
   see also Board of Manufactures
Exposition Universelle, Paris 1878, 177–8,
   207

Fala Dam, 81–4
Falkland House, 144–8
fern decoration, 111–12
Fife, 114, 150–1
First World War, 95, 199, 218, 225–6
Fletcher, F. Morley, craft educator, 206
flexible specialisation, 6, 213
folk craft, 79, 214
Frayling, Christopher, 2–3
furniture, 30, 37–8, 40–1, 43, 46, 99–100,
   101–2, 110, 123–5, 139–40, 142, 145,
   149, 150, 152, 173
   James Dowell, cabinetmaker and
      auctioneer, Edinburgh, 40–1
furniture makers and retailers

Caledonian Cabinet and Chair Works, Beith, 101
James Shoolbred & Co., London, 149
Scott Morton & Co., art furnishers, Edinburgh, 44–5, 151
Strattan & Mackay, Glasgow, 53–4
Wheeler, William, art furniture maker, Fife, 150
Whytock & Reid, art furnishers, Edinburgh, 44–5, 63, 151, 168
Wylie & Lochhead, house furnishers, Glasgow, 54, 150, 153
see also cabinetmakers, chair makers, upholsterers

Galt, John, novelist, 9
Galashiels, 107–8, 138
Geddes, Patrick, craft educator, 200–1, 205
gifts, 108, 120, 127, 188, 192
Glasgow, 8, 27–8, 29, 52–74, 134–5, 150, 204, 218–19, 226
East End Exhibition 1890, 73, 204
Industrial Exhibition 1865, 180–2, 203
International Exhibition 1888, 61, 102, 162–3, 170, 174, 176
International Exhibition 1901, 67–8, 166
Kelvingrove Museum and Gallery, 166
Kyrle Society, 200
Maryhill, 72–4
Museum and Polytechnic Exhibition 1866, 181
Scottish Exhibition of National History, Art and Industry 1911, 176
Society of Lady Artists, 177
glass workers, 31, 64–7, 72–4, 171,182, 214, 218–19
Adam, Stephen, glass stainer, Glasgow, 72–4
Cottier, Daniel, glass stainer, Glasgow and London, 72
Dumbarton Glass Works Co., 64–5
F. & C. Osler & Co., Birmingham, 65
Holyrood Flint Glass Co., Edinburgh, 65–6, 112, 170–1
Hunter, Richard, glass cutter, Edinburgh, 171
Miller, David, glazier, Fife, 146, 148
goldsmiths, 10, 54, 166, 169; see also jewellers, silversmiths
Hamilton & Inches, Edinburgh, 35
Heriot, George, Edinburgh and London, 10

Great Exhibition of 1851, 7, 29, 111, 146, 147, 161, 166, 202
Greenock, 12, 55, 64

Haddington, 179–80
handloom weavers, 30, 56–60, 88–90, 100–1, 119–20
Blair, Matthew, Paisley, 177
Brotherstone, Peter, Dirleton, 160
Hammond, William, Glasgow, 56–7, 60
McIndoe, George, Glasgow, 59–60
Muir, William, Glasgow, 56–7
Munro, Angus, Inveraray, 90
Sharp, John, Crieff, 119
Tannahill, Robert, Paisley, 56–7
Thom, William, Inverury, 88–9
William Wilson & Sons, Bannockburn, 59
see also Harris tweed, linen industry, woollen industry
Harmony House, 140–3
Harris, 122–3
Harris tweed, 120–1, 123, 162
Harrod, Tanya, 3
hat makers, 28, 126
Hawick, 93–5, 122
Handicraft and Industrial Exhibition 1887, 95, 167–8
Hebrides, 89
Helensburgh, 149–50
Heritage Crafts Association, 3–4
Heritage wood, 109–15
Highland Home Industries Association, 120–1, 122, 162; see also Home Arts and Industries Association, Scottish Home Industries Association
Highlands, 84–8, 115, 135, 175–6, 191, 215–16
Hill House, 149–50
Home Arts and Industries Association, 199–200; see also Highland Home Industries Association, Scottish Home Industries Association

India, 61, 144, 172, 173–4, 213
Industrial Museum of Scotland, 7
Innes, Gilbert, craft sponsor, 16–17
international comparisons, 213–14
international exhibitions, 61, 67–8, 100, 124, 127, 159–82, 194, 202
Invercreran Estate, 86–8, 143
Inverness, 91, 127
Inverurie, 88, 89

Iona Celtic Art, 118–19
Irish peasant industries, 162, 175

Jamaica, 39, 86, 140–3
jewellers, 7, 19–20, 36, 54, 115–19
    Jamieson, William, Aberdeen, 19
    Macgregor, David, Perth, 163
    Marshall & Sons, Edinburgh, 126,
        166–7, 168
    Morton, Robert, Edinburgh, 20
    Rettie & Sons, Aberdeen, 117,
        169, 219
    Ritchie, Alexander and Euphemia, Iona,
        117–19
    Scott, Robert, Glasgow, 54
    Westren, Peter, Edinburgh, 173
    Wilson, P. G., Inverness, 127
    see also lapidaries, goldsmiths,
        silversmiths
joiners, 29, 84, 94–5, 140, 146, 148
    Simpson, James, Fala Dam, 84
    see also carpenters, wrights
Journal of Modern Craft, 5

Kellie Castle, 124, 150
Kelso, 142
Kilbarchan, 90
Kinloch Castle, 148–9
Kirkcaldy Linoleum Co., 170
Kirkwall, 123–6
knitters, 3, 89, 120, 122, 162, 164–5,
    174–5, 190, 191, 215
    Ross, Mrs and Miss, amateurs, Tain, 190
Korn, Peter, 2

lace and embroidery workers, 120, 160,
    163, 181, 214; see also needleworkers
lapidaries, 117, 192
    Gray, Lord Francis, amateur, Perthshire,
        192
Lauriston Castle, 44, 154
Lavery, John, artist, Glasgow, 172
leather workers, 28–9, 100, 102, 223
    Fallas, John, saddle maker, Dumfries,
        100
    W. & J. Milne, Edinburgh, 29
    Wilson, Walker & Co., Leeds, 29
    see also boot and shoemakers
linen industry, 14, 61, 112, 163
Liverpool, 11, 19, 55, 62
Lockhart, J. G., biographer, 138, 142
London, 10, 11–13, 17–20, 30, 31, 62, 69,
    136, 140, 169, 179, 180

Macgill, William, craft retailer, Edinburgh,
    194
McIlwraith, Andrew, patternmaker,
    Ayrshire, 95–7
McKenzie, Sir James of Scatwell, country
    house owner, 39
machine making, 53, 95–7, 164, 222
Manchester, 44, 45
Mar Lodge, 151–3
marble workers, 16–17, 142, 145, 147
    Campbell, Thomas, Edinburgh, 16–17
    Joseph Browne & Co., London 145, 147
    Ness, David, Edinburgh, 145
    Thomson, James, Leith, 142
Maryhill Burgh Hall, 72–4
masons, 93, 138, 160; see also building trades
    Black, John, Kirkcaldy, 146, 147–8
    Miller, Hugh, Cromarty, 4, 90–3, 115
Mauchline wares (treen), 110–15
    Caledonian Fancy Wood Works, Lanark,
        112
    Morton, Thomas and Rachel, box
        decorators, Cumnock, 112
    Smith, Andrew and William, Mauchline,
        110–11, 165
mechanics institutes, 34, 69, 96, 198
Melrose, 114–15, 137, 140
metal workers, 63, 179, 221, 222
    Carron Iron Co., 31, 61–2
    Hadden, Thomas, Edinburgh, 63,
        151, 227
Miller, Hugh, mason and geologist, 4,
    90–3, 115
modernism, 3, 227
Montrose, 192
Mount Stuart, 153
Murphy family, textile workers and
    inventors, Glasgow, 217
Musselburgh, 37–40
    Industrial Exhibition 1908, 205

National Galleries of Scotland, 14, 165
needleworkers, 3, 97, 102–3, 120, 160, 162,
    164, 181–2, 188–90, 193–4, 217
    Dalrymple, Jenny, embroiderer,
        Edinburgh, 160
    MacKay, Margaret, seamstress and
        sewing mistress, Perthshire, 85
    Spiers, Lady Anne, amateur, 193
    White, Nicholas, amateur quilt maker,
        Dundee, 188
Newbery, Francis, craft educator, 206
Newhaven Fish Wives, 175

Ogilvie-Gordon, Maria, apprentice guide author, 220–3
opticians, 55
Orkney, 123–6

painters and decorators, 72, 146, 147, 152, 182
    Bonnar & Carfrae, Edinburgh, 147, 168
    Hamilton, John, Edinburgh, 178
    Hay, David Ramsay, Edinburgh, 138, 147
    Traquair, Phoebe, 63
Paisley, 56, 68, 177
Paisley shawls, 5, 68–9, 176–7
'pals' regiments, 226
Parker, Rozsika, 3
patents, 12, 29, 112; see also copyright
pattern makers, 62, 95–7
Perry, Grayson, 2
Perth, 32, 121, 163
Perthshire, 45, 85, 87
photographers, 82–3, 93, 124
    D. & J. McEwen, Stirling, 207
    Hill and Adamson, Edinburgh, 92
    Kent, Tom, Kirkwall, 125
    Lothian, Robert, Fala Dam, 82, 83
    Ross, John, Tain, 190
    Smith, William, Tain, 98–9
    Webster, Alexander McCallum, Argyll, 86–7
plasterers, 32, 146
    James Annan & Son, Edinburgh and Perth, 146
plumbers, 44, 133, 151, 152, 179–80, 222
    Inglis, James M., Edinburgh, 151
    Ross, Tommy, Haddington, 179–80
pottery workers, 10, 11–13, 55, 61, 169–70, 171–2, 223–4
    Bell & Co., Glasgow, 61
    Bird, John, London and Glasgow, 11–12
    Delftfield Pottery Co., Glasgow, 11–13
    Doulton & Co., London, 61
    Dunmore Pottery, Airth, 169–70
    Gardener, Peter, Stirlingshire, 169–70
    Groom, Alice, Glasgow and Lambeth, 171–2
Princess Louise, craft sponsor, 90, 121, 123
printers and engravers, 27, 32–3, 63–4, 224
    James Kirwood & Sons, Edinburgh, 32–3
    Miller & Richard, Edinburgh, 64
    Robert Scott & Sons, Edinburgh, 33
    Thomson, Charles, Edinburgh, 33
    Wilson, Alexander, Glasgow, 63
Prestonpans, 16

Queen Victoria, craft sponsor, 115–16, 121, 151, 163, 170, 171, 191

Reid, William R., interior designer, 44, 153–4
'Repair Shop', 4
Roseberry, earl of, craft sponsor, 120–1
Rosehaugh House, 39
Ross and Cromarty, 98
Royal Institution (Royal Scottish Academy), 14, 68, 161, 168
Ruskin, John, author, 63

Sanquhar carpets, 102, 122
scientific instrument makers, 54–5
    Alexander Dick, Glasgow, 54
    McGregor, Duncan, Greenock, Glasgow and Liverpool, 55
    Whyte, Thomson & Co., Govan, 55
Scotch pebbles, 115–17, 169, 192
Scott Morton, William, cabinetmaker and designer, 44–5, 168
Scott, W. R., economist, 215–16
Scott, Walter, novelist and poet, 34, 109–10, 137–40, 143
Scottish Art Manufacturers Association, 7
Scottish Committee of the Council of Industrial Design, 128
Scottish Home Industries Association, 89, 124, 175; see also Home Arts and Industries Association, Highland Home Industries Association
Select Committee on Handloom Weavers, 60
Select Society, 160
Sennet, Richard, 2
Shetlands, 120, 164–5
silversmiths, 20, 28, 35, 54, 117–19, 163, 219, 223
    Edward Barnard & Sons, London, 219
    Marshall & Sons, Edinburgh, 166–7, 168
    Ritchie, Alexander and Euphemia, Iona, 117–19
    Storr & Mortimer, London, 144–5
    see also goldsmiths, jewellers
Society of Antiquaries of Scotland, 111, 166–7, 192
souvenirs, 107, 108–9, 111, 113–15, 126–7, 128; see also tourists
spinning wheels, 121, 190–1
Stirling, 109, 111, 207
Stobs Castle, 93–4, 95
stonemasons, 90–3, 141

Stowe, Harriet Beecher, anti-slavery campaigner and tourist, 114–15
Sturt, George, wheelwright and author, 2, 79–80
Sun Alliance Insurance, 36–7

tailors, 53, 86, 93, 223
  Goodfellow, William, Galashiels, 138, 139
  Herkes, Peter, Fala Dam, 82
Tain, 98–100, 190
tartan, 11, 120
Taymouth Castle, 139, 143–4
technical innovations, 59–60
technical schools, 71–2
temperance movement, 187, 205
Thoms, Sheriff George, exhibition sponsor, 123–4, 175
toolmakers, 59, 94, 221–2
tourists, 107–28
  accommodation, 107–8
  clothing, 121, 123, 127
  guidebooks, 107, 109, 126, 127
  postcards, 58, 83, 119, 124–5
  travel, 108, 121
  workshop visiting, 113
  see also souvenirs
trades houses, 5, 8, 219
trades unions, 56, 64, 67, 101, 102, 218, 221, 225
travel case makers, 28–9
  J. Stephenson, Edinburgh, 29
Trotter, William, country house owner, 153
Turkey red printed cotton, 6, 60–1, 188
Tynecastle Tapestry, 45

upholsterers, 9, 41–3, 46–7, 53–4
  Allan, Francis, Edinburgh, 139–40
  McKennon, Angus, Edinburgh, 36–7
  Thomson, Danny, Tain, 99–100
  Watson, James, Edinburgh, 41–3
  see also cabinetmakers, chair makers, furniture makers and retailers

village crafts, 79–84

Waal, Edmund de, 2
Wallace Memorial, 111

watch and clock makers, 15, 28, 53, 59, 146
  Begg, John, Glasgow, 15
  Macvicar, Archibald, Glasgow, 59
  Symington, Andrew, Fife, 146
Watt, James, entrepreneur and inventor, 12–13
Waugh, Robert, country house owner, 140–3
Wedgwood, Josiah, entrepreneur, 13
wheelwrights, 79–84
  Stoddart, Walter, Fala Dam, 83
  Sturt, George, Surrey, 79–80
Wilson, Charles Heath, craft educator, 70
workshops
  costs, 34–5
  employees, 11–13, 40, 42, 46–7, 65, 83, 101–2
  fires, 31–2, 35, 40, 101
  layout, 35–6, 37–8, 40–1, 58, 65–6, 72–3, 83, 99–100
  size, 13, 35, 45, 55, 72–3, 113, 153
  theft, 36
women's industry displays, 68, 162, 164, 174–5
woodcarvers, 33–4, 192–3, 224
  Cairns, Peter, amateur, Dalkeith, 207
  Gordon, duke of, amateur, Morayshire, 192
  McNeill, Sir Malcolm, amateur, Edinburgh, 193
  Scott Morton & Co., Edinburgh, 44–5, 151
  Steell, John, Edinburgh, 33–4, 194, 198
  see also carvers and gilders
woollen industry, 59, 60, 89–90, 102, 218
  William Wilson & Sons, Bannockburn, 59
wrights, 29, 31, 85, 141
  Baxter, Andrew, Edinburgh, 31
  Robertson, John, Perthshire, 85
  Rogers, William, Edinburgh, 15
  Smith, George, Falkirk, 62
  see also carpenters, joiners

yarn bombing, 4